Advance Praise for *Embracing Auschwitz*

"As the Holocaust shifts from living wound to fitful memory, the urgent question is not just how to remember but why. In *Embracing Auschwitz*, Rabbi Joshua Hammerman gives us a compelling and provocative answer. His 'Torah of Auschwitz' celebrates the life-affirming values of heroism, persistence, faith, Jewish unity and defense, and universal justice. *Embracing Auschwitz* is an essential contribution to our understanding of what we as a people need to carry from the 20th into the 21st century."
—**Yossi Klein Halevi**,
Senior Fellow, Shalom Hartman Institute, Jerusalem
author, *Letters to My Palestinian Neighbor*

"I hate the title of this book and there are tens of passages which make me wince and grit my teeth in order to go on. Yet this is an important book and should be read by every Jew who cares about Judaism—because its central point is true and it offers wisdom to guide us into the Jewish future.

"Hammerman's fundamental thesis is that the Holocaust must be incorporated into the fabric of Jewish religion. Our understanding of every tradition and ethical commandment must be reshaped by its light. This book shows how to do this. Thankfully, he makes clear that the correct application of this concept is not to magnify death and the feeling of victimization. Rather it is to respond with greater intensity of human responsibility and to savor life even more for its fragility and vulnerability.

"This is not to mention other exciting challenges in the book. Take his bold proposal—for the sake of creating an indissoluble bond—to grant every Jew in the world a vote in Israel. I don't agree but this is a proposal that makes waves and is worth fighting over.

"In short, damn the torpedoes and wrecks along the way. Full speed ahead. Read this book. Criticize its faults. Absorb its truths. The life you inspire may well be your own."
—**Rabbi Dr. Irving "Yitz" Greenberg**,
founding director of the President's Commission on the Holocaust,
Chair of the Holocaust Memorial Museum
founding President of the Jewish Life Network

"With immense insight and unstinting honesty, this work looks hard at the Holocaust's enduring meaning for Jewish identity and the world. In examining the past in all its complexities, Rabbi Hammerman suggests a hopeful path for our complex Jewish community. Like many of Rabbi Hammerman's sermons and other writings, it is eye opening and thought provoking. *Embracing Auschwitz* will make you think and feel—no walk in the park, but a journey well worth taking and embracing."
—U.S. Senator **Richard Blumenthal**

"A powerful meditation on what Judaism could be in this time."
—**Peter Beinart**, author, *The Crisis of Zionism*

"Starting with a jarring book title, Joshua Hammerman captures our imagination and re-pivots our approach to dealing with the horrors of the Holocaust. As a gifted journalist and spiritual leader, he makes his case with a clear voice and open heart, showing us that we can fulfill the biblical mandate to 'choose life' by doing so with new forms of joy and sanctity.

"Hammerman's brave new vision challenges us and demands our attention."
—**Gary Rosenblatt**, editor at large, The Jewish Week

Embracing Auschwitz

Joshua Hammerman

Ben Yehuda Press
Jewish Arguments

Published by Ben Yehuda Press
122 Ayers Court #1B
Teaneck, NJ 07666

http://www.BenYehudaPress.com

To subscribe to our monthly book club and support independent Jewish publishing, visit https://www.patreon.com/BenYehudaPress

Ben Yehuda Press books may be purchased at a discount by synagogues, book clubs, and other institutions buying in bulk. For information, please email markets@BenYehudaPress.com

ISBN13 978-1-934730-89-8

20 21 22 / 10 9 8 7 6 5 4   20200514

Dedication

This book is dedicated to my in-laws, Gloria and Howard Aisenberg. Howard (of blessed memory), in every respect a member of the Greatest Generation, was a highly decorated survivor of the Battle of the Bulge who experienced the devastation wrought by Hitler up close. In some manner, I hope this book can pay tribute to his memory and ease the pain of all those who bear the deep scars of World War II and the Holocaust. We have become their witnesses.

Contents

There are three ways in which we respond to sorrow. On the first level, we cry; on the second level, we are silent; on the highest level, we take sorrow and turn it into song.
　—Abraham Joshua Heschel

Chapter One

THE TORAH OF SINAI AND THE TORAH OF AUSCHWITZ

Let me get this out there right from the start, so that there will be absolutely no confusion: *There was nothing good about the Holocaust.* What happened during the period of Nazi hegemony over Germany and Europe, from 1933-1945, was the nadir of human history. No other historic event is remotely comparable, and it is hard to conceive of any future atrocity being so maliciously designed and meticulously carried out on so vast a scale.

So, if the title of this book tempted you to toss it—because you think it is somehow disrespectful to view the Holocaust in positive terms, but for some reason you still decided to glance at this page—you are now aware that I am in no way glorifying this catastrophic event. An "embrace" is not an endorsement, nor is it a directive to "get over it."

But why not "get over it?" It *has* been over seventy years. Isn't it time to move on?

No—it's not.

In fact, it is time—*to embrace it.*

The Holocaust was bad, no question about it. But that doesn't preclude it from leading to something good; many things, in fact. You'll read about some of them in this book.

It is time to embrace Auschwitz. Not to get over it and not to become desensitized to what took place. On the contrary. It's time to fully incorporate its lessons into our souls; to recognize that in fact the Holocaust is not only part of our story, it frames our story; it *is* our story—and our greatest responsibility and honor is to bear witness and to share that story.

While this is true primarily for Jews, it is also true for many others for whom the Holocaust has become a cultural and historic touchstone; a benchmark for how low civilization can go and a warning about the human susceptibility to perpetrate extremism and tolerate evil. While this book primarily addresses the Holocaust from a Jewish perspective—I am a rabbi, after all—in no way should it be seen as excluding fair-minded people who wish to understand how this epochal event can bring about positive change today.

Incidentally, when I speak of *Auschwitz*, I am speaking in symbolic terms, as that single death camp complex has over the decades come to represent the Holocaust as a whole.

And by the way, if you are an anti-Semitic conspiracist convinced that Jews just made the whole thing up, you will find no fodder for your crazy speculations here. No, the Holocaust was not good, nor was its unimaginable evil imaginary. It really happened, and its impact continues to ripple across the world. But for the rest of you, those open to a conversation about how we can place Auschwitz before our eyes as a lodestar of meaning, moral guidance and, yes, ultimately even joy, join me on this journey to the darkest places ever known to humankind and to the light that is beginning to glimmer ever so faintly at the end of the tunnel.

For most of my life, I felt that the Holocaust took up far too much Jewish bandwidth, that it smothered joy and suffocated Jews with guilt and resentment. It posed questions that were unanswerable. It eclipsed centuries of Jewish achievement and it brought out the worst in people. It gave us an excuse to hate—and it gave our children the excuse to opt out of being Jewish altogether. Who would want to be part of such a hopeless, hapless people?

So here is the conundrum that has prevailed among Jews since at least the 1970s, when preoccupation with the Holocaust became pervasive, as survivors began to discover their collective voice and many people began to take notice. It was necessary to place the survivors' experience front and center, especially as Jews fought anti-Semitism on so many fronts, particularly in the Soviet Union and at the UN. We craved to live lives of joy, love, acceptance, community, hope and faith. But as Jews looked out there at the cultural landscape, what did we see? Everywhere we turned, being Jewish and the Holocaust became virtually inseparable.

I've spent the better part of my career as a rabbi and writer trying to reframe Judaism in positive terms, which for me meant steering the conversation away from the Holocaust, lest my faith tradition wither on the vine. But recently I've discovered that the opposite is true. Judaism is now being interpreted anew through the prism of this epochal event, filtered through the experience of Auschwitz, with surprisingly positive results.

I was born more than a decade after the end of World War II, part of the baby boom generation of American Jews for whom the Holocaust was both as distant as a grainy black and white movie, yet as close as the tattooed arms of so many of my Hebrew school teachers. We were subjected to the unex-purgated newsreel footage of heaps of corpses being tossed into deep pits for mass burial, in films like the 1956 French documentary *Night and Fog*, which became as much a part of my childhood as Superman comics and baseball cards. I recall one scene depicting Jewish fat being carved into soap and skin turned into lampshades. These days, *Night and Fog* would never be shown to middle schoolers, and to high schoolers only with therapists present. Not back then. Even when they weren't teaching about the Holocaust—and rarely did we hear the actual word "Holocaust"—most of my Hebrew school teach-ers were habitually angry, stern, and mistrustful. Israel's miraculous victory in 1967, when I was in fifth grade, only made them worry more... *"Oy! Now they'll really get us!"* Despite it all, I loved being Jewish, but the shadow of the Holocaust weighed heavily on me and my generation.

Fast forward a half century to November, 2018: the 80th anniversary of Kristallnacht, the "Night of Broken Glass." I stood before a few dozen He-brew school students and asked them what they knew about the Holocaust. We hadn't shown movies like *Night and Fog* to kids for many years, so the atrocities were left to the imagination. Hands shot up—they knew a lot but wanted to know more. Lots more.

How did Hitler succeed in capturing the minds of an enlightened nation?
Why did the Jews not escape when they could?
What happened to the free press?
What about the political opposition?
What did the world do?
Did they really experiment on twins?

These were middle schoolers—and younger—and their understanding of the Holocaust exhibited a sophistication far beyond their years; it was a topic that clearly had been discussed at the dinner table, with little of the *"Shush! They'll hear you"* that I had heard in my day. There was none of the shell-shocked shame that afflicted my contemporaries when we were their age, none of the sadness or fear—this even though several of them reported swastikas scrawled on lockers at school and other experiences of hate, during a year when anti-Semitic incidents skyrocketed and just after the horrific murder of eleven Jews at prayer in the Tree of Life synagogue in Pittsburgh. These kids never lacked for questions, but when the Holocaust came up—the topic that my generation had wished would go away—their interest level soared, way beyond what it might have been had I started a conversation about, say, the Sabbath, or Israel, or the Yankees. It was reassuring that it still mattered to them, without the need for cinematic shock therapy, and it was refreshing that it mattered in such an uncomplicated way.

And no wonder they are so interested:

The Holocaust has become ubiquitous in American culture.

The Holocaust has entered mainstream American culture in a big way. It's in the news constantly, saturating conventional and social media. Increasingly, politicians, entertainers and newsmakers with Holocaust-related family stories are characterizing these accounts as an emblem of honor, rather than viewing their forbears' victimization as a badge of shame, as was the case a generation ago. The roster of witnesses at the Trump impeachment hearings in late 2019 included E.U. Ambassador Gordon Sondland, who proudly announced at the beginning of his testimony that his parents fled Germany during the Holocaust. "Like so many immigrants, my family was eager for freedom and hungry for opportunity. They raised my sister and me to be humble, hardworking, and patriotic, and I am forever grateful for the sacrifices they made on our behalf," he said. Similarly, Marie Yovanovitch, former Ambassador to Ukraine, proudly proclaimed in her opening statement that her parents fled Europe during the Holocaust.

Just a few months earlier, at the 2019 Emmy Awards, best supporting actress Alex Borstein thanked her mother and grandmother, both Holocaust survivors, during her acceptance speech: "My grandmother was in line to be shot into a pit," Borstein said. "She asked a guard 'what happens if I step out of line?' and he responded, 'I don't have the heart to shoot you, but somebody will.'" Because of that, Borstein added, "I am here and my children are here. So step out of line, ladies! Step out of line!" she told the audience, appending a #MeToo era message to her family story.

It is no surprise Google tracks a significant increase in literary references using the terms "Holocaust" and "Hitler" through the early years of the 21st century.

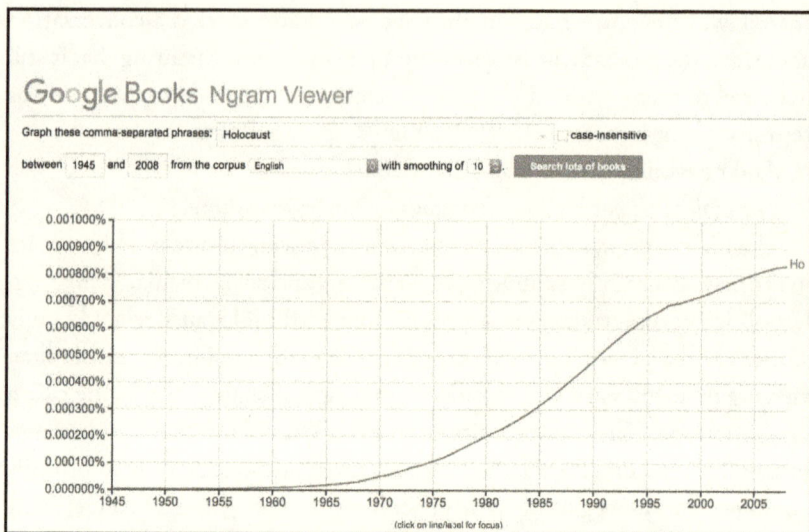

Chart of the usage of the word "Holocaust" since 1945.

Those two terms have been brought into so many political arguments, on all sides of the spectrum, that a new rule was created: Godwin's Law, stating that if a discussion continues long enough, inevitably someone or something will be compared to Hitler.

Everywhere you turn, it's all Holocaust all the time. In school, Jewish kids—even those from ultra-assimilated backgrounds—are expected to be Holocaust experts, BFFs with Anne Frank. Whenever a swastika appears anywhere, every Jew suddenly is expected to be an authority on the history of that creepy black spider. The Holocaust is also gaining more traction in theaters, on TV, in books and in popular conversation. A landmark exhibit of Auschwitz artifacts that opened on May 8, 2019 at New York's Museum of Jewish Heritage, attracting more than 110,000 visitors during its first five months, including more than 36,000 students. It was extended until the following May, by which time it was expected to draw more than 200,000 visitors, more than doubling the museum's typical attendance for that time span.

As the actual events have receded into history, the Shoah has only become more relevant. And while it has become less emotionally daunting for a younger generation now two generations removed, the decreased chronological proximity has rendered it increasingly compelling—not just for Jews but for much of the world. Time may heal all wounds but the memory persists;

and for the Holocaust, time is also bringing into sharper focus the many ways that this event affects our lives today.

Turn on PBS, and you get Black History Month; Puerto Rican Heritage Month; Gay Pride Month; Polish Heritage Month—and for the Jews? For many years all you got was Holocaust Remembrance Month, because for many Americans, including many Jews, being Jewish and the Holocaust have become virtually inseparable. It is only recently that Holocaust Remembrance Month was changed to Jewish American Heritage Month. Even so, turn on public television during the month of April and Auschwitz is ubiquitous.

As the Holocaust has evolved from epochal event to timeless symbol, there has been a proliferation of Holocaust museums and memorials, from Poland to Peoria (yes, there is a Holocaust memorial in Peoria), tailoring the event to fit the needs of each locale. According to Edward Jacobs, a consultant on many of these projects, Holocaust museums need to "expand the narrative" in encouraging people to evaluate human rights in their own countries and stand up for victims today. Jacobs tells the *Times of Israel* that to perpetuate Holocaust memory, the next generation of museums is symbolically connecting the genocide to events that took place in, for instance, southeast Texas, or on the streets of Skokie, Illinois. For museums built far from Europe, this shift helps localize, and personalize, the narrative of the Holocaust.

Years ago, Elie Wiesel, in his work *Legends of Our Time*, bemoaned, "No cocktail party can really be a success unless Auschwitz, sooner or later, figures in the discussion." If anything, the Holocaust has permeated casual conversation even more since then. The trivializing of the tragedy has always been a danger, but there's no denying the growing influence of all things Holocaust.

If we needed more proof of the Holocaust's massive impact on popular culture, there was the release in late 2017 of the video game, *Call of Duty: WWII*, the long awaited next installment of the *Call of Duty* series that has, since its initial release in 2011, sold 30 million units worldwide. What makes this one different is that it depicts the Holocaust graphically, something that prior WWII video games have rarely done. In this game, the player controls an American soldier fighting in the European theater. In addition to shooting Nazi soldiers, players also experience racism directed toward Jews and African Americans within their platoon.

"We absolutely show atrocities," the game's senior creator Bret Robbins said to Mashable. "It's an unfortunate part of the history, but you can't tell an authentic, truthful story without going there."

Call of Duty is not alone in bringing the Holocaust into the mainstream of popular culture. And if you are more into old-fashioned board games, a recent hit is called *Secret Hitler*, which simulates the rise of fascism. It's been a top seller on Amazon. Now I could say it's in bad taste to depict the Holocaust as a video game. But the ubiquity of Holocaust references in our culture is something that Jews should embrace. While I'm not a great fan of video games, thanks to *Call of Duty*, millions of people who otherwise may not learn about the Shoah will now bear witness, hopefully with some accuracy, to the greatest crime ever perpetrated on humanity—and hopefully they will convert that gamer's rush into a renewed commitment never to let such hatred prevail again.

Back in the 70s, Elie Wiesel disparaged the groundbreaking TV miniseries "Holocaust"—he called it "untrue and offensive." But that series, as pedestrian as it as was, accomplished two very important things: 1) it helped to launch the career of Meryl Streep; and 2) when it was shown in West Germany, it changed everything. It was seen by 20 million people—half the population of the country. After the programs aired, panels of experts helped explain what happened, as thousands of shocked and outraged Germans called in. *"Did we do THAT?"* This led to massive reforms in the German educational system, including the popularization of the term "Holocaust" itself, and that has made all the difference.

Despite the Holocaust's ubiquity in our culture, a survey published in April 2018 by the Conference on Jewish Material Claims Against Germany raised red flags about some disturbing gaps in Holocaust literacy, especially among millennials. Of all respondents, 66% did not know where Auschwitz is, and 22% of millennials conveyed that they either hadn't heard of or were not sure whether they had heard of the Holocaust. More disturbing, perhaps, is that 31% of all adults and 41% of millennials incorrectly think that two million or fewer Jews were killed. Additionally, although 84% of adults surveyed knew the Holocaust happened in Germany, just 37% knew that it took place in Poland too. But while much educational work needs to be done, still, the survey's revelation that 89% of all Americans have heard of the Holocaust means that the literacy glass is much more than half full.

If this book is a page-turner—and I hope it is—it's not so much a who-dunit as a "how-*does*-it?" We all know whodunit—no mystery there: the

Nazis and their legions of complicit co-conspirators, including many Poles, Hungarians, and people of almost every European background.

But the questions I address have less to do with the past than with the present and future: How *does* the Holocaust propel us forward today to addressing the big questions we all face, like climate change, racism and "fake news"? How *does* the legacy of the Holocaust help all of humanity come together as one family while at the same time helping Jews become a more unified people? How *does* the evil that we faced seven decades ago help us to confront our own dark sides: our anger, our fear, and our resentment? How *does* a new generation properly bear witness to this evil when the last of the actual witnesses are leaving the scene? And last but not least, how *do* we generate new visions of faith and hope in the face of what appears to have been God's utter disappearance from the course of human events?

The "Holocaustization" of Jewish life

In the summer of 2017, I led a group of my congregants on a pilgrimage to Auschwitz and other sacred sites in Europe and then explored some of these themes in a series of High Holidays sermons when we returned. Those sermons were the inspiration for this book.

Previously, back in 2010, I visited these places for the first time, escorting a group of teens on the *March of the Living*, an annual pilgrimage of thousands of Jewish teens who gather at Auschwitz on Holocaust Remembrance Day and march the approximately 1½ miles from Auschwitz I (the original camp) to Birkenau (also known as Auschwitz II). That first visit was transformative for me. As the bus from Krakow passed small villages on the hour-long route, it was hard to believe we were approaching the place I had heard about all these years. Auschwitz I was originally a Polish military training camp, so the facilities seem almost livable when first approached. Built of an orangey-colored brick, they are less evocative of hell-on-earth than some neighborhoods in Queens. So ordinary—a first glimpse of what Hannah Arendt called "the banality of evil," though what went on inside those buildings was simply the greatest crime against humanity of all time. We saw up close the machinery of mass murder and walked into a gas chamber, staring up at the vents through which the killers spewed Zyklon B into the room.

Despite seeing these horrors, the *March of the Living* has a celebratory nature to it that might be considered disrespectful to the dead; but in fact it is just the opposite. As more than ten thousand teens from fifty countries mingled in the alleyways, trading pins and sweatshirts with the logos of their regional groups, the great death camp was transformed into an Olympic village of sorts, complete with all the excitement that you would expect to find at a high school mixer just before Thanksgiving. And the millions of dead, wherever they lay, seemed to be celebrating along with us during this astounding display of teenage Jewish hormones in full bloom; this ultimate repudiation of the Nazis, right in the heart of the valley of the shadow of death. The Final Solution had turned out to be not so final after all.

Seven-plus decades after Auschwitz, something is happening. Something new is emerging. This book contains the first peek into what that "something new" looks like.

The "Holocaustization" of Jewish life—and to only a slightly lesser degree, of American life in general—might sound ominous, but I contend that precisely the opposite is true. In fact, for a Jewish people currently being ripped apart along political, religious, demographic and geographic fault lines, a deepened connection to the Holocaust is just about the only thing that everyone shares. It is what Jews are most passionate about. Pilgrimages to Poland, such as the one I experienced with my congregants recently, are now taking their place alongside trips to Israel on the bucket list of world Jewry. In the pantheon of sacred places, the Western Wall is being joined in this "Wall of Fame" by the walls surrounding the Warsaw Ghetto and the gate at Auschwitz proclaiming "*Arbeit Macht Frei.*" Berlin, with its abundant Holocaust memorials and welcoming atmosphere, has now become a magnet for Jews—including many Israelis—seeking a locale promoting inclusiveness and accountability.

Embracing Auschwitz might be just what the doctor ordered. Embracing Auschwitz could save the Jewish people. It could save Judaism. It could save Israel. It could, by extension, save all of humanity and save our planet. And it could even save God.

And I'm not exaggerating. Except maybe for the God part.

Maybe.

What, then, do I mean when I say that it is time for Jews to "embrace Auschwitz"?

Two things, really:

First, Jews need to embrace our obligation to be surrogate witnesses as the last of the actual witnesses, the survivors, depart.

Jews are living links to the greatest crime ever perpetrated on humanity, and this is the most important role Jews can possibly play in the world today. Humanity, hungry for moral leadership at a time when fascism and hate are on the rise, is turning its lonely eyes to us.

Something of fundamental importance is happening. Auschwitz was liberated over seven decades ago, but the Holocaust refuses to recede from view. On the contrary, its overwhelming power has only deepened, its popularity has increased dramatically, its lessons have never been more relevant, and its stories never more resonant to a wider audience.

This fact was driven home to me during that 2017 congregational trip to Poland, Hungary, the Czech Republic, and Germany—a momentous pilgrimage that will be highlighted in several chapters of the book. We saw death camps, of course; but also small villages where Jews used to live and a few places where Jewish life is being revived. We spoke to Righteous Gentiles and the descendants of the collaborators; to Poles, Hungarians, Czechs, and Germans—and Jews. We saw cemeteries and synagogues, museums and memorials; and we saw anti-Semitism and fascism rearing their ugly heads once again in these countries.

Our return was followed almost immediately by the neo-Nazi march in Charlottesville, Virginia, which stirred up dormant anxieties among American Jews and amplified interest in the Holocaust among the general population. During that horrific Sabbath, at a synagogue in that city, Jews feared for their lives while neo-Nazis shouted epithets outside. Some escaped out the back door. Worst of all, those who marched with or alongside the Nazi banner were called "good people" by the president of the United States—and a startling number of Americans supported this outrageous remark.

A couple of weeks after Charlottesville, a congregant of mine was in Oxford, Mississippi on business. He heard that a Holocaust survivor, a Jew named Marion Blumenthal Lazan, was scheduled speak at a chapel on the campus of the University of Mississippi, and he was curious to see what type of crowd she would draw. Let me insert here that the Jewish population at Ole Miss is so tiny that if you go on the International Hillel website, it is listed at zero percent of the overall student body. There are, after all, only thirteen synagogues in the whole state.

The place was packed. Hundreds were in the room. People were standing three-deep on the sides and they were sitting in the center aisle. And, according to my congregant, even though the acoustics were not great, there was no problem hearing Lazan since everyone was so captivated and moved by what she had to tell. Outside there was only one campus police car parked and no protesters or hecklers in sight.

Again, this was just after the Nazi-led match on Charlottesville.

Something very important was happening on that college campus that day, something that transcends party politics or religious affiliation. A sacred story was being shared, one that the world has never needed to hear more than it does right now—and not only was she heard, but she was embraced; and not only was she embraced, but her message was equally embraced.

Marian Blumenthal Lazan and other survivors are fast leaving the stage of history. Elie Wiesel said that anyone who hears the account of a witness becomes a witness. With Wiesel himself also now gone, who will stand up to presidents who schedule visits to SS graves or who ignore genocides in Rwanda or Bosnia? With no survivors left, who will speak truth to power and call out hate from a place of conviction and authenticity? Who will be the conscience of the world? Yes, the world set in place safeguards after World War II, such as the Fourth Geneva Convention, which in 1949 protected noncombatants from deportation, pillage, degradation, and execution. International norms seem to be fraying right now along with globalism itself, victims of a worldwide outbreak of nativism.

In 1940, a high Nazi official stated, "The fifth commandment, 'Thou shall not kill,' is not God's commandment at all: It is a Jewish invention." Long before the war, Hitler is said to have uttered words that the world should have heeded: "Conscience is a Jewish invention. It is a blemish, like circumcision….I am freeing men from the restraints of an intelligence that has taken charge; from the dirty and degrading modifications of a falsehood called conscience and morality."

What Jews were charged to do at Sinai—to have conscience, to be pillars of morality, to be a nation of priests—and what Jews were charged by Isaiah, to be a "light unto the nations"—now takes on an added urgency after Auschwitz. Jews need to learn how to tell the witnesses' story, with love and conviction. We need to embrace it with bursting pride at the incomprehensible acts of heroism and faith that we have witnessed. We need to celebrate who we are—and *that is* who we are.

Which brings me to the second reason why Jews need to embrace Auschwitz at this time:

Because the Holocaust has taken its place at the very core of what it means to be Jewish.

The 2013 Pew survey of American Jewry had plenty of revelations. But what stood out above anything else was the response to the question, "What does it mean to be Jewish?" "Respondents were asked about which of nine suggested Jewish activities and attributes are "essential" to what being Jewish means to them." They could choose as many as they wished.

Of those surveyed, nineteen percent said, "Observing Jewish law." So much for Judaism of Sinai. "Being part of a Jewish community" was the answer from twenty-eight percent of respondents. Forty-two percent said, "Having a good sense of humor." Just forty-three percent said, "Caring about Israel." Fifty-six percent said, "Working for justice and equality," and sixty-nine percent said, "Leading an ethical and moral life."

But leading the way, was "Remembering the Holocaust," at *seventy-three* percent.

You can't get three quarters of American Jews to agree on *anything*—except for that. Not whether to fast on Yom Kippur, light Hanukkah candles, or what to put on a bagel. If there is a core to our self-image as Jews, a common story, that teaching is far more likely to come from Auschwitz than from Sinai.

We may not be comfortable with that fact, but we cannot deny it.

Want to hear something even more amazing? Ask *Israeli* Jews the same question. Well, Pew did. And we know that Israeli Jews and American Jews don't agree on much these days. And when you ask, "What is an essential part of what it means to be Jewish?" there are lots of differences. Just nine percent of Israeli Jews say, "Having a sense of humor." But for Israeli Jews, just as for American Jews, the Holocaust ranks by far the highest: sixty-five percent—twenty points higher than the second choice, living an ethical life. We can see from this that despite the growing differences between American and Israeli Jews, the Holocaust is the greatest common denominator. Park that tidbit away—we'll get back to it in chapter 12.

U.S. Jews more likely to see ethics, justice as essential to being Jewish

% of Jews who say ... is an essential part of what it means to be Jewish

	Israeli Jews	U.S. Jews
	%	%
Remembering the Holocaust	65	73
Leading an ethical and moral life	47	69
Observing Jewish law	35	19
Living in Israel/ caring about Israel*	33	43
Working for justice and equality	27	56
Eating traditional Jewish foods	18	14
Being intellectually curious	16	49
Having a good sense of humor	9	42

Source: Survey conducted October 2014-May 2015. Data on U.S. Jews from survey conducted February-June 2013.

*Question was phrased as "Caring about Israel" in the U.S. and "Living in Israel" in Israel.

PEW RESEARCH CENTER

As the decades have passed, the Holocaust has ceased to be simply a fundraising tool for federations and advocacy groups. It has become much more. It has also ceased to be solely secular. It has become rooted in the Jewish psyche. *Any modern expression of Judaism to emerge out of this era must place the Holocaust experience directly at its core,* or it will not be authentic; it will fail to speak to our need to confront the blackest black hole in history. But just as it cannot ignore or deny the abyss, to be authentic, any modern expression of Judaism must also speak to the need to affirm joy, beauty, renewed life and at least the possibility of a responsive divinity, or it will not survive.

Two Torahs

The Torah of Sinai, the backbone of rabbinic Judaism, now has a companion narrative that I call the *Torah of Auschwitz*, a series of sacred teachings and practices that enable us to confront the darkest demons of seven decades ago. At the same time, this narrative is filled with positive and life-affirming lessons that can have an enormous impact on not just the Jewish people, but the entire world.

I use the term *Torah* with deliberate irony—it is intended to provoke thought, not to show disrespect. For in the broadest sense, the word *Torah* means "sacred teaching." It is also a verb, connoting an ongoing, evolving process of discovery. I contend that that process of sacred discovery has been stirred by the epochal events of seven decades ago, in a manner that is dramatically changing the face of Judaism and the Jewish people, with profound implications for humanity as a whole.

This *Torah of Auschwitz* is analogous to the New Testament in how the Gospels adapted the Hebrew Bible to the radically changed world experienced by the early Christians. At exactly the same time that the Gospels were composed, rabbinic Judaism was retrofitting the Hebrew Bible as well, enabling it to speak to the vastly changed realities they confronted. When I talk about the Torah of Sinai, in fact, I'm talking about the Hebrew Bible, also called the "Written Torah," as understood by the rabbis of the first six centuries of the common era.

Jeremiah, in chapter 31, envisions the creation of a "New Covenant," and this passage is used by Christians, Jews and Muslims to validate their post-biblical additions to the sacred canon. But the prophecy fits even better as a harbinger of the *Torah of Auschwitz*, in this mashup of relevant verses:

> "Behold, I will bring them from the north country, and
> gather them from the uttermost parts of the earth, and
> with them the blind and the lame, the woman with child
> and she that travails with child together; a great company
> shall they return hither…Behold, the days come, says the
> LORD, that I will make a new covenant with the house
> of Israel, and with the house of Judah; not according to
> the covenant that I made with their fathers in the day that
> I took them by the hand to bring them out of the land of
> Egypt…And there is hope for your future, says the Lord."

So now, I'm claiming that a new, radical re-visioning of the Jewish canon, the *Torah of Auschwitz*, is still in its infancy—as yet unedited and far from canonized, but with some of its key lessons and seminal stories now coming clearly into view.

And what a narrative it is!

Just as the evil perpetrated by the Nazis has no historical parallel, so does the valor of the Holocaust era dwarf anything we see in the Hebrew Bible. When it comes to pure courage and unfathomable love, Joshua, Miriam, and David can't hold a candle to the stories of Janusz Korczak, Mordechai Anielewicz, and Hannah Senesh. It's not just about the most noticeable stars. I conduct lots of funerals for Holocaust survivors, and each life story is filled with courage the likes of which I can't begin to fathom. And the prophetic proclamations of Jeremiah and Isaiah are mirrored—and perhaps surpassed—by the immortal words of such modern-day prophets as Elie Wiesel and Primo Levi. As the decades pass, these supernovas will further brighten the midnight sky as their stories merge into the collective, sacred chronicle. Anne Frank is our modern Dina (Jacob's innocent and victimized daughter). As for Oskar Schindler and Raoul Wallenberg and over 11,000 Righteous Gentiles honored at the Yad Vashem Holocaust Memorial—well, as we'll see in chapter 7, the modern-day Righteous Gentile really has no parallel in the Hebrew Bible's precursor of the Holocaust, the Exodus from Egypt; and therein lies a tale.

How can one not burst with pride at the poetry composed by those living in the midst of hell; at the small deeds of heroism; the scraps of food shared; the secret Seders; the impossible escapes; the beautiful children of Terezin; how the victims were able to maintain their dignity and humanity in the most inhuman conditions, protecting their loved ones—even falling in love? What makes Anne Frank so eternally appealing is her very ordinariness, her capacity to have remained a child in the most sinister of conditions. Frank has already become a universal symbol of innocence and steadfast optimism in the face of pure evil, eclipsing ancient heroines like Ruth and Esther in our collective imagination, inspiring multiple dramas, films, and novels and drawing 1.3 million visitors to her secret annex in 2016 alone. In a thousand years, people will still speak reverently about Anne Frank. Only now are we beginning to understand how her most famous proclamations have become bumper stickers of hope for a generation that rarely picks up a prayer book.

Her pure, optimistic utterances might seem absurdly naïve when taken out of context, but when coming from someone who lived *there*, who persisted in her positivity despite *that*, these quotes have become all that separates so many of us from succumbing to the nihilistic despair that a post Holocaust dystopia might otherwise demand.

As the decades pass and the enormity of Auschwitz sinks in, we should, by all rights, simply be tossing aside all pretense and giving up on human possibility. But how can we, when Anne Frank's diary proclaims these stunning declarations:

"I keep my ideals, because in spite of everything I still believe that people are really good at heart."

"How wonderful it is that nobody needs wait a single moment before starting to improve the world."

"Think of all the beauty still left around you and be happy."

"Whoever is happy will make others happy too."

"I don't think of all the misery, but of all the beauty that still remains."

The *Torah of Auschwitz* that is now emerging will feature Anne Frank's wisdom as its book of *Proverbs* and Elie Wiesel's *Night* as its book of *Job*. Auschwitz was the Nazis' attempt to extinguish the human spirit. The *Torah of Auschwitz* has reignited that sacred torch.

Two Judaisms

My contrasting of classical, rabbinic Judaism with "Holocaust Judaism" is nothing new. Scholars have been doing that for decades.

During the weeks prior to the Six-Day War in 1967, Israel faced a mortal threat that evoked genocidal nightmares of what had taken place only a couple of decades before. This was a time when such nightmares were commonly suppressed and the term "Holocaust" was still rarely employed. But all that changed in 1967, as fear was replaced by euphoria following Israel's stunning victory. At that point, the Holocaust emerged from the closet and took center stage in American Jewish civic life.

A few years later, when I was an undergraduate at Brown University in the 1970s, I studied with Jacob Neusner, the renowned and prolific historian, who explained that there are essentially two Judaisms for the American Jew. On the one hand, there is what he called the Judaism of Sinai; and on the other, the Judaism of Holocaust and Redemption—with the birth of the State of Israel being the harbinger of that redemption. As Neusner described it, these two visions of Judaism are, on the surface, irreconcilable: the Judaism of Sinai—with its Adam and Eve; Abraham, Isaac and Jacob and Sarah, Rebecca, Rachel and Leah; its slaves in Egypt; Moses on the mountain; sanctification in the here-and-now and salvation at the end of time—flourishes alongside the Judaism of Holocaust and Redemption, of Auschwitz and Israel. The Judaism of Sinai plumbs the depths of being created in God's image, and the Judaism of Holocaust and Redemption reaches into that sore surface of Jewish life. One speaks of a universal redemption, with the Jewish people being agents and catalysts; the other speaks of the Jewish people being redeemed from the clutches of the outside world. One world view is based on a God who hears us and saves us from Egyptian bondage; the other is based on a silent God, who either chose not to help us or was incapable of doing so. One is essentially optimistic and hopeful, with universal messianic aspirations; the other is insular, gloomy and particularistic, reeking of victimhood and proclaiming, "Never Again."

Essentially, we have a glass-half-full religion, the Judaism of Sinai, for a glass-half-empty people, contemporary Jews preoccupied with Auschwitz/Israel.

In a seminal essay written in 1982, "Auschwitz or Sinai?", philosopher David Hartman came down solidly on the side of Sinai, writing, "I believe it is destructive to make the Holocaust the dominant organizing category of modern Jewish history and of our national renewal and rebirth. It is both politically and morally dangerous for our nation to perceive itself essentially as the suffering remnant of the Holocaust. It is childish and often vulgar to attempt to demonstrate how the Jewish people's suffering is unique in history." Hartman adds:

> The model of Sinai awakens the Jewish people to the awesome responsibility of becoming a holy people. At Sinai, we discover the absolute demand of God; we discover who we are by what we do. Sinai calls us to action, to moral awakening, to living constantly with challenges of building a moral and just society which mirrors the kingdom of God in history. Sinai creates humility and openness to the demands of self-tran-

scendence. In this respect, it is the antithesis of the moral narcissism that can result from suffering and from viewing oneself as a victim. Because of Sinai, Jewish suffering did not create self-pity but moral sensitivity: "And you shall love the stranger because you were strangers in the land of Egypt."

Hartman concludes, "Auschwitz, like all Jewish suffering of the past, must be absorbed and understood within the normative framework of Sinai. We will mourn forever because of the memory of Auschwitz. We will build a healthy new society because of the memory of Sinai."

In the three-plus decades that have passed since Hartman wrote that, that absorption has begun to occur. Where I differ—and he could not have possibly known this back then—is in the recognition that Auschwitz is bringing something positive to the table, or at least something authentic, that has utterly transformed Sinai in the process of that absorption.

Hartman's and Neusner's ideas still resonate, but as the decades have passed, the *Torah of Auschwitz* has taken root to the point where it now is no longer joined at the hip to Zionism, and the idea of Israel as Auschwitz's redemptive antidote has become increasingly problematic for many.

Additionally, while Auschwitz resides at the core of the new generation's Judaism, it has taken on different shades of meaning. Just as the exodus from Egypt must be reinterpreted *b'chol dor vador* (in every generation), so must the Shoah. As the immediacy of the event recedes, the bitterness is dissipating. New generations are grappling with Auschwitz in new ways, with added irony and even with humor. It is hard to imagine anyone coming to reaffirm joy through these darkened binoculars, but that is precisely what is taking place. The Judaism of Sinai and the Judaism of Auschwitz are merging, resulting in new visions of Judaism that are only beginning to take shape. Our perceptions of God are being transformed in the process, as are Jewish holidays like Passover and Yom Kippur and values like social action, environmentalism, peoplehood, Israel, intermarriage and the shifting boundaries between Jews and non-Jews.

In this light, I don't view this new, post-Holocaust vision as a reinforcement of Jewish peoplehood, particularity and exclusivism. In that sense I agree with religion scholar Shaul Magid, who has written masterfully about Judaism as now being "post-ethnic." But I do see an important place for peoplehood in the *Torah of Auschwitz*, as well as possibilities for greater solidarity among Jews, which I explain in chapter 12. What I reject is when peoplehood and Holocaust become synonymous with victimization.

While the Holocaust continues to be a tool for demagogues to manipulate and Chicken Littles to fundraise, and while memorials and museums often exploit it to promote narrow agendas, something else is happening. No longer does Auschwitz appear as a phenomenon grafted onto the imagination— like a tattoo on our souls. Now that tattoo appears to have been there since birth, a natural projection of who we are and how we look at the world, our inherited collective memory.

It's part of us.

Each of the chapters of this book outlines an aspect of this work-in-progress, this *Torah of Auschwitz*, and we will see just how the ways of Sinai are being recast, the old wells re-dug.

Abraham Joshua Heschel, perhaps the greatest Jewish visionary of the post-Holocaust era, who escaped Europe and bridged the Torahs of Sinai and Auschwitz, said two things of particular significance to this book. The first was the call from his masterpiece of biblical exposition, *The Prophets*: "In a free society, some are guilty; all are responsible." No statement better sums up the clash of civilizations between what the Nazis stood for and what Judaism demands. Contrast it to Hitler's rant freeing humanity from the restraints of a "falsehood called conscience and morality," and the battle lines are clearly drawn. The *Torah of Auschwitz* stands, like the Jewish people itself, as a living refutation of Hitler's pathological nihilism. To remember the Holocaust without a social conscience is not to remember it at all. As Elie Wiesel said in his Nobel acceptance speech, "Wherever men or women are persecuted because of their race, religion, or political views, that place must—at that moment—become the center of the universe."

The second Heschel quote, with which I opened this book, paraphrases the nineteenth Rebbe of Kotzk, whose life-embracing brand of Hasidism enabled shell-shocked Jews to take the already hostile Polish landscape and turn it into an incubator of spiritual growth and enchantment:

"There are three ways in which we respond to sorrow. On the first level, we cry; on the second level, we are silent; on the highest level, we take sorrow and turn it into song." And Heschel adds, "The love of life despite its absurdity holds out the certainty of a meaning that transcends our understanding."

Jewish survival will not be assured until the grandchildren of survivors and others of their generation can begin to take the darkness of the Shoah and turn it into a song, absorbing the absurdity of a silent God while loving life nonetheless. That would be the most fitting memorial to the martyrs and a guarantee that their precious memory will be preserved. It's precisely what's happening right now—and considering the state of our world, not a moment too soon.

This book takes the spirit of the *March of the Living* and applies it to the Holocaust as a whole. The Holocaust is no longer an unbearable burden but a source for instruction, inspiration and even exuberance. The words of Ecclesiastes have never been more apt: There is "a time to weep, and a time to laugh: a time to mourn, and a time to dance."

The time to weep is ending; the time to dance has begun.

So now, let's carefully open up the *Torah of Auschwitz* to see what wonders await us on its sacred pages.

Chapter Two

THE BOOK OF SURVIVAL
The Candy Man and Elijah Girl

In mid-August of 2017, one of the most remarkable news stories I've ever seen came across the wires. The oldest person in the world—Guinness-certified as the oldest for over a year—had died at the advanced age of 113. He would have turned 114 just a few weeks later. His name was Yisrael Kristal, and Yisrael lived in Israel. A nice touch, but none of that is what was most remarkable.

He had celebrated his "bar mitzvah plus-100" a year before, when he turned 113, which *also* was not the most remarkable thing. In fact, this second bar mitzvah was really his first, because when he had turned thirteen a hundred years before, during World War I, his mother had just died and his father was fighting in the Russian army. Oh, and he was observant and prayed every morning after his thirteenth birthday. Amazing—but still not the most amazing thing.

Yisrael also had a sweet tooth and made a living running a candy factory in Haifa. And in his younger years, he had owned a candy factory in Lodz. During the Holocaust, he was the candy man of the Lodz ghetto. Remarkable.

But here's what's most amazing. Yisrael Kristal, the world's oldest man, was a survivor of Auschwitz. When he was liberated, he weighed all of 81 pounds. His wife died there and his children died in Lodz, but he survived, moved to Israel and began a new life. Like a modern-day Job, he married again, had more children, died "old and full of days," and he felt so blessed that he never stopped praying—which, come to think of it, might be just as remarkable as his having survived Auschwitz.

Deuteronomy, chapter 30, presents us with a stark choice:

> "See, I set before you today life and prosperity, death and destruction…life and death, blessings and curses. Now *choose life*, so that you and your children may live…For the Lord is your life…" (Deut. 30:19)

Curiously, "Choose life!" is not listed among the 613 Commandments of the Torah as delineated by Maimonides in the twelfth century. Some similar laws are included in the list, including the injunctions against murder and standing idly by if someone's life is in danger, but not "Choose life." Rabbi Eliot Kukla has noted, "When the Torah states that God puts life and death before us, our tradition is not telling us to decide whether to live or die, but that every choice we make from birth to death matters. These choices range from how we treat our loved ones to how we spend money; from whom we bring into our world view, to how we choose our food. In each of these choices, we should choose life."

Here's where the *Torah of Auschwitz* veers from the Torah of Sinai's path. It's all well and good to speak of life-*affirming* activities; or that, as my teachers Rabbis Yitz Greenberg and Neil Gillman taught me, the ultimate goal of Judaism is to defeat death and enable life to emerge triumphant.

But the *Torah of Auschwitz* takes that gem of advice from Deuteronomy 30 and interprets it in the manner more akin to Woody Allen, who wrote, "I don't want to achieve immortality through my work; I want to achieve immortality through *not dying*. I don't want to live on in the hearts of my countrymen; I want to live on in my apartment."

The *Torah of Auschwitz* teaches that "Choose life!" calls upon us *literally* to choose life in the face of death, to seek the path that will engender survival, despite any odds, and that survival itself is victory. It goes beyond simply making each moment of life as full as possible, as Psalm 90 implores: "Teach us to count our days that we may gain a heart of wisdom." The *Torah of Auschwitz* goes beyond that, imploring us simply to add to life by continuing to live, and thereby make our lives into a statement of persistence and courage.

Everything was laid out for Yisrael Kristal to make such a choice; he had seen the pinnacle and the nadir of human potential. Having been born three months before the Wright Brothers' first flight, he had witnessed remarkable progress. But he had also borne witness to the world's darkest hours; and yet, despite it all, *he chose life*. He was lucky to live, very lucky, surviving not only Auschwitz, but wars, pogroms and the Lodz ghetto—not to mention all that the state that bears his name has endured for the past seven decades. But he could easily have allowed himself to die. Instead, Yisrael chose life. And not just life—but life with a cherry on top.

What was the secret of his survival? Maybe it was his chosen profession.

For Yisrael, life literally was a box of chocolates. And his grandson noted that when Yisrael was twelve, during World War I, he was also a booze smuggler: "He used to run barefoot in the snow for miles every night, smuggling alcohol between the lines of the war."

Is it conceivable that the living hell that was Auschwitz propelled this man to cherish life so much that he could break through the physiological barriers of a normal life span and become the oldest living human? Could a man who was larger than life have been propelled to fame by having to survive a place that was darker than death?

The Holocaust is filled with remarkable stories of survival, even among those whose survival may have been temporary, people who are exemplars of what it means to choose life.

Although his story of survival is extraordinary on an individual level, Yisrael is also a fitting symbol for the entire Jewish people, not only because of his extraordinary perseverance, his yen for sweetness and the fact that his name also became the very name of the Jewish state, but because of an additional ironic twist involving his name. In August of 1938, the Nazis enacted the "Executive Order on the Law on the Alteration of Family and Personal Names," requiring all German Jews bearing first names of "non-Jewish" origin to adopt an additional name: "Israel" for men and "Sara" for women. German Jews were required to carry identity cards with those names, and then, in the autumn of 1938, all Jewish passports were stamped with an identifying red letter "J." The name that later came to be emblematic of Jewish singularity, Israel, was employed by the Nazis to rob Jews of their individuality, to make it easier later to isolate them and herd them into ghettos for eventual liquidation. "Israel," the brand of death, later became the trademark of rebirth. Yisrael Kristal survived it all, and through it all, he just kept on making candy.

After seven decades of grief for what was lost—and so much was—Yisrael's tale of triumph over tragedy, of life over death, is an early indication that the Holocaust narrative is beginning to shift, from a story of abject despair to one of astonishing, incredible and miraculous (though not necessarily divinely ordained) survival.

Yisrael Kristal might be *Exhibit A* that, for the Jewish people, at least, what doesn't kill us makes us stronger.

Exhibit B is Rywka Lipszyc, a 14-year old Jewish girl, orphaned and surviving in the Lodz ghetto. From October 1943 to April 1944, she recorded her thoughts, feelings, hopes and dreams in a diary. Along with 67,000 other inhabitants of the Lodz ghetto, Rywka was deported to Auschwitz-Birkenau in August 1944. Nearly a year later, in June 1945, her diary was found in the ashes of the crematoria by a Soviet army doctor.

Like Anne Frank, Rywka was a simple teenager living a simple teenage life. But Anne Frank wrote from the relative safety of her secret annex in Amsterdam—and although that security was fleeting, it could not compare to the hell that Rywka endured in Lodz.

The 112-page diary details Rywka's activities at work and in school, her relationships with her friends and family and events in the ghetto. Despite the devastating conditions she confronted, Rywka wrote poetry, participated in literary clubs, kept studying and focused her aspirations on a time when things would get better—and on her own maturation process. In entry after entry, this remarkable resolve, this true grit, is played out in the frail body of this fourteen-year-old. As she wrote in an entry dated March 7: "I've fallen… or rather I'm falling. I have to lift myself up. It's important."

Much of the diary dwells on everyday activities, the nobility of normalcy. But there are times when her ability to find light in the darkest of nights is absolutely stunning. In one entry, she talks about a book she is currently reading, Victor Hugo's *Les Misérables*. As I read this, I was sitting there wondering whether the dark world of Hugo's Parisian sewer system was somehow escapism for her. Did she see herself as starring in some sort of sequel? Did she imagine herself as young Cosette, waiting for her Jean Valjean to come and rescue her?

The next day, March 5, she thinks of her mother and begins to well up. "I can't write because of my tears," she exclaims. "Oh, I'm suffocating. I'm choking. My dear God, what will happen to me?" Then she immediately collects herself. "Enough. It's always the same. I have to do an examination of conscience…to persevere."

On April 11, 1944, she writes:

"Thank you, God, for the spring! Thank you for this mood! I don't want to write about it, because I don't want to mess it up, but I'll write one very significant word: hope!"

That passage is just under 140 characters long—maybe the most inspirational pre-Twitter tweet ever. This was at a time when she was still deeply grieving the loss of both her parents.

Here's her final entry, written the very next day:

"At moments like this I want to live so much. There is less sadness, but we're more aware of our miserable circumstances, our souls are sad and… really one needs a lot of strength not to give up. We look at this wonderful world, this beautiful spring, and at the same time we see ourselves in the ghetto being deprived of everything…. How hard it is! Oh God, how much longer? I think that only when we are liberated will we enjoy a real spring. Oh, I miss this dear spring."

That's where it ends.

We know that Rywka survived Lodz and that she also survived Auschwitz. Then she survived the death march to Bergen-Belsen and she lived to see the liberation. She was too ill to be evacuated, however, and the record of her life ends.

Her final whereabouts remains a mystery, which perhaps is as it should be. Her name last pops up in records of a hospital in Germany. So, who knows? Like the immortal prophet Elijah, Rywka may still be among us, hopping from Seder to Seder, looking for her mother. Her diary's recovery was itself miraculous—her own survival would be even more so.

Rywka's diary's publication itself tells an inspirational tale. In the spring of 1945, a Red Army doctor was rummaging around the ruins of the crematoria at Auschwitz-Birkenau. She bent down and discovered the diary among the ashes. After the war, she took it with her to her home in remote Siberia, stashed it away, and it remained with her until her death in 1983. Her son took her possessions to his apartment in Moscow, where the diary stayed with him until he died in 1992 and then it remained with his wife after that. Their daughter, who had emigrated to San Francisco, found the diary during a 1995 visit back home. She immediately understood its significance and brought it back with her to the States, where, after a long and convoluted process, in 2015, exactly 70 years after it was discovered, the astonishing diary of fourteen-year-old Rywka Lypszyc was published in English translation.

Rywka's long-lost diary was found—and with its publication, Rywka's name was redeemed from oblivion.

In another entry, Rywka writes:

"A few years ago, in my dreams, when I was imagining my future, I could see sometimes: an evening, a studio, a desk, there is a woman sitting at the desk (an older woman), she's writing…and writing, and writing…all the time…she forgets about her surroundings, she's writing. I can see myself as this woman…. Some other time I can see: an evening, a modest room with lights, all my family sitting at the table. It's so nice…so warm, cozy…Oh, it's so good! Later, when they all go to bed, I sit at the sewing machine and I'm sewing…sewing…it's *so sweet*, so good…so delightful!"

Seeing sweetness in life seems to be a key to survival, for Rywka, as for Yisrael.

Dan Barber, a chef and writer, writes about an experiment he ran on a special kind of vegetable, a Mokum carrot, which he was able to grow outdoors in the middle of cold, cold February. When it was ripe, he ran something called a Brix test, which measures the sugar content. It came to 13.8. He compared it to an organic carrot purchased from a Whole Foods, presumably grown in a much less hostile environment. That carrot measured 0.0. on the same scale.

No sugar detectable.

Why such a dramatic difference? He explains that the carrot is feverishly converting its starches to sugars because, in those hard freezes, it doesn't want ice crystallization.

And why is that?

Because if it gets ice crystallization, it dies.

"What you're tasting is sweetness," he states. "But what the plant, the root vegetable is telling you, is that it doesn't want to die."

Talk about mindful eating. Maybe that's why Jews make such big *tzimmis* about *tzimmis*, the consummate carrot casserole eaten especially on the High Holidays, a time when, tradition has it, our lives hang in the balance. The sweetness we're tasting is survival itself.

Have you ever noticed how the sweetest things are produced under the greatest duress? The State of Israel has never known a single day of complete peace. Yet perennially it lands near the top of all the nations in the world in the happiness index, most recently eleventh out of 156 countries. The US places fourteenth. Basically, ahead of Israel, you've got Australia, New Zealand, Canada and the nations of Scandinavia, where the closest they've come to war in recent decades was when Prince Hans Westergaard tried to usurp the throne of Arendelle in "Frozen."

And then you have Israel: calamitous, terror-filled, polarized Israel, with the crazy bus drivers and rude bank clerks. It's also the country where the tomatoes are more flavorful, the falafel crispier, the sunsets more spectacular, the people more welcoming, the children more playful and life is simply sweeter.

We appreciate life more when we see how fragile life is, then take those lessons and photosynthesize them into love. That same proclivity for sweetness was the key to candy man Yisrael Kristal's longevity and the orphaned Rywka's resolutely positive perspective.

Psalm 115 asserts "The dead do not praise the Lord, neither do those who go down in silence." It is only by staying alive that one can praise. And Psalm 150 adds, "All who have breath praise God." That exclamatory verse from Deuteronomy 30, calling on us to *choose life,"* adds, in the next phrase, "*Ki Hu Hayyecha.*" "For God *is* life."

If you take any prayer and substitute the term "Life Force" for "God," you end up with a palatable post-Holocaust theology. After the Holocaust, many can no longer believe in the same God that our great grandparents believed in. Elie Wiesel in his book *Night* echoes the notion shared by many, that the God of Sinai died at Auschwitz. But perhaps a different understanding of God was born there. Perhaps God's essence can be seen in this life force, this unfathomable survival instinct, as expressed through each breath.

I'll propose more ways we can imagine God post-Holocaust in future chapters, but for now, let me assert simply that if God can be associated with the sheer will to live, then Yisrael Kristal and Rywka Lipszyc are God's prophets—as are so many survivors.

Choosing life doesn't come without cost. Many survivors have lived with an immeasurable degree of guilt. Those feelings are understandable, but for those of us who were born after the guns went silent, we are in awe of their resilience. The label "survivor" is not a mark of shame, even if for many years after 1945 few chose to share their experiences. Their persistence is a badge of courage, the likes of which the world has never seen. Wiesel's God may have died in the crematoria, but through that incomprehensible life force, something sacred lives on in those who somehow survived.

Psalm 126, speaking of survivors returning from a prior genocidal onslaught, the Babylonian exile, states, "Those who sow in tears will reap in joy." The Hebrew word *zorim* is derived from *zera*, or "seed," and it could plausibly be speaking not of sowing crops, but of sexual procreation. I never cease to be amazed at how those who survived the lowest episode in human history could somehow have had the spiritual wherewithal, the audacious *chutzpah,* to marry and have children. Why bring kids into a world like this? Why *choose* to procreate? Why, given all that they had seen, would a survivor not stop at simply "choosing life," but also choose to make that choice for a new generation, to continue life beyond their own lives?

So the *Torah of Auschwitz* interprets that verse from Psalms anew:

Those who procreate in tears shall witness the end of their suffering, as they reap the sweet joy of their first fruits, and against all odds, a life imbued with hope continues with a new generation.

And we can now understand Deuteronomy 30:19 from the perspective of the survivor: *"Choose life, so that you and your children may live."* For the survivor, the directive is to choose life in the most literal sense, by having children.

Here's one more way the commandment from Deuteronomy 30, to "choose life," plays out in the *Torah of Auschwitz*: through the survival of Yisrael—not Yisrael Kristol the individual—but through Israel the collective, the Jewish people.

In the *Torah of Auschwitz*, when Jews proclaim *Am Yisrael Chai*, "the people of Israel lives!" it is no longer merely an amusing circle dance popularized at bar mitzvahs and solidarity rallies. *Am Yisrael Chai* has become an *imperative*, a collective fulfillment of the commandment to "Choose Life," a mission to keep the Jewish people afloat, against all odds.

We are seeing that play out in our day.

One of the highlights of my congregation's 2017 pilgrimage to Central Europe was our encounter with the Jewish community of Budapest. We joined with one of the city's most active congregations, the Frankel Synagogue, for a Friday night service, and before that, we spent about a half hour conversing with Rabbi Tamas Vero and his wife, author and educator Linda Vero Ban. The congregation comes from a branch of Judaism unique to central Europe, called Neolog—sort of a fruit salad of Orthodox and Conservative Judaism.

We came away from that evening amazed at the vibrancy of the community—and equally concerned for its future. Before the Shoah, nearly a quarter of Budapest's population was Jewish. But during the war, of the more than 800,000 Jews living in Hungary, nearly 620,000 died or were deported. In Budapest, Jews had a somewhat better chance of survival at first, until the notorious Arrow Cross—those rabid Hungarian nationalists who tried to out-Nazi the Nazis—took over, herded Jews into the ghetto beginning in December 1944, took as many as 20,000 out to the banks of the Danube, shot them and threw their bodies into the river. We saw the memorial that has been set up right by the riverbank, a sculpture depicting the shoes that were left behind. It's exceedingly moving, but equally problematic, because the memorial does not specify that the victims were Jewish.

The current Jewish population is about 100,000—they think. That number is based on those who have received reparations for the Holocaust. But no one really knows, because the majority of Jews are afraid to be identified. They remain in the closet, at times literally, because many still remember hiding there from that proverbial knock on the door. While physical attacks are rare, anti-Semitism is plainly practiced by the extreme right-wing government and is embedded in the culture. Vandalism of Jewish gravestones and synagogues is commonplace. While we were there, the government rolled out a nationwide anti-Semitic poster campaign scapegoating the Hungarian born Jewish financier George Soros. I asked the rabbi whether he wears a kippah in public, and he said no. Most Jewish children encounter anti-Semitism in school from a youthful age. The word "Jewish" is often used as a curse word in the vernacular.

And then, beyond the pervasive anti-Semitism, there is Jewish illiteracy. After the Nazis were defeated in 1945, the country was "liberated" into nearly half a century of communist rule, where anyone living an openly Jewish lifestyle was subject to ridicule and discrimination. After the horrors of Auschwitz, most Hungarian Jews had little place for God in their lives anyway, so while the practice of Judaism wasn't expressly *forbidden*, it was for all intents and purposes *forgotten*.

Yet despite all this, what we saw during our visit was remarkable: Jewish life is rising in Budapest like a phoenix from the ashes.

There is a thriving summer camp called Szarvas near the city, which serves Jewish communities all over Europe. Some campers recall being dropped off and asking their parents why they were being sent to a Jewish camp. At that point, the parents would tell them, while driving off, "By the way, you're Jewish."

The Shabbat service at the synagogue was one of our most cherished moments on the trip. There were a number of young families with kids there—well over a hundred people in all. The rabbi mentioned that very few Jewish groups from America visit them, so they were curious to meet their guests. Most Jewish tours of Eastern Europe only visit the dead; we were determined to visit living communities too. We were there to tell the Jews of Budapest that they are not alone.

And at the end of the service, we joined together to chant the Sabbath table prayers typically done at home. So why were they being done at the synagogue, even though there was no meal? Because, the rabbi explained to me, few of the congregants know how to do Shabbat at home.

In Deuteronomy 32:7, Moses instructs the Israelites, "Ask your father and he will tell you, your elders and they will explain." But for Hungarian Jews, there are often no grandparents to ask, because most were murdered by the Nazis or Arrow Cross. Even more to the point, Budapest's Jews don't do the rituals at home because so many are *afraid* to. Their Jewish lives are confined to their synagogue, a building so heavily barricaded that it is not visible from the street. The *Torah of Auschwitz* would amend that verse from Deuteronomy, to this:

Ask your elder how they somehow were able to survive. If you encourage them patiently and gently, eventually—hopefully—they will explain.

Despite all the challenges placed before them, the Jews of Hungary have survived, like those legendary gingko trees that somehow withstood the nuclear attack on Hiroshima and thrive there to this day. How did the gingkoes manage to overcome the fallout of a nuclear blast? It's because they have very deep roots.

Jewish roots are unnaturally deep as well.

Any other people would have given up after the Shoah, but I saw in Budapest that the Hungarian Jews have chosen life. They have opted to see *Am Yisrael Chai* not as a song, but as a summons.

In the *Torah of Auschwitz*, Deuteronomy 30 is a clarion call:

Choose life, because actual physical survival is victory.

"Who shall live and who shall die?" is a refrain constantly repeated during the High Holidays. Well, we know that we're all going to die, eventually. It's like the Buddhist coroner who lost her job because, when she was filling out the forms, whenever she came to "cause of death," she would write, "birth."

But for the Jewish coroner, the cause of death would better be put as "heroic struggle against impossible odds."

It is now a commandment for the Jewish people to live, not to spite Hitler, but to teach the world what Hitler did—and to guarantee that it doesn't happen again. It is essential to the future of the world that Jews survive—in order to tell our story.

Choose life, so that you—and all of humanity—may live.

At a small museum in Krakow that displays photos and artifacts from the formerly thriving Jewish communities of Poland, there is a photo of a stone tablet, similar to decorative tablets that were quite common in synagogues throughout Poland before the war. It says, in Hebrew, a verse from Psalm 16: *Shiviti Adonai l'negdi tamid,* "I have set God before me always."

What makes this find so important is that this is the only such pre-war tablet to have survived intact in Polish Galicia.

What makes it so astonishing is that this simple, pure statement of faith and continuity, the only one to have survived intact, this gingko tree (and Yisrael Kristol) of unbroken decorative stone tablets, a stone tablet that not even the Nazis could destroy—nor Moses, for that matter, the all-time tablet shatterer, who destroyed the tablets of Sinai at the slightest provocation—*this* tablet was found at the last remaining synagogue in the pretty, tree-lined Polish countryside town of Oświęcim.

You might know its German name: Auschwitz.

Just one mile from the hell that nearly destroyed the Jewish people and all of human civilization, somehow this reminder of a bygone, simpler era withstood the fallout of the moral detonation that took place right down the street. Maybe the discovery of this preserved tablet teaches us that in the *Torah of Auschwitz*, Psalm 16 is calling on us to place *Auschwitz itself* before us always. No, not the place of death and destruction, but the place of renewal and hope, the place that now exists to forever remind us where hate ultimately leads, the place visited by more people every year than were killed there, the place of pilgrimage for heads of state and leaders of all faith traditions—and a place where thousands of Jewish youth congregate every year for Jewish youth's annual Spring Awakening, the *March of the Living*.

That Auschwitz.

For thousands of years, the holiest place for Jews has been the very spot where one of the Bible's most infamous, shocking acts occurred, Abraham's near murder of his son, Isaac. Later legends countered that image with stories of selfless fraternal love taking place on that exact spot; but the tip of Abraham's knife remains at the heart of Moriah's power. In the Holocaust, one third of the Jewish people were murdered. If Abraham had succeeded in his reflex-driven "I follow orders" deed, the yield of victims would have been one hundred percent. The entire Jewish future would have been wiped out.

But it was on that very spot of infamy that God was seen for the first time. The location of Isaac's binding was renamed *Adonai Yir'eh*, "The Place Where God is Seen." And it was on that very spot that the Temple was later built.

From catastrophe comes sanctity.

In the *Torah of Auschwitz*, perhaps Auschwitz *itself* must be the place where a true divine vision can best be seen—not the Auschwitz that existed in 1944 but the Auschwitz that today exists for the sole purpose of remembering that prior incarnation. In "placing God before us always," Psalm 16 can now be a reminder that the lessons of the Holocaust must reside eternally before our eyes.

We are all survivors—and maybe God is a survivor too. But after Auschwitz, perhaps the God of Psalm 16, the one whom we place before us, is survival itself, that life force that drives us to breathe and to love and to find hope among the ashes, if only we will choose life.

In the *Torah of Auschwitz*, the life force is embodied by an innocent, precious girl, whose diary was found next to the crematorium—the frail girl who lost both parents in Lodz and had little chance of living, but who allowed a gorgeous spring day to supplant her gloom. The Jewish knack for survival is embodied in that fragile fourteen-year-old who survived Lodz AND Auschwitz AND the death march AND Bergen-Belsen—and, in our dreams, at least, this young Cosette may still be alive today.

In the *Torah of Auschwitz*, Rywka Lipszyc is our new Elijah, a prophet who attained his status in Jewish folklore in large part because in the Bible he is never recorded to have died. Rywka is now the one to visit every Seder, even if she is still under age for the wine. She is the one to make us care about the lonely and the forgotten, while she searches longingly and innocently for her mother, like the baby bird in P.D. Eastman's beloved children's book.

Rywka wrote these wise words in her diary, words that I believe complement Anne Frank's assertion, "Despite everything, I still believe that people are really good at heart."

Rywka wrote:

"I am just a tiny spot, even under a microscope I would be very hard to see—but I can laugh at the whole world because I am a Jew. I am poor and in the ghetto, I do not know what will happen to me tomorrow, and yet I can laugh at the whole world because I have something very strong supporting me—my faith."

Whether or not she is still alive, Rywka has had the last laugh on her tormentors. Whether she is still alive, she *chose* life, and she is directing our gaze, with hope, to the future—which is exactly what the Holocaust is at long last able to help us do.

We place life before us always, ever mindful of the gift that is life and the responsibility that survival implies. Survival is victory only if we earn it, by translating it into a life of service. And if we do, Yisrael Kristal, that 113-year-old modern Methuselah would tell us, that life, in the end, is like a box of chocolates.

You never know what you're gonna get. But survival sure is sweet.

The Candy Man and Elijah Girl have taught us to thoroughly enjoy every bite, anticipating with mouthwatering expectancy whatever will come next.

So, we have our first commandment: Choose Life!

But as we begin to unscroll the *Torah of Auschwitz*, beyond this Book of Survival, we need to unpack the complex relationship Jews have had with a tormented history. We need to peek at the dark side of the Jewish psyche to perceive the light that is beginning to seep back in.

Chapter Three

THE BOOK OF DARKNESS AND LIGHT
The Mark of Abel

On a Tuesday morning in the late summer of 1999, my synagogue's executive director pulled me from the hall into her office, her face drooping and troubled. "There is something in our parking lot," she said. "A package of medical waste with swastikas." Together we walked out to the corner of the lot, where our custodians had already cordoned off the area with traffic cones, as if to contain the contamination, not so much of the bloody syringes but those dastardly drawings. The swastikas were crudely scribbled in marker, small, almost dainty spiders, like the stick-figure drawings a first grader brings home. I counted two or three—I couldn't get close enough to know for sure. I didn't want to.

Only later did I feel the anger. My first sensation, astonishingly, was just the opposite. For the first time in my life, I felt utterly connected to the essence of the Jewish condition. Suddenly the eternal dialogue between God and the Jewish people now ran through me. I was no longer a bystander. I had become, in the eyes of at least one crazed individual, the Other.

Finally, it had happened.

"At last we meet," I thought. "I've been waiting for you."

All my life I'd read the stories and seen the pictures of anti-Semitism, but had never experienced it so close at hand. I'd heard the ravings of the haters and even invited their websites into my home. Jewish suffering long ago had become a part of me, even though I had hardly suffered myself. I walk with the slightly hunched look of an ex-slave. I'd learned the shrug, the Jewish shrug with eyes slightly raised heavenward, which has helped us to shoulder the pain, and at times even laugh a little in spite of it. I'd spoken to other rabbis who have had the evil insignia spray-painted on their synagogues, or worse. If it wasn't to be my Jewish rite of passage to experience hate firsthand at some point, at least I figured it to be a rabbinic one. At last, there it was, the Angel of Death in the corner of my synagogue's parking lot, in the form of a pathetic scribbled swastika.

Others wait for lady luck to come their way. Jews wait for the black spider.

Recall that world of mid-1999. It was a summer of fear all across America, but particularly for Jews. In the shadow of the Columbine massacre (it's hard to recall when school shootings were rare and unspeakable atrocities) lurked the figure of Dylan Klebold, grandchild of proud Jewish community benefactors in Ohio who became not a Jew but a hater of Jews, who admired Hitler and white supremacists. Then there was Buford Furrow, who attempted to murder Jewish preschoolers in Granada Hills, Calif., then proudly turned himself in proclaiming, "I killed the Jewish children." To those outrages were added the torching of synagogues in Sacramento and Long Island.

Within hours of the discovery, TV trucks from Hartford and New York filled the parking lot. I began receiving calls of condolence and support from fellow clergy and politicians—sincere, heartrending expressions of sadness and regret. I received a letter of stunning humility and shock from Bishop Edward Egan, then based in Bridgeport, who followed up with a personal phone call. The local interfaith council immediately organized a rally of community support for local Jews. Hundreds of people came to the event, and community leaders and pastors signed a scroll of tolerance that was presented to my congregation. The chief of police vowed to upgrade patrols as the High Holy Days approached. No efforts would be spared to apprehend the fiend.

I was exceedingly moved by these gestures. I recall sitting at the rally listening to the speeches of love and support for Jews, imagining how history could have been changed if this same scene had played out in Germany in 1933. Not to compare Heidelberg and Munich to my neighboring communities of Greenwich and Darien, but I could not help but wonder how miraculous it is—and how simple—that former bastions of prejudice can so quickly be turned into citadels of sympathy. It was if the person who intended to defile our sacred space had instead brought about a mass communal exercise in atonement.

I accepted these condolences numbly, uncomfortably. I didn't feel that I had suffered a loss. On the contrary, I felt at last complete, utterly at one with the Jewish experience. The pain I felt was not so much for myself as for those in my congregation who had seen this spider before, at mid-century, during its terrifying initial run as a symbol of doom. I'm sure most of my Christian friends could not imagine a scenario where they would see such a blatant message of hate on their front doors. What they didn't understand is that long ago in Hebrew school I had learned how to imagine the unimaginable—and to expect it.

At last, I was one with Anne Frank, Alfred Dreyfus and Natan Sharansky. I was a victim, which in turn gave me license to choose—and to hate—a villain.

Dancing with Amalek

Four days after the incident, by which point the news caravan had followed the black spider to another synagogue somewhere else, I sat at services trying to make sense of the last section of the Torah read that day, describing the great evil done to Israel in the wilderness by the rogue nation Amalek. There we read that we are to remember what Amalek did to us, never to forget to blot out their name. Up until now I had considered this a summons to arms, imploring Jews to wage an eternal war against evil. But I now understood that the old commandment from Sinai had a new twist.

In fact, *zachor*, which means "remember," can be understood in a number of ways (as I'll demonstrate in upcoming chapters): one way is to see it not as a commandment at all, though it appears to be one in Deuteronomy 25:17 and it is counted as such on Maimonides' list of 613 commandments. In the *Torah of Auschwitz*, it can be seen as both condemnation and a shrugging acceptance of our dreaded destiny to remember—not out of obligation, but as an existential necessity. For we know that, no matter what we do, Amalek won't let us forget Amalek. Lest I might have forgotten about that dreaded embodiment of evil, the spider was there to remind me. Lest my most assimilated congregants might have tried to forget; the spider was there to call them back to the fold.

The swastika isn't just among us—it is part of what makes us, *us*.

For Jews, the swastika has become our national tattoo, burned into our souls like the number on a survivor's arm. It is spray-painted on the doorposts of our homes and upon our gates. It is our hovering Angel of Death. We are a people born of blood on a door in ancient Egypt. We now subsist hand in hand with bloody syringes and Amalek's blood-stained hands.

Wherever we look, the evil is there. The passage is not "You shall remember what Amalek did," but rather, "You *will* remember, because you'll have no choice," for Amalek has never ceased its murderous activity and we have never ceased resisting it.

What the *mezuzah* was to the Torah of Sinai, the swastika has become to the *Torah of Auschwitz*, in a perverse, inverse fashion—a talisman of fear rather than a sign of our escape from the Destroyer, who in Egypt passed over those doorposts marked in lamb's blood. Jews mark that bloody spot with a *mezuzah*, while anti-Semites scrawl a swastika. One chases evil away, the other invites it in. (Stay tuned, because in chapter 11, I'll present an entirely different slant on the swastika.)

Does this give a victory to the haters, to allow their swastikas to torture us so? No, the victory is not theirs; they are not the ones who ordained that this tortured dance continue through the ages, from the days of Moses until today. It's not Amalek's fault that Amalek is still among us and that we suffer from this particularly Jewish form of arachnophobia.

Nor is it *our* fault—it is our *fate*. As King Saul discovered in his day and Mordechai in his, there is something in the very nature of the universe that won't allow us to destroy Amalek completely, even if we could. For we know, deep inside, that the day Amalek truly departs from the scene, the dance will be over, that Paschal blood on the door will become dry, brittle and meaningless, and the Jewish people will, devoid of their eternal foil, disappear.

The blood in my parking lot has long since been washed away, and the container with the swastikas has presumably been destroyed. The place was sterilized, but the stain just won't disappear, this indelible Mark of Abel, the everlasting badge of victimhood.

Yet there is something about it all that was comforting for me, at last to have joined in the dance with Amalek.

There is, however, more to this story.

Several weeks after the incident, the perpetrator was apprehended—and shockingly, he turned out to be a Jew. Not only that, but at one time he had been a member of my own congregation. Alan Lorenz was a salesman of containers used to dispose medical waste and, through some bizarre logic, he had apparently perpetrated this outrage as a publicity stunt to improve business.

When the arrest was made, I found myself in an awkward position. Demonizing an unknown perpetrator had enabled the community to come together as never before. So much good had come from this united crusade against this latter-day Amalek, the biblical incarnation of evil. And now Amalek, it turned out, was one of us.

But Amalek is always one of us, I realized, because something of Amalek resides within each of us. The biblical Amalek, in fact, was Esau's grandson, the great great grandchild of Abraham and Sarah; therefore a member of the family, one who was explicitly rejected and turned away. The battle against hate is internal as much as external. Ironically, Lorenz was charged with the federal civil rights crime of obstructing persons in the free exercise of their religious beliefs. In fact, his act had brought people to a deepened awareness of their faith attachments. Service attendance had increased substantially after the incident.

He had also clarified for us the battle lines, redrawn every generation, between victim and villain. Everything was crystal clear; that is, until his identity became known. I could feel myself backpedaling as I told the local reporter that "we still must fight bias, whatever the source," but my discomfort was acute. It was embarrassing.

For Lorenz it was far worse. He sought and received psychiatric help. Acquaintances later informed me of his general instability and his distress over what had transpired. I never met him. Two years later, he died, an apparent suicide.

Long before the Holocaust, Jews were already a glass-half-empty people. Born of slavery, perpetually exiled and perennially hated, there is good reason for Jews to be prone to cynicism and despair. We have a dark side and it is not something that can be easily exorcised—this is a major lesson of the *Torah of Auschwitz*. But within the Jewish psyche there has always been a healing force, constantly striving to transform victim into vision, the Mark of Abel into the Mark of Able. That dynamic is always at work, as it was even during the darkest hours of the Holocaust itself.

The electrified fence

A BBC story appeared in 2014 about a group of about 300 deer living on the frontier between Germany and the Czech Republic. According to the report, fully a quarter of a century after the iron curtain fell, the deer still seem to believe there is an electrified fence spanning what is now a totally open frontier. You don't even need a passport to go from one country to the other. But, as confirmed by GPS-equipped collars placed on the herd, the German deer stay on the German side, the Czech deer stay on the Czech side, and never the twain shall meet. A biologist noted that this is remarkable because the average life expectancy for deer is 15 years—meaning that none living now would have encountered the barrier when it was operational.

The report adds that scientists believe that fawns tend to follow mothers for the first year of their lives and develop a pattern in their movements, so the same area remains the habitat for each new generation. It is so easy to remain the captive of ancient fears.

In Czechoslovakia, in the spring of 1944, not far from that same border, a young man named Michael Flack looked out toward the lovely, spring-like countryside surrounding Terezin and wrote:

> The sun has made a veil of gold
> So lovely that my body aches.
> Above, the heavens shriek with blue
> Convinced I've smiled by some mistake.
> The world's abloom and seems to smile.
> I want to fly but where, how high?
> If in barbed wire, things can bloom
> Why couldn't I? I will not die!

Behind an electrified fence, more than a generation ago, a young Jew dreamed of flight. The spirit of freedom never died within him. Like the deer thirsting for water witnessed by the author of Psalm 42, this imprisoned soul refused to allow his life force to succumb to grim realities.

Flack ran the children's home in Terezin, caring for about sixty children aged four to nine, many of them orphans or who had arrived in the ghetto without parents.

And now, a full human lifespan after the Holocaust, we ask ourselves, are we like Michael Flack, who looked around in the depths of hell and saw beauty and let his spirit soar?

Or are we like those deer in the floodlights, who, though they never themselves knew the pain of that barbed wire, confine themselves in a virtual prison, their souls imprisoned simply by force of habit? Is the Mark of Abel, the imprimatur of the victim, so indelible as to be eternally irreversible?

Two kinds of Jews and the *sitra achra*

Many years ago, the American Jewish activist Leonard Fein wrote that there are two kinds of Jews in the world:

There is the kind of Jew who detests war and violence, who believes that fighting is not the Jewish Way, who willingly accepts that Jews have their own and higher standards of behavior, and not just that we have them, but that those standards are our lifeblood, what we are about.

And then there is the kind of Jew who is convinced that we have been passive long enough, who is convinced that it is time to strike back at our enemies, to reject once and for all the role of victim, who will willingly accept that Jews cannot afford to depend on favors, that we must be tough and strong.

And the trouble is, Fein, added, that most Jews are both kinds of Jew.

At times we are like Michael Flack, allowing our spirits to soar with idealism and hope. And at times we are like the deer, weighed down by a burden of fear, a habit, by our anger, our feelings of victimhood, unable to transcend the shadows of the past.

A wise man once said, "If we had two hearts like we have two arms and two legs, then one heart could be used for love and the other one for hate. Since I have but one heart, then I don't have the luxury of hating anyone."

The challenge is not to be able to rid ourselves of this dark side, but to acknowledge it, recognize its allure and power, channel its destructive urges through the prism of wisdom and thereby ultimately to control it—not only to control it, but to use our experience to model for the world how to live positive lives while eternally dancing with Amalek.

The rabbis of the Talmud had a name for this, speaking of the *sitra achra*—literally the "other side," a force for ill within each of us that succumbs to temptation, greed, self-delusion and fear. We are advised to confront it head-on, much as Jacob wrestled with his dark side at the Jabbok River upon his return to Canaan. Only when we confront those demons can we become whole, though for Jacob that battle resulted in a permanently maimed hip. Only a wounded Jacob could become a spiritually healed and worthy "Israel." It's hardly a coincidence that *Star Wars* calls those who battle the dark side, "Jedi," which is basically the Hebrew word for Jew, inspired by the wise Yoda, whose name in Hebrew correlates to wisdom. Jews have been fighting their internal and external dark sides for a lot longer than Obi Wan Kenobi (and incidentally, Kenobi translates from Hebrew to "as a prophet.")

Once, when my family was visiting a national park out west, we were given some advice by a park ranger on what to do in the off chance that we encountered a bear or mountain lion: never run. Grab the children, put them on your shoulders, stand tall and wave your arms wildly. If it attacks, wrestle with it. Never run or the animal will catch you and kill you. That's easy for Mr. Ranger to say. But the same lesson holds true for this adversary called Amalek. It's important to confront our fears one-on-one, never to run and hide—because there really is nowhere to hide.

It's not easy to continue to dance when a third of your people was inciner-ated a generation ago. There have been many catastrophes in Jewish history, but Auschwitz was uniquely catastrophic. How could we possible wrestle against a *sitra achra* on steroids.

Jews are indeed a glass-half-empty people, a traumatized, damaged, per-petually neurotic, scared-of-our-shadow, groundhog nation. These qualities have coarsened over centuries of exile and persecution and the Holocaust has sealed it into our souls. There is no getting rid of it. But there's no getting rid of *us* either, and sometimes that fact alone is enough to help us confront the despair.

For the darkest part of the Jewish dark side is neither anger nor hate nor the thirst for vengeance, but fear itself. Just as we need to confront our innate hatred, we need to confront our inbred insecurities.

The Torah of Auschwitz commands us to come face to face with our darkest impulses, the hatred that persists toward the Other—and the fear that persists within ourselves.

When my family was touring Europe in 2004, we found ourselves a bit uncomfortable proclaiming our Jewishness in public. In this crazy world, well, you never know. Amazingly, even in Israel, our first stop, the official at immigration control seemed to understand the perpetual paranoia of the wandering Jew, offering to stamp a separate piece of paper rather than my passport. I would have none of it; I'm proud of the many Israeli stamps in my passport. It did occur to me, however, that the Israeli seal could become some sort of a scarlet letter in Europe.

Our next stop was Rome, where every time we said "Israel" in public, we had this irrational sensation that the entire place was looking at us, much like the old E.F. Hutton ads. So, we developed a strategy (our Jewish survival instincts at work): Whenever we wanted to say "Israel," we replaced it with "Ireland."

As in, "You know, the falafel we had in *Ireland* tasted much better than this."

"Yes, and I really miss Ireland right now. Especially the sunset over the golden walls of ... ah ... *Dublin*."

It became our own little secret code.

We were sitting next to a lovely couple one day at lunch while touring Pompeii. We asked where they were from and they replied, "We're from Ireland."

This threw us off completely and made me a little ashamed of our ruse. It's as if we were having an illicit affair with Israel. Just because the entire world seems to hate us, why should we hide?

We think of modern Jewish terror victims like Daniel Pearl and Nicholas Berg, who, like the Maccabean martyrs of old, proudly proclaimed their Jewishness despite the dangers.

Berg was a freelance radio tower repairman who was decapitated by terrorists in Iraq in 2004. Not only did he have an Israeli stamp in his passport when he went there, but according to family sources, he also brought his *tallit* and *tefillin* (phylacteries) with him. Friends spoke of his having developed a deeper interest in his Jewish faith, one that could possibly have fed his idealistic yearning to participate in Iraq's reconstruction before he met his brutal end.

Pearl, a journalist, was kidnapped and killed by Al Qaida in Pakistan in 2002. His last words, delivered on videotape before his neck was slit were an affirmation of his identity:

"My name is Daniel Pearl. I'm a Jewish American from Encino, California, USA. I come from, uh, on my father's side the family is Zionist. My father's Jewish, my mother's Jewish, I'm Jewish. My family follows Judaism. We've made numerous family visits to Israel."

If they could overcome the fear under the most extreme duress, so can we.

The Mezuzah Gouge

My squeamishness in Europe did not keep us from visiting Jewish sites. One was the old ghetto in Venice dating back to 1516. Very few Jews live there anymore, but many once did. You can tell because the doorposts are made of stone and you can still see which houses once had *mezuzahs*, those inscribed amulets affixed on the doorposts of most Jewish homes. There is a long, angular gouge in the stone where the *mezuzah* was affixed.

So, I went on a continent-wide hunt for *mezuzah* cavities, first in the ghetto, then across Venice and then everywhere else. I found scores of gouged-out *mezuzah* holes in plaster and stone and telltale indentations in wood. I began to notice distinctive styles—some longer, some thicker, some painted over, some plain.

All these houses shared two things: 1) Jews once lived there; and 2) Jews don't live there anymore.

It was depressing, until somewhere in Venice a smile crept upon my face, as I realized that even when the Jew is gone, the residue of Jewish life remains. I imagined some Venetian homebuyer moving into his new home and trying somehow to carve it away, to wipe off the damn *mezuzah* spot like Lady Macbeth—or like that bloody medical waste in my synagogue's parking lot—but the gouge won't go away. It can't be washed off like yesterday's swastika. Call it the Jewish stain. The indelible Jewish stain. It's a history that outlives its own people. While Jewish numbers in Europe continue to dwindle from the Parthenon to Paris, the residue of Jewish presence only deepens and expands.

My smile broadened as I realized that I can't screw up this continuity thing. Somehow the Jews survive even where there are no Jews around. We have the astounding capacity to outlive even ourselves. We just won't go away. We aren't merely indestructible, we are ineffaceable.

Plus, to achieve this triumph, we do not have to defeat anyone in battle. We don't need to vilify or demean. All we need to do is openly announce that we are Jews by carving a mezuzah into our homes, and that implant in the plaster will ensure that our presence will be forever sustained.

My fear of being identifiably Jewish in Europe melted away.

It turns out I am not the only hunter of mezuzah imprints. The *Torah of Auschwitz* tells the tale of a pair of Jewish entrepreneur artists living in Poland, Aleksander Prugar and Helena Czernek, who created the Judaica design brand *Mi Polin* (from Poland) a few years ago. They are marketing mezuzahs molded from gouged doorposts they have discovered in dozens of former Jewish communities all over that country. The Jews are gone, but their imprint remains forever. And in this case, some Jews, like Prugar and

Czernek, are back.

As they describe it, "This project commemorates the Jewish life of pre-war Poland by taking *mezuzah* casts from the door frames of once Jewish homes. Wax imprints are taken from the door frames where the *mezuzot* were removed and are then hand-cast in bronze to create a three-dimensional replica of the scar left on the buildings whose original Jewish tenants are long gone. They symbolize the emptiness of now vacant homes, the remembrance of those who lived there, and the reclaiming of the *mezuzah*, which for years remained empty but now can fulfill its role in Judaica at home."

Now, Jews everywhere can have a little piece of pre-war Jewish Poland on their doorposts, and suddenly the *mezuzah* has taken on new meaning. It's not merely an amulet designed to remind us of God's ways and to invoke divine protection, as the Torah of Sinai would have it; now it's a reminder of our deep roots in a place that was utterly destroyed, and an assertion that the Jewish stain, that Mark of Abel, still, somehow, remains.

And not only that. The gouges are being cared for by artists who have revived Jewish existence in this colossal graveyard.

In the *Torah of Auschwitz*, the *mezuzah* has been transformed from a security blanket into a time capsule, a herald of heroism from a dark past, beckoning us toward a brighter future.

After I left Venice on that family trip in 2004, I visited London, where, catching a show on the West End, I went out to stretch during intermission. I was thinking about the courage it takes to affix a *mezuzah* on unfriendly soil and how such acts are similar to other indelible signs of Jewishness—like circumcision. Think of how brave it was for Jews to ineffaceably mark their baby sons as Jews, when that tiny bit of surgery could become a mark of ridicule—or death—later on.

As I was walking back into the theater I suddenly heard a voice:

"*Rabbi Hammerman?*"

Oy. Here? *Even here?*

My cover was officially blown.

Turned out it was a young family that had moved from Connecticut to London. I recognized them and glanced over at their two kids, who looked to be about 7 and 10.

"Do you remember him?" the mother said to her older child, gesturing my way. "He was at your bris."

Indeed, I was. Yes, I felt like telling the kid, I was there when your penis was altered forever, and you were tattooed with what the Torah of Sinai calls the sign of the Covenant with God, but that now has become the ticket to a destiny that is as inescapable, for a people that is indestructible; and nothing, no one, not even an army of anti-Semites, not even Al Qaida or Isis or White Supremacists, not even "the Reich that will last for a thousand years," will ever be able to make that ineradicable sign of Jewishness go away.

There is something about Judaism that goes far beyond our lifetimes. We are part of it, and it is part of us. All we have to do to tap into that unimaginable power is gather the strength to declare proudly, in our minds and hearts, upon the doorpost of our homes, on our passports, on our private parts: "I am, for all eternity, a Jew."

Sacred Memorabilia

The eternal dance with Amalek has taken on various symbolic forms, some of which have been added to the iconography of the *Torah of Auschwitz*. There's the swastika, and the crematorium, to be sure; the cattle car, and the cast-iron gate marked "*Arbeit Macht Frei*." There are Torah scrolls that survived the Holocaust, which have taken on added sanctity even as they are no longer kosher to be used ritually. My synagogue possesses one. There also is the lampshade and the soap, the shoes and the hair, the butterfly and the stale bread. The Holocaust has introduced an entire line of sacred memorabilia.

In Israel, a stark reminder of our precarious existence—and the legacy of the Holocaust—is the sealed room, where Israelis gather when there is fear of a gas attack. Unfortunately, they have had little opportunity to gather dust.

I was flying back from Israel in the early 90s, shortly after the first Gulf War, sitting by the window as the dawn arose. You might recall that as the time when Israelis huddled in safe rooms while awaiting Saddam Hussein's Scuds, that Amalek button was pushed once again for Jews all over the world; as each of these thirty-nine "flying Auschwitzes," (as activist Arthur Waskow called projectiles carrying instruments of mass murder) landed, Jews held their collective breath wondering whether any contained lethal gas. The nation was still steeped in trauma when I visited.

My red-eye route back to New York took me close to the Arctic Circle, where the summer's sun never sleeps. The sun chased us across the horizon, but it never quite caught up. The sky was filled with gorgeous hues of pink, light and royal blue, gradually brightening, then receding as the plane turned south across Newfoundland. Soon it was all blackness again.

No wonder Jewish days always begin with evening, I reflected. No matter how hard we try, night seems always to overtake us. Light cannot penetrate the darkness in our hearts.

Like it or not, I thought, leaning my head on the window, we Jews are the Sons of Darkness, and we can never go long without confronting that perpetual shadow that envelops us. If you are looking for happily-ever-after, if you want quick and easy answers to life's perplexities, it would be best to avoid the Judaica section of your local bookstore. We Jews trudge through existence straining to elevate ourselves from the depths of victimhood; but we can't fully douse the embers of Auschwitz.

This is our Mark of Abel, I wrote in my journal that night, that segment of our collective soul filled with shame, guilt, fear, and a heavy dose of neurosis. We try so hard to sugarcoat the Jewish experience; this darkness is such a turn-off, after all. It petrifies people right out of the Jewish fold. So, we write lots of happy books and Jews of all denominations conjure up many happy Messiahs who can give us many happy endings. And we stress joy, above all: happy-faced, have-a-nice-day saccharine, shallow smiley stuff that doesn't fool anyone and comes out looking like almost every other religion but ours. Those faiths all give us happily-ever-after, most of them without much travail. Our ending will be happy too, I believe, but not without incredible struggle—a struggle that is primarily internal. To deny our dark side is to deny who we really are.

But to succumb to it is to deny what we really can become.

The gas mask is a piece of the Jewish experience now, like the gas chamber before it, and the blood libel, and the Black Plague and expulsion after expulsion that we have tried and failed to expel from our psyches. My generation tried so hard to suppress it, from the moment the feel-good *Jewish Catalog*, a Jewish version of the *Whole Earth Catalog*, appeared during the Woodstock era, but a half a century later the demon still hasn't gone away. That is why the face of Jewry has looked so dour, so aged, for so long. We are weighed down by this lethal memorabilia.

What I wrote on that flight still holds today. We cannot neglect our *sitra achra*. If we acknowledge and even embrace the fear and the anger that still pervades our lives, perhaps we can keep it from controlling us. For this dark side, unleashed, not only brings us to premature panic; it drags us down in so many other ways. The Mark of Abel turns board meetings into screaming sessions and causes us to terrorize our closest friends with malicious gossip; it prompts us to humiliate our women and emasculate our men. The Mark of Abel unleashes hatred against those who are different, including other Jews. The Mark of Abel has, in the eyes of many, transformed the state of Israel from a "Light among the Nations" to a penned-in shadow of its founders' prophetic visions. The Mark of Abel inevitably turns us against ourselves.

We are the Children of Darkness.

But we are also the Children of Light.

Moments later, I turned to the window again, and not only did I see another spectacular rising dawn, but beneath it, in a single panorama, the entirety of southern New England, my lifelong home, from Gloucester to Cape Cod to New Haven, a breathing map, glittering below. It was magical, so much so that I searched for a prayer. And then I wondered, when could I say the morning prayers, anyway? If morning comes twice, when does morning really come?

Sometimes we don't really know when the dawn really begins and ends. The Hebrew term for dawn is fraught with darkness and ambiguity. *Shachar* is derived from the term *Shachor*, which means black, and it also means "to seek" or "to long for." *Shachar* is the time when the angel who wrestled with Jacob, that *sitra achra*, turned, blessed him and fled. *Shachar* is when David lamented in Psalm 22, "Oh Lord, why have you forsaken me?" The break of day is our most vulnerable time, when dreams melt into reality, when we often awaken with great fear, sorrow and loneliness. But *Shachar* is also when new hope arises with the sun. It is the fuzzy passage from past to future.

This ambiguity of passage is instructive as we confront many changes in the world around us. Every day, it seems, someone is proclaiming the beginning of a new era—a "sea change," a "break from the past." Jews should know better. Yes, the new day will come, but we're not exactly sure when it will begin. Or perhaps it has already begun and we've just been too busy living it to notice. I believe that to be the case regarding the Holocaust. But even if the dawn has arrived, the dawn will always have some darkness left in it and sometimes the sun will recede before returning for the long haul.

Our souls will continue to retain some darkness too. Even as we struggle to forge a feel-good vision for a new age, we will never stop dancing with Amalek. Perhaps that is for the best, because we've gotten pretty good at it, and we can teach others how to keep those dark forces of resentment and victimization in check.

A story from earlier in the Jacob cycle of Genesis is instructive. When he awakens from his famous dream in Genesis 28, where he envisions the angels ascending and descending a ladder, he exclaims, "God was in this place and I…I had no idea." He names the place Beth El, the House of God, which has become a standard name for synagogues and churches worldwide. In traveling from Beersheba in the south on his way out of the country, and in stopping at Beth El, which is just north of what was to become Jerusalem, he bypassed Mt. Moriah, the very place where his father was nearly murdered by his grandfather, the place of the *Akedah*—his family's greatest trauma. Contemporary Bible scholar Avivah Zornberg writes:

> I suggest that, for Jacob, the *Akedah* is the unreachable place. His prayers cannot find inspiration in the thought of that terror. But, having unwittingly traveled past Mount Moriah, guilt assails him: "How could I have passed by the place where my fathers prayed, without praying there?" He sets himself to return, and finds himself abrasively hurtling against that place, that darkness. A new prayer is born: *arvit* (the evening prayer), which represents an unimaginable possibility—that divine light can be revealed in the dark. The world of darkness, of sleep and dream, of loss of consciousness, vulnerability, passivity—all this is associated with the Akedah and his father's helplessness from which he has long recoiled.

Yes, Jews are a glass-half-empty people with lots of baggage. No one would choose to have been born into such a people. But there is something curiously beautiful about those mezuzah gouges and circumcised anatomies. Scarred from birth, we have been cursed and blessed to have been handed, at Mount Sinai, a glass-half-full religion.

Golda Meir once said: "Pessimism is a luxury a Jew cannot allow himself." But we are also a people who can't seem to take "yes" for an answer." This despite the fact that our tradition has provided us with a chance to permanently transform that "oy" to "joy." And now, paralleling the Torah of Sinai's journey of Jacob from darkness to dawn, more than seven decades after Auschwitz, the joy is beginning to, at long last, re-emerge.

Dawn is breaking.

We are an ever-dying people. But now, with the killing fields of central Europe having been blanketed nearly eighty times by winter snow and springtime sunflowers, something remarkable is happening. The *sitra achra* is receding, and Jews are moving on, stepping forward ever so gingerly with Jacob's limp. Miraculously and surprisingly but remarkably on schedule, after seven decades, the hate, the anger, and the fear are receding, and the ever-dying people is coming alive again.

Zachor is not a commandment at all, as interpreted by the Torah of Auschwitz—it is our destiny.

But now that we've seen how Jews are learning how to cope with the psychological burdens of victimhood, let's explore why now is precisely the right time for the wounds of the Holocaust to begin to heal, ushering in a time of astonishing creativity and promise.

It has happened before.

Chapter Four

THE BOOK OF DREAMERS
The Sabbatical Decade

The *Torah of Auschwitz* is filled with visionaries who could imagine a world beyond the darkness of their bleak horizon, heroes like Artur Berlinger, who was born in Wurtzberg, Germany in 1889. After Kristallnacht in 1938, he was able send his kids to safety to England on the *Kindertransport*, while he and his wife were deported to Dachau and eventually to Terezin, an hour from Prague.

Terezin was as hellish as any other camp, but for propaganda purposes, Jews there were given more opportunity to express themselves through the arts. The aptly named Artur was an artist of many talents, a Judaic scholar, cantor, painter, and calligrapher. He was also a visionary; in Terezin, he could put all his talents to work. In 1943, after miraculously being removed from a transport to Auschwitz at the very last minute, he discovered a small room with a vaulted ceiling in the secluded yard of a prisoner house. There he created a secret prayer room, decorating the walls and ceiling with stars, candles and calligraphy.

In March of 2000, I traveled to Prague as part of a group of thirty rabbis representing the full geographical and denominational spectrum of North American Jewry. We journeyed there to fulfill a vision—several, actually. We went to accept a genuine offer of reconciliation from church and government leaders, concretized by a contritely worded plaque placed alongside an anti-Semitic icon on the Charles Bridge. We also went to demonstrate an authentic model for unity amidst diversity. Members of our group offered a class to the Prague Jewish community—the first ever in Eastern Europe taught by rabbis of three different denominations. And we went to pay respects to the victims of Terezin.

At the end of a long and emotional tour of the camp, the guide brought us to Artur's secret synagogue, which had only recently been discovered. It was an oasis of holiness in the midst of hell, never defiled by the Nazis—a place where the condemned could utter ancient prayers and dare to hope. On the walls are Hebrew liturgical inscriptions, beautifully inscribed by

The secret synagogue of Terezin, 2017

Berlinger to assist the prisoners, since no prayer books were available. Two of these inscriptions absolutely floored me. One says, "Know before whom you stand," a verse found in synagogues everywhere, but one that took on a whole new meaning in that place; for on the other side of that wall stood the S.S. guards. They hoped in their hearts, perhaps, that the One before whom they really stood was God, a sovereign whose very existence they certainly had every reason to doubt. Despite it all, at least Artur appears to have believed. But it was the second inscription, the one right up front, that stunned me the most. One of the most visionary lines from the daily liturgy—a verse, in fact, *about* vision:

"*V'techezena aynaynu b'shuvcha l'tziyon berachamim*,"
"Let our eyes envision God's merciful return to Zion."
Return to Zion?

In the Terezin synagogue:
"Let our eyes envision God's merciful return to Zion."

The prisoners' eyes could envision no such thing. They likely knew what lay ahead for them. But somehow, led by this single, heroic individual, they could convert their living hell into an oasis of hope. With the SS lurking just outside, inside this secret synagogue their world was transformed.

Hazon in Hebrew means "vision" and that word is embedded in the in- scribed verse. Note that the prayer doesn't ask that the people themselves be whisked to Zion. The Jews of Terezin were not so quixotic as to imagine that they themselves would ever see the spectacular sunrise over Jerusa- lem. They didn't pray for their *own* return to Zion but for *God's*. Hidden away for a moment of sanity amidst the madness, these heroes had the audacity to pray that God and the Jewish people survive the Holocaust, even though they knew that they themselves most likely would not. They not only saw the light at the end of the darkest tunnel in human history, they shined it toward a distant future that no sane person could possi- bly have imagined, a future that all but certainly would not include them. We were in tears. Spontaneously my rabbinic group prayed the afternoon service, although very few of us had prayer books. It didn't matter. The prayers were calling out to us from those walls. It suddenly didn't matter to my Orthodox colleagues that there was no partition separating the men from the women or, for me and my liberal colleagues, whether the language was gender-neutral. Nothing mattered but that we were Jews, praying together, the living fulfillment of Artur's aspirations. Then I read aloud two selections from that classic collection of children's poetry written in Terezin, *I Never Saw Another Butterfly*, and I felt like a pilgrim on the steps of the ancient Temple in Jerusalem, reciting psalms. The poems were all about the joy of being alive. If these residents of hell could find the vision to see butterflies and pray for God's renewal, how dare we allow ourselves to become mired in cynicism and negativity, I thought. The words of the prophets were written on these subterranean walls, by a true prophet of the *Torah of Auschwitz*, Artur Berlinger. I was reading a sacred text in a very holy place.

On September 28, 1944, Berlinger was transported to Auschwitz, where he was murdered. His daughter Rosie, who moved from England to America and now lives in Detroit, says this secret synagogue shows that her father never lost his faith in God.

I don't know whether Artur eventually lost faith in God; I can only say for sure that no one who visits this place will ever lose faith in Artur. And whenever I come to that prayer in the *Amidah*, I think of him and others weeping for salvation in that holy space, people who dreamed of a future that they knew they would never see. We are not merely their witnesses—we are the fulfillment of their dream.

In the midst of the inferno, Berlinger and his people were able to be "as dreamers," imagining a world that would not emerge until long after they had passed.

There's a classic Talmudic tale of a man named Honi, the Jewish Rip Van Winkle. Throughout his life, Honi was always bothered by the verse from Psalm 126, which speaks of the triumphant return to Zion by the exiles from Babylonia:

Shir ha-ma'alot: be-shuv adonai et shivat tzion, hayinu ke-cholmim.

"When the Lord returned the exiles of Zion, we were as dreamers."

He asked, is there anyone who dreams for seventy years? In other words, is it possible that the whole seventy-year Babylonian exile would seem like a dream?

One day, Honi was walking down the road when he saw a man planting a carob tree.

Honi said to the man, "How many years will this tree need to produce fruit?"

The man answered, "Seventy years."

Honi said, "Is it so clear to you that you will live seventy years?"

The man answered, "I found carob trees in the world. Just like my ancestors planted for me, I plant for my children."

Honi sat to eat some bread, and fell asleep. A pile of rocks and dirt rose around him, and he was hidden from sight. He slept for seventy years. When he woke up, he saw the same man picking (carobs) from the tree. Honi said to him, "Are you the man who planted this tree?"

The man answered, "I am his grandson."

The Talmud is teaching us to take the long view. We should always be "as dreamers," envisioning what the world will look like seven decades from now, as the exiles did in Babylonia. Given the advantages of vision and sufficient time to heal all wounds, both of which the Jews have always had an ample supply, a nightmare can be transformed into a more positive dream. Wait a generation, and even exiles can become "as dreamers."

Disaster + 70 = Renewal

How much time constitutes a generation? In the book of Numbers, it takes 40 years of wandering for that generational transition to occur. But for a group of ex-slaves coping with life in the desert, it makes sense for the time frame to be compressed. For the Torah, the key is that enough time needs to have elapsed for all the ex-slaves to die off, save for Joshua and Caleb, the two spies who gave a positive report. Psalm 90 gives a more commonly accepted answer regarding a typical lifespan, stating "Our days may come to seventy years, or eighty, if our strength endures," indicating that 70 or 80 years would constitute a full lifespan.

That is precisely where we are now in relation to the end of the Holocaust.

Seventy is a powerful, mystical number, the combination of two sacred numbers in Judaism, seven and ten. Seven is especially important regarding the Jewish calendar and lifecycle rituals. Traditionally at Jewish weddings, the bride circles the groom seven times (I often do a modified egalitarian version) and a funeral procession makes seven stops on the way to the grave. A circumcision is held on the eighth day—that is, seven plus one, a full cycle of Creation plus one more day. As for seventy, in rabbinic and mystical literature, there are seventy members of the Sanhedrin court, seventy elders to support Moses, seventy words in the Kaddish, seventy faces of Torah and seventy names for God. In numerology, seventy is equivalent to the letter *ayin*, which means "eye," symbolizing the eye that can see hidden mysteries and connections. Seventy is the number that sees not only what's on the surface, but what lies beneath.

So, it makes perfect sense that after seventy years, the equivalent of a lifetime, we can at last envision new possibilities and remove ourselves, ever so slightly, from the traumas of the past.

And indeed, seventy years has borne itself out throughout Jewish history as precisely—or at the very least approximately—the amount of time needed to fully recover from a catastrophe. Often, that period of recuperation has been followed by a burst of creativity, sort of a reversal of Joseph's interpretation of Pharaoh's dreams, where the seven years of famine were *preceded* by years of plenty.

It has been axiomatic in Jewish history that approximately seven decades after an enormous disaster has occurred (and there have been many), new, creative expressions of faith surface as a new generation comes of age. It's uncanny how often this "seven-decade rule" has borne itself out.

As the Honi story indicates, it was seventy years after the first temple was destroyed in 586 BCE that an edict of King Cyrus restored a glimmer of hope to a Jewish people primed to return to Jerusalem, following the city's utter devastation and the exile of a significant number of the population. In 520, following the conquest of Babylonia by Cyrus the Great of Persia in 538, the sacrificial cult resumed in what was to become the Second Temple, whose construction was completed in 515—precisely 70 years after the original temple was destroyed. Judaism underwent tremendous transformation as those seven decades passed, including, according to many scholars, the editing of biblical sources into a written canon.

Psalm 126's dreamy return to Zion must have been as euphoric as the Six-Day War of our era, but the greatest miracle was survival itself. By all measures of logic, a people whose entire history was based on residence in a single land (after their initial return from Egyptian slavery) and whose worship was based on a sacrificial cult based in a single holy site, would have no chance of surviving the forced departure from that land and the complete destruction of that site.

As they entered their captors' capital, the Jewish exiles from Jerusalem sat by the rivers of Babylon and wept for the home that was no more. Their weeping is recorded in Psalm 137:

> By the rivers of Babylon, there we sat down, we also wept, when we remembered Zion. We hung our lyres on the willows in its midst. For there those who carried us away captive required of us a song; and those who tormented us required of us mirth, saying, Sing us one of the songs of Zion. How shall we sing the Lord's song in a foreign land? If I forget you, O Jerusalem, let my right hand forget her cunning. If I do not remember you, let my tongue cleave to the roof of my mouth; if I do not set Jerusalem above my highest joy.

Ancient Babylon, with its hanging gardens and spectacular ziggurats, was a metropolitan marvel. Herodotus, a historian in 450 BCE, wrote, "Babylon surpasses in splendor any city in the known world." But for the Jews, brought there after the destruction of the first temple in 586 BCE, this was their first dispersion, the first exile. King Nebuchadnezzar's Army Corps of Engineers had constructed a massive network of canals and aqueducts feeding from the Euphrates. These were the "Rivers of Babylon," where the Jews sat and wept for Zion. This system of canals, ironically, ultimately proved the city's undoing when the army of the Persian King Cyrus was able to conquer Babylon fifty years later. Because the massive rivers had been drained in order to create these canals, the Persians were able to wade in the waist-deep waters and enter the city.

The Psalmist probably was aware of that when Psalm 137 was written. For this Psalm doesn't just leave the victims to wallow in their misery, it takes the Jews on a journey from exile to restoration, from powerless and homelessness to the promise of return. It begins by those Babylonian rivers, where the tormentors forced the Jews to sing songs of their home. But singing those songs was just what they needed. For in doing so, they learned how to sing the songs of God on alien soil. It's not easy to do that, but they did. They set up entirely new institutions so that they would not forget Jerusalem, which came to be called synagogues. They set up Hebrew schools. They wrote down from memory all the stories and laws that had sustained them back home, all those things they took for granted all those centuries. They painted verbal pictures of what life was like back there in Jerusalem, so their children would not forget. They collected all these stories and laws into a single scroll, which they called the Torah.

And these people came to be known by an entirely new name—they were called Jews.

All this happened by the rivers of Babylon. In the face of utter homelessness, they faced Jerusalem and held it up above their foremost joy. Disregarding their sorry lot and defying their tormentors, they forged a new destiny. And then—at last—the enemy was destroyed and redemption was at hand. Psalm 137 is truly a snapshot of a single moment of triumph in Jewish history—the moment when the home team learned how to win on the road.

Scholars date this Psalm to a time just after the return to Zion, since it speaks of Babylonia as "there," not "here." But the recollections are raw and vivid enough to reflect a survivor's experience. This creative masterpiece, then, was a product of the renaissance of the return. Following that homecoming, the public reading of the Torah became a central feature of a reimagined Judaism. While the centrality of the temple and its sacrificial cult were reestablished, seeds were planted for a more portable faith, one that could be practiced at local synagogues that would soon spring up throughout the Mediterranean.

After the destruction of the first Temple, this astounding rebirth came to fruition seven decades later.

The second great cataclysm to impact Jewish life was the destruction of the Second Temple by the Romans, in the year 70. It was in the seventh decade after that calamity that Judaism's most revolutionary reinvention took place, triggered by a revolt in the 130s that ended all hope for the Temple to be rebuilt yet again. It is quite possible that the rabbinic leaders of that period in the second century looked to the Babylonian experience as a historic model and anticipated a redemption analogous to the Persian conquest and return to Zion, so as the seventh decade began, they became more restless. The Bar Kochba revolt in 132-135 resulted in a disastrous defeat for the Jews, decimating the population to the tune of at least half a million killed. This debacle was exacerbated by the onerous decrees of the Roman emperor Hadrian, designed to eradicate Jewish life in Judea and erase all hope of a restoration of the Temple. The leaders of the revolt, among them famous rabbis, including the greatest of them all, Rabbi Akiva, were summarily executed.

During the first two decades of the third century, precisely seventy years after the quashing of the Bar Kochba revolt, Rabbi Judah ha-Nasi completed his codification of the Mishnah, and rabbinic Judaism came of age—replacing the temple sacrificial cult with prayer, acts of kindness, and an array of laws and rituals based in moveable centers like synagogues and homes.

That's how Jews created something dynamic and new after surviving the second most horrific catastrophe in Jewish history. And so it went throughout the Middle Ages, as this equation of *Disaster + 70 = Renewal* continued to appear.

The First Crusade of 1096 resulted in the killing of tens of thousands of Jews. With the passing of seven decades, dramatic changes began to revolutionize Jewish philosophy and law. Maimonides' first religious masterpiece, his *Commentary on the Mishnah*, was finished in 1168. In poetry, there was the work of Judah Halevi, who died in 1141; a little later, in mysticism, Moses De Leon wrote the Zohar in the thirteenth century. Some of the most famous religious poetry recited on the High Holidays was written out of the ashes of the traumatic massacres of the Crusades, including the Rosh Hashanah imagery of the Book of Life.

Seventy years after the expulsion from Spain in 1492, which displaced 200,000 Jews and resulted in tens of thousands of deaths, Jewish life was replanted in Safed, Palestine. It came to full flower with the publication of the great law code, the *Shulchan Aruch*, in 1565. The year 1648 was a dark one for Eastern European Jewry, as a Cossack revolt killed upwards of 100,000 Jews in Poland. Almost exactly 70 years later, the Baal Shem Tov introduced the Hasidism to Polish Jewry. In early Hasidic literature, his followers specifically draw a line from the ordeals of 1648 to their teacher's career, asserting that this charismatic leader "awakened the people Israel from their long coma and brought them renewed joy in the nearness of God."

The folklore of the early Hasidic masters demonstrates that that the Cossack massacres were still very real to them, well over a century after they occurred. Those tales are filled with the pathos of illness and poverty and loss—but they took that sadness and transformed it into song. They could not succeed in doing that until a full generation had come and gone and few, if any, actual witnesses were left. Otherwise, to sing and dance, as they did all the time, would have been to sing and dance on someone's fresh grave. The Hasidim were considered radicals by the Jewish establishment, but their ability to innovate in the face of profound disruption is what enabled their form of Judaism to strongly influence modern Jewish movements across the religious spectrum, from Chabad to Renewal.

So, based on historical precedent, it makes perfect sense that after seventy years, the rabbinic equivalent of a lifetime, we can begin to envision new possibilities and remove ourselves from the traumas of the past.

With that magic number now having been surpassed since the liberation of Auschwitz, we ask: where is *our* Torah, *our* Mishnah, *our* Shulchan Aruch? Where is Honi, who can remind us of our duty to focus on the future? Perhaps his message is embedded in Artur Berlinger's visionary handwriting on the wall.

Our ancestors could move on; but can we?

Yes, we can.

But the Holocaust is unique, right? Isn't it still *too soon*? According to the Urban Dictionary, "too soon" is "a phrase used to respond to someone making a comment that was intended to be funny, but touches on subject matter that shouldn't be joked about, usually because it was a recent event (being in the last decade or so).

When a joke is no longer considered "too soon," we know that a threshold has been passed. That might be the best indicator that we've reached a different moment, a point of inflection, in the perception of an event.

It might forever be "too soon" to joke about certain elements of the Holocaust. In some ways, the Holocaust **is** unlike other tragedies. But the same thing might have been thought regarding the Lincoln assassination until someone uttered sometime in the 1950s, "But how did you like the show, Mrs. Lincoln?" Some say the joke came from a New Yorker cartoon, other say it was from a comedian like Tom Lehrer or Bob Newhart in the early 60s. Either way, we're talking about nearly a century since that night in Ford's Theater before it was not "too soon" to joke about that national trauma.

With the Holocaust, that moment might have come in November of 2017, when Larry David went on Saturday Night Live and talked about the difficulty of coming up with good pickup lines at a concentration camp. The monologue was met with considerable shock from the Jewish community, even though it hardly is the first time the Holocaust had been a source of humor by Jews—including Larry David—but most of the prior jokes had been told at the expense of the perpetrators rather than the victims (like Mel Brooks' Shoah-stopping "Springtime for Hitler," which had its share of detractors, though many more for the 1967 movie than the 2005 musical).

When I heard Larry David's quip, I recoiled at its insensitivity, instinctively saying to myself, "too soon." But then I reflected for a moment about whether the shock I was feeling that this joke was "too soon," because survivors are still among us, or did I gulp so hard precisely because the real shock was not the joke itself, but rather the realization that the "too soon" moment had just passed before our eyes? It was no longer "too soon" to usher the Holocaust into the realm of normalcy, to treat it as history, to begin to remold it and rethink it, and in doing so, to reinvent the Judaism that the victims bequeathed to us.

In fact, Larry David's monologue was just the most visible eruption of something that has been slowly boiling beneath the surface as a new generation of writers and artists has come of age. In Shalom Auslander's angry, narcissistic, yet shockingly brilliant memoir, *Foreskin's Lament*, published in 2007, he describes the horrible way his parents inflicted guilt as "going Holocaust" on him, as in, "Do you know how many Jews died at the hands of the Nazis so you can keep kosher?" The Holocaust itself becomes a character in the narrative: "Mr. Holocaust," he calls it, the bearer of eternal Jewish trauma. Auslander is numbed by the naked bodies in the newsreel footage he watches at school assemblies. He struggles with the horror even as he trivializes it, out-Rothing even Philip Roth in his cynical detachment. Similarly, in the documentary *Kike Like Me*, also released in 2007, Jamie Kastner takes us on a sophomoric, self-indulgent road trip through the Jewish world, culminating with a visit to Auschwitz. It is an infuriating yet revealing window into the YouTube generation at its most cynical and most shallow. Borat meets Buchenwald. Kastner, like Auslander, is simply one lost young Jew trying to figure out how this big Holocaust piece fits into the rest of the puzzle known as Jewish identity. It's a big piece, but it's just another piece. Even Larry David might have recoiled to read this bit of "humor" from David Deutch, as quoted in *Heeb* magazine: "So I guess you don't think the

Holocaust is funny. But I gotta tell you, it killed them back in Poland."

And back when he was writing *The Producers*, even Mel Brooks might have questioned the wisdom of employing a slapstick-silly Adolf Hitler as the secret friend of a German boy in the critically praised 2019 film, *Jojo Rabbit*. Where *The Producers*, a pure comedy, mocked Hitler while avoiding the more substantive issues of the Holocaust, *Jojo* goes straight from scenes with prancing Adolf to ones featuring hidden Jews and hanging collaborators. Also in 2019, Netflix streamed a comedy series that included a comedic roast of Anne Frank, featuring Adolf Hitler as one of the roasters. It was slammed by critics; but the fact that it aired at all indicates that the "too soon" era is passing as we speak.

In the Torah of Sinai, on the seventh day, God rested. In the *Torah of Auschwitz*, at the conclusion of the seventh decade, the dead began to rest in peace. A joke was told on national TV by a Jewish comic at their expense— and the world kept on spinning.

The Holocaust has receded far enough into history to begin its assimilation into the larger Jewish story. This process was inevitable and for the most part beneficial. When we lose a loved one, the grief eventually gives way to "normalcy"—but not normalcy as it was before the person died. Instead, a new equilibrium forms, an altered worldview, in which the story of that departed relative becomes one with our own, imbuing our lives with added meaning.

We have reached that point from which there is no return: seven decades after the most disruptive event of Jewish history. It's a reverse Sabbatical. God counted to seven, in days, and rested. Human beings count to seven, in decades, and awaken. We awaken "as dreamers," with restored hope and clarity of vision.

The Seventy Year Rule has been born out with shocking consistency as catastrophes have come and gone. Something new is emerging.

Chapter Five

THE BOOK OF REMEMBRANCE
An Arm and a Name

In chapter 3, I spoke about Deuteronomy 25:17-19, which commands us to remember (*zachor*) what the Amalekites did to Israel in the wilderness, when they attacked the meek and innocent. "Never forget to blot out their memory," the Torah of Sinai says, paradoxically, then repeats emphatically, "Never Forget." I'd like to look at that same commandment in this chapter, but from different perspectives, because the *Torah of Auschwitz* has much more to say about it.

In the book of Exodus, after the crossing of the Red Sea, the Torah describes an epic battle in the wilderness between Israel and a unique enemy. The Amalekites attacked them from behind, killing women, the elderly and children, terrifying the weakest among them. They were the biblical version of modern-day terrorists who strike the young and defenseless and embed themselves within civilian populations.

And Israel was commanded to wipe them out. Not simply to wipe them out, but to wipe out the *memory that they ever existed*.

Tradition has it that all enemies of the Jewish people can trace their lineage back to Amalek, and the command to wipe out Amalek is seen as a directive to defeat all our enemies, those who seek to destroy us in every generation.

"Never Forget" became perhaps the rallying cry and first commandment of the *Torah of Auschwitz*, alongside its corollary, "Never Again."

As we've seen, for many centuries, *zachor* has been interpreted as a call for vigilance in the face of evil. It still is. It has also been the rallying cry of victimhood—a justification to avenge the murders of our brethren. *Zachor* was the inspiration for Baruch Goldstein's murderous spree in Hebron on Purim of 1994, when he took the commandment, which is inextricably connected to that holiday, and played it out in grotesque fashion by murdering 29 Muslims at prayer. After that horrific distortion of even the most extreme interpretation of *zachor*, Jonathan Sacks, Chief Rabbi of Great Britain, added:

"Such an act is an obscenity and a travesty of Jewish values. That it should have been perpetrated against worshippers in a house of prayer at a holy time makes it a blasphemy as well . . .Violence is evil. Violence committed in the name of God is doubly evil. Violence against those engaged in worshipping God is unspeakably evil."

So *zachor* has never really been about bloodthirsty revenge, even though it speaks of wiping out the memory of an enemy. Through the centuries, commentators like Maimonides looked for ways to reinterpret this call so that it would not appear so, well, genocidal, by stating, among other things, that since Amalek no longer exists as a nation, the command to entirely wipe out a national population is no longer operative.

Early Hasidic commentators tried to internalize Amalek, *Pogo*-style: They met the enemy, and the enemy is us. Rabbi Levi Yitzchak of Berdichev wrote:

"Not only are Jews commanded to wipe out Amalek, who is the descendant of Esau, but each Jew has to wipe out that negative part that is called Amalek *hidden in his or her heart*. When the power of evil in each of us arises, Amalek is present in the world."

In chapter 3 I spoke of our dance with Amalek and the need to confront our fears. But the Amalek within is more than that: It's that part us that succumbs to the impulse to take advantage of people's weaknesses; that is cruel and angry and derisive and out of control; that force within us that sees every encounter as a means to an end; that objectifies other human beings as if they were pieces on a game board, instead of as fellow living, breathing souls created in God's image. That battle against our *sitra achra*, our internal dark side, is more than a need to honestly address neurosis and trauma—our collective and individual Holocaust-based PTSD. It's also a fight against temptation and evil, whatever the source: not just neurosis, but also brainwashing, peer-pressure, genetics, cable news talking head incitement—you name it. It's all the Amalek within.

Zachor reimagined

But, aside from the *sitra achra*, the *Torah of Auschwitz* presents us with three additional ways to approach Deut. 25:17-19, all of them gaining increasing urgency in our day:

1) When the *Torah of Auschwitz* speaks of the command to remember the evil of Amalek, it is speaking to our generation specifically about keeping alive *the memory of the Holocaust itself*. Often the Yiddish term used for

zachor is: *G'dank!* געדענק, with precisely that connection in mind.

2) *The Torah of Auschwitz* emphasizes *zachor*, not as a call to punish the villains—even those that reside within our psyches—or simply to remember the Holocaust as a singular event. Rather it is a call *to remember the victims*—each individual—and not merely the victims of the Holocaust itself. Our task is to ensure that *never again* should a cry from the depths of despair, danger and loneliness go unheeded—from *anywhere and anyone.*

3) The call to remember, *zachor*, is not simply a call to preserve the memory of one dark chapter in history, but *to preserve historical memory,* period. *Never forget* means to remember always that there is an authentic basis for experienced truth, that *facts matter* and we should be accountable to them. I'll cover this in chapter 10, on post-Holocaust ethics.

For now, let's look at how the *Torah of Auschwitz* reinterprets *"zachor"* as it relates to remembering the Holocaust.

My congregation's 2017 visit to Auschwitz and other "Holocaust centers," (to employ Sean Spicer's unartful term) taught us the essential meaning of that commandment, *zachor*. A catalyst for the trip was the Trump Administration's act of Holocaust denial in leaving out references to Jewish persecution in their infamous January 2017 Holocaust Day proclamation. If ever the world needed to be reminded of the uniquely Jewish dimension of the Holocaust, it was during the first days of the Trump administration.

Fackenheim's 614th Commandment

"Because I remember, I despair," Elie Wiesel said. "Because I remember, I have the duty to reject despair." But in either case, memory is the key.

The Jew has an obligation to remember, but then to shed confining casing of resentment and despair, and to transform the disaster into an embrace of life and a relentless pursuit of justice and dignity for every human being. For a Jew is responsible not merely to be a witness, but to dream, to imagine a better future—despite the darkness that surrounds us. Shimon Peres said we should use our imagination more than our memory. "Optimists and pessimists die the exact same death," he said, "but they live very different lives!"

The Jew has an obligation not only to remember the Holocaust, but to remain Jewish. So said the twentieth century philosopher Emil Fackenheim, who introduced the concept of a 614th commandment, building from the traditional notion of the Torah of Sinai containing 613. This commandment is to prevent Hitler from gaining a posthumous victory. We have many reasons to bear witness, ranging from the particularistic (preserving the Jewish people) to the universal (to prevent genocide from happening anywhere). Fackenheim's injunction emerged as part of an awakening he had to the precariousness of the Jewish condition during the perilous run-up to the Six-Day War. It has greatly influenced post-Holocaust Jewish thought, including my own—I took a class with him when studying at Hebrew University during my rabbinical school year in Israel. Since Fackenheim's *Voice of Auschwitz* was a prime inspiration for my *Torah of Auschwitz*, let's take a closer look at it:

"What does the Voice of Auschwitz command?" he asks in a 1978 book, *The Jewish Return into History: Reflections in the Age of Auschwitz and a New Jerusalem*.

"We are, first, commanded to survive as Jews, lest the Jewish people perish. We are commanded, second, to remember in our very guts and bones the martyrs of the Holocaust, lest their memory perish. We are forbidden, thirdly, to deny or despair of God, however much we may have to contend with him or with belief in him, lest Judaism perish. We are forbidden, finally, to despair of the world as the place which is to become the kingdom of God, lest we help make it a meaningless place in which God is dead or irrelevant and everything is permitted. To abandon any of these imperatives, in response to Hitler's victory at Auschwitz, would be to hand him yet other, posthumous victories."

Fackenheim asserts: "For a Jew hearing the commanding Voice of Auschwitz, the duty to remember and to tell the tale is not negotiable. It is holy. The religious Jew still possesses this word. The secularist Jew is commanded to restore it. A secular holiness, as it were, has forced itself into his vocabulary.

"Jews after Auschwitz represent all humanity when they affirm their Jewishness and deny the Nazi denial . . .The commanding Voice of Auschwitz singles Jews out; Jewish survival is a commandment which brooks no compromise. It was this Voice which was heard by the Jews of Israel in May and June 1967 when they refused to lie down and be slaughtered.

"For after Auschwitz, Jewish life is more sacred than Jewish death, were it even for the sanctification of the divine Name. The left-wing secularist Israeli journalist Amos Kenan writes: 'After the death camps, we are left only one supreme value: existence.'"

Within this seminal passage, three distinct commands emerge (which parallels Maimonides' division of the passage into three of his 613 Torah commandments): to survive, to remember, and not to despair. Notice how Fackenheim subtly shifts the focus of remembrance from the perpetrators to the victims. No longer is it specifically Amalek, the Other, that we need to remember, much less to avenge. Anger and resentment only feed into the despair and nihilism that he is trying to allay. We don't need to remember *them* at all. *Zachor* refers primarily to *us*. The ultimate vindication occurs when we assure Jewish survival.

An Arm and a Name

In the decades that have passed since Fackenheim articulated his 614th Commandment, the focus of *zachor* has turned to honoring the survivors and recalling the individual victims of Amalek, rather than avenging them. This shading of *zachor* can in fact be traced back to the Hebrew Bible, to second Isaiah, who, unlike the Isaiah who pontificates for the first 40 chapters of the book, lived after the destruction of the first temple, at a time when the Jews in Babylonia were aching to return and still mourning their losses. Isaiah comforted the exiles with prophecies of a mass gathering and return.

In chapter 56, Isaiah makes it clear that it's not just the Jews who will be gathered together in this rebuilt Jerusalem. Isaiah is also including gentiles in this mix—all foreigners and others typically on the outside. God blesses the outcasts here, including the lowest of the low, specifically eunuchs, who have no possibility of legacy, no offspring to ensure a future for their family name.

We read in Isaiah 56:5, as he speaks of the eunuchs: "To them I will give within my temple and its walls *a memorial and a name*, better than sons and daughters; I will give them an everlasting name that will endure forever."

In the Hebrew transliteration, you might be able to pick out a familiar phrase:

"*V'Natati Lahem B'vayti YAD VASHEM tov, mibanim u'banot; shem olam eten lo, asher lo yikaret.*"

The great memorial to Holocaust victims in modern Jerusalem, "Yad

Vashem," got its name from that verse.

It is fitting that Yad Vashem is the name of the depository memorializing those who have no one to carry on their name after death—much like the childless eunuchs of Isaiah's day. Isaiah is affirming that despite their status, eunuchs would still achieve a measure of immortality with the Lord. No one would be forgotten; not just those unable to have children, but also strangers—gentiles. All will merit the promise of everlasting remembrance.

Yad Vashem means "a memorial and a name." But in fact, the word for memorial, *Yad*, literally means an arm. *An arm and a name.* The image is of someone lending a hand, helping someone who has fallen.

Dear Evan Hansen, the Tony-winning musical that dwells on the topic of teen depression and suicide, also features an arm and name. Without giving too much away, the title character is a high school student whose profound social anxieties cause him to live a very isolated and lonely life, to the point where, when he falls from a tree and breaks his arm, he waits for an unbearably long time writhing on the ground before anyone hears his cry. No one hears him. It's as if he doesn't exist.

The musical constantly returns to that place and that image of the unheeded human, all alone, fallen in the forest—and, while the musical is morally complicated, one clear message is that *no one deserves to be forgotten*. No one—not the dead nor the living—deserves to disappear. And the plot is propelled by a name inscribed on the cast covering Evan's arm.

Names are the currency of memory. To have a name is to be unique, to be loved, to belong and to be connected. The book of Proverbs states that while most things in life are transitory, a good name lasts forever.

The relationship between memory and names goes back to the very beginnings of the Hebrew language. In fact, as biblical critic Robert Alter has pointed out, the Hebrew noun for "remembrance," *zecher*, the expression used in Deuteronomy and Exodus in regard to Amalek, also means "name." The etymological link is also gender-based (*zachar* means "male"), which accounts for the historical Jewish obsession for males to have sons to say the mourner's *Kaddish* after they have died, and to carry on the family name. In traditional Jewish circles, a first-born son is even called a *Kaddish*.

So in those circles, a Jewish child learns early on that now that he has been born, his dad can die in peace. And you wondered why Jews are neurotic?

In the Holocaust, Jews and other victims were denied their names, and therefore their humanity, their individuality, and their uniqueness. Well before they were sent like sheep to the slaughter, victims were stripped of their human dignity. Their names were replaced by numbers. Their shoes, jewelry and clothing were ripped from them. Even their hair, perhaps a human's most distinct, individuating feature, was shorn.

See these words from Livia Bitton Jackson, who was deported to Auschwitz from Hungary in 1944. She speaks of how it was her long golden locks that saved her from death during the selection. But then, after she was clipped like an animal, she says:

"...The haircut has a startling effect on every woman's appearance. Individuals become a mass of bodies. Height, stoutness, or slimness: There is no distinguishing factor—it is the absence of hair which transformed individual women into like bodies. Age and other personal differences melt away. Facial expressions disappear. Instead, a blank, senseless stare emerges on a thousand faces of one naked, unappealing body. In a matter of minutes even the physical aspect of our numbers seems reduced—there is less of a substance to our dimensions. We become a monolithic mass. Inconsequential."

At the museum in Auschwitz, you can see the piles of hair. As the decades have passed, these inert strands have lost all life, all color, all individuality. Before the Russians liberated Auschwitz in early 1945, the Nazis got rid of most of the hair that they had been storing. Only seven tons remained, a tiny fraction of what had been shorn from the heads of Jews. The rest was sold to German companies that transformed the hair into mattresses and felt—something to think about when checking into that quaint B and B next time you are driving through the Bavarian countryside.

So the commandment *zachor*, as filtered through the *Torah of Auschwitz*, has come to mean that we've got to remember and to cherish the uniqueness and sanctity of every human being, down to even the smallest shreds of their existence—every strand of hair, every single letter of every name. Which, incidentally, is why Nazis hate Jews—then and now. While Nazis have always been more about numbers, Jews have always been more about names. The second book of the Torah is called "*Shmot*," "names." True, there is also a book called "Numbers," but the original Hebrew name for that book is not Numbers, it's "*Bamidbar*," "In the Wilderness," and the census held at the beginning of the book is specifically seen as an exception to the rule. Jewish tradition frowns on counting people; it cherishes individuality and uniqueness—precisely what the Nazis tried to obliterate.

Jews refuse to forfeit the distinctiveness of each human being.

Jews refuse to degrade anyone's sanctity, body and soul.

In fact, the Hebrew word for soul, *neshama*, has the word *shem*—name—right at its heart. Jews are, after all, Semites—descendants of Noah's son Shem—so Jews are literally "*Name-ists*." And the hater of Jews is, by definition, an anti-*Shemite*—the "*Denier of names*." One who defiles God is one who perpetrates what is called a "*Hillul ha-shem*," a desecration of the Name; and one who dies the holiest of deaths, as a martyr, dies, "*Al Kiddush hashem*," in an act of ultimate sanctification of the Name.

To be named is to be—and even more, to be *holy*.

When Jews say the Mourner's Kaddish, after Auschwitz there is an added purpose. We are praying not only to restore the sanctity of God's name in the traditional sense, but also to affirm the infinite value of each human life. The words of this ancient prayer call for the restoration of cosmic wholeness in the face of a shattered present, and that wholeness can only be achieved through the renewal and re-sanctification of "the Great name." Post-Auschwitz, there are six million more Great Names to be redeemed.

When we recall a human being individually, as someone who was unique and loved, we are redeeming them from oblivion. When we say the second blessing in the daily prayer known as the Amidah, calling upon the Divine to revive the dead, the *Torah of Auschwitz*, which might question the efficacy of a God who acts in history, is calling upon us to muster that spark of divinity that is within each of us, in order to redeem them.

In camps like Majdanek and Plaszow, in Poland, the Nazis used dislodged gravestones to pave roads, a way of erasing Jewish names from history. By making pilgrimage to those places, our group saw those stones, and in doing so, we redeemed those victims from oblivion.

In Krakow after the war, the few Jews who managed to return began to piece their world together by gathering overturned gravestones and assembling them into a memorial wall in the back of the main cemetery. My 2017 group saw that wall, and those names, and in doing so, we helped to redeem them from oblivion. In Krakow, in fact, we saw names everywhere. In 1939, over 60,000 Jews lived in that city. But only 2,000 Jews from Krakow survived the war, and most of *them* left the country. By 1968, there were no Jews left. A small community has grown since then and now there are about 1,000.

Several synagogues have been restored, and Jewish style restaurants cater to tourists, complete with klezmer music.

We sat in the Tempel Synagogue and danced with an Israeli group we happened to meet there. Then, like two Jewish ships passing in the night, we went our way and they went theirs. As we got up from the pews to leave, I asked members of our group to think for a moment about the people who used to sit in those same seats, all of whom are gone.

"No one deserves to be forgotten," they sing in *Dear Evan Hansen.* "No one deserves to fade away. No one should come and go and have no one know he was ever even here. No one deserves to disappear."

In the *Torah of Auschwitz*, a mitzvah that nearly equals the one to "Choose life" in importance is that every lost or abandoned person must be found.

It's interesting that in the Nazi march on Charlottesville in August of 2017, the white supremacist haters shouted, "*Jews* will not replace us." But in Krakow, we *did* replace them. We replaced the Nazis, who during the war used the Tempel Synagogue as an ammunition storage area. So, yeah, we replaced them. But strangely, on one level, the neo-Nazi chant in Charlottesville spoke to one demented group's fear of being left behind. Of being forgotten.

But white supremacists do not deserve our pity; for the cry "*Jews* will not replace us" also speaks of a ravenous desire to intimidate, isolate and destroy those who are different. That is what the Nazis did in the 1930s and 40s and that is what their cowardly heirs still want to do—and what in fact happened to the Jewish community of Charlottesville. Those who were in synagogue on that fateful Sabbath were terrified in a manner unprecedented for Jews in this country—only to be topped a year later in Pittsburgh, when fear turned into carnage. In Charlottesville, Jews had to escape their synagogue through the back door, as neo-Nazis carrying semi-automatic rifles streamed past their sanctuary, calling out "*Oy, gevalt,*" in mocking Brooklyn accents. In Pittsburgh, for the victims there was no path to escape at all, as the weakest—the elderly, some adults with special needs—were mowed down from the behind, precisely how Amalek attacked the Israelites in the Wilderness.

There is no place for white supremacy in America.

Notably, Deutero-Isaiah included the stranger in the Yad Vashem passage. Isaiah's motto—our motto—is not "*Jews will not replace us.*" It is, instead, to paraphrase Evan Hansen, "*Jews will be found.*" And non-Jews will be too.

My group rode through the forests of Poland—with the omnipresent birch trees (Birkenau *means* birch, in fact)—where Jews fell like trees, shot by SS commandos or gassed at Belzec, Treblinka and Majdanek. When a Jew falls in the forest and no one is around, do they make a sound?

Yes, because we remembered them.

We drove through the storybook mountains of Slovakia, with gorgeous sunflower fields—and I thought of Simon Wiesenthal's story when he was a prisoner in one of the camps.

One day, he and his work detail were sent to clean medical waste at an army hospital for wounded German soldiers. He writes:

"Our column suddenly came to a halt at a crossroads. I could see nothing that might be holding us up but I noticed on the left of the street there was a military cemetery . . . and on each grave, there was planted a sunflower . . . I stared spellbound . . . Suddenly I envied the dead soldiers. Each had a sunflower to connect him with the living world, and butterflies to visit his grave. For me there would be no sunflower. I would be buried in a mass grave, where corpses would be piled on top of me. No sunflower would ever bring light into my darkness, and no butterflies would dance above my dreadful tomb."

We saw the sunflowers, imagined the Jews who once lived in the neighboring shtetls, and we remembered them.

And I remembered as well that classic poster of the Vietnam era, with the words, "War is not healthy for children and other living things" scrawled in innocent childlike lettering, all surrounding a sunflower. Sunflowers add a touch of innocence and hope wherever they appear, but never more than when they appear on bloodstained, war-torn landscapes. Central Europe is covered in those landscapes, and in sunflowers as well, which, like Jews, know no borders and always seem to crave a return to the innocence and promise of a new dawn. Sunflowers are also the only herbage with a memory, or what seems like a memory. And like Jews, they wake every morning and pray facing east.

In Prague, we saw the priceless Jewish artifacts that the Nazis collected to show the world the people that they planned to destroy. We saw those ornaments and Torah scrolls, and we remembered the people who once proudly marched around the sanctuary with them.

By a quirk of good fortune, the Nazis in Czechoslovakia, prompted by Prague Jews in 1942, opted to preserve large numbers of Jewish ritual objects, even as the synagogues that housed them were vandalized and destroyed.

They envisioned housing them in a museum to celebrate the destruction of the Jews. More than 100,000 artifacts from over 100 congregations—gold and silver and ritual textiles, books, Torah scrolls, even clocks and pianos—were brought to the city's Jewish Museum and stored in over 40 warehouses. Among the items were 1,564 Torah scrolls. After the war, the scrolls were acquired by a member of London's Westminster Synagogue and they were later distributed throughout the Jewish world for memorial displays. On Rosh Hashanah 1982, my synagogue in Stamford dedicated one such scroll, officially entitled Czech Memorial Scroll MT#1272. Even the scroll has a name. While it is no longer kosher for ritual use, this Torah from Sinai by way of Prague serves an equally important purpose. It is a silent witness, not only to the horrors of the Holocaust, but to Jewish heroism, courage and hope.

One synagogue in Prague, the Pinkas synagogue, contains a list of all the names of those from Bohemia and Moravia who were killed. It covers the walls of several rooms. 77,297 Jewish victims.

In Berlin, there are memorial plates in the ground for those who were deported—stumble stones, they are called, because when you stumble over them you **have to notice**—and everywhere you go there are reminders of who once lived in that place. There are 56,000 *stolpersteine*, as they are called, throughout Germany.

In Leviticus 19:14, the Torah of Sinai says that we should not place a stumbling block before the blind. But the *Torah of Auschwitz* says, *Yes, you should place these stumble stones everywhere a victim lived, to remove blinders from the eyes of those who try to forget their suffering.*

The *Torah of Auschwitz* commands, *You **should** place a stumbling block before the blind—those blind to the suffering of others.*

Stolpersteine in Berlin

In the leafy neighborhood where Einstein lived, called the Bavarian Quarter, there are signs on every street showing how the Nazis systematically denied the Jews any semblance of dignity, before denying them life itself. Before they were killed, Jews were methodically robbed of even the smallest dignities of daily life, like working in their professions, buying newspapers, buying fresh milk, owning pets. This testimony from 1943 appears on one sign:

> "We used to have a canary. When we learned of the
> law prohibiting Jews to keep pets, my husband simply
> could not part with the bird. (...) Maybe someone in-
> formed on him, because one day my husband was called
> in for questioning by the Gestapo. (...) After many weeks
> of agony I received a note from the police that, for the fee
> of 3 Reichsmark, I should pick up my husband's urn."

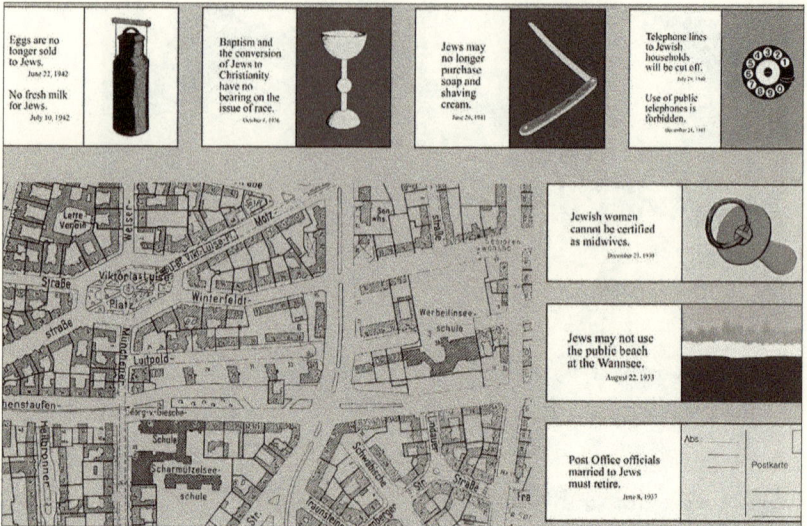

Some of the signs in the Bavarian Quarter,
showing genocide's incremental creep

As we walked through that neighborhood, we happened upon a ceremony where German elementary school children were standing in the courtyard of a destroyed synagogue and dedicating individual bricks to memorialize Jewish children who once lived there, or who shared their first name. Brick by brick, they were building a memorial. A memorial with names—their own *Yad Vashem*. This ceremony was not staged for the tourists. We just happened upon it. We *stumbled* upon it.

This was the anti-Charlottesville. These children were proclaiming, "*Jews will **not** be forgotten! We will replace hate with love!*"

And they were proclaiming this—in the heart of Berlin.

It brought me to tears.

As Jews, we believe that when you've fallen in a forest and there's no one around, you *will* be found. We love forests. The Hasidim in pre-Holocaust Poland would dance and sing there. Hey, even our *trees* have names. Just ask the JNF what happens with all those certificates we give out at Bar Mitzvahs. (On second thought, maybe don't).

The orphans of Warsaw were found by Janus Korczac. My group visited the orphanage where this great hero nurtured and protected those who were most vulnerable. On the fifth of August 1942, Korczac and his 200 children were rounded up and sent walking to the Umschlagplatz, where the trains would take them from the ghetto to the camps and certain death. Many living in the ghetto remembered the haunting silent procession of Korczac's kids from one side of the ghetto to the other, "carrying blankets, walking hand in hand led by Dr Korczac, a stooped aging man."

Korczac was considered a national treasure by the Poles for his pioneering work on child rearing, so although he was a Jew, whose original name was Henryk Goldszmit, he was offered a chance to escape deportation. But he chose to remain with "his" children, as he comforted them right to the very end. Because of that, an act so noble as to be beyond the capacity even for Abraham—who nearly killed *his* child—neither Korczac nor those children will ever be forgotten.

All of which demonstrates how the heroism in the *Torah of Auschwitz* dwarfs anything we read in the Hebrew Bible.

That passage from Isaiah, where he talks about the forgotten, the stranger, the victim who seem hopelessly alone, ends with this verse:

"Even *them* I bring to My holy mountain, and make them joyful in My house of prayer; their burnt-offerings and their sacrifices shall be acceptable upon My altar; for My house shall be called a house of prayer for all peoples."

A month after our 2017 trip group returned, my congregation participated in a ceremony of remembrance on Rosh Hashanah. I handed out lists of names taken from the Yad Vashem database, including particularly the names of children. Everyone in attendance had a unique list, so in all, there were about 15,000 different names in the room. I asked people to read aloud, simultaneously, the names on the page each person was holding. The resulting cacophony was the most intense moment of prayer many of us have ever experienced. In the twenty-first century, and as carried forth by the *Torah of Auschwitz*, this, I thought, is what authentic prayer looks and sounds like.

I asked people to take the lists home and do some research about the names they had recited—and also to dedicate themselves to one act of world repair to perform in remembrance of that victim, so that their victim will, in a real sense, be redeemed from oblivion—and be "found." If ever I needed proof that the Holocaust has become an increasingly potent and powerful force in American Jewish spiritual connection, this was it.

Here are a few of the responses I received that week:

Dear Rabbi Hammerman,

I have seldom been more moved than when standing with hundreds of others reading the names of children who perished and knowing that there were thousands more such lists. I think the emotional outreach that recitation provided might well benefit us if it is part of our service each year.

You asked that we each reach out over the years to the children we remembered. I would like to honor some of those children by acquiring a number of books appropriate for children about the Holocaust. I will then create a small personalized remembrance bookplate label with a child's name on it to go inside the front cover.

Dear Rabbi,

I've spent a great deal of time on the Yad Vashem website since your sermon on Rosh Hashanah. Growing up Catholic, I never really gave a great deal of thought to the Holocaust until I met my husband and got to know his family. His father fought in WWII in Patton's third army and was a part of many of the major battles toward the end of the war. I also know that not all of his family immigrated to the US from Romania, so I used the database to look up the last name. There were numerous names of those who were persecuted and murdered, and many more who they did not know what happened to them. It left a lump in my throat and a feeling of innate sadness.

Reading the stories of the children were heartbreaking...some of the children had pictures attached to their memorial page. The absolute enormity of the waste of these beautiful children's potential was overwhelming. I do not know yet how to best honor their memory. I do know that this year on Kristallnacht, I will post once again that we must NEVER forget and I plan to scan in one of those lists and mention to my friends who have children, "What if this had been YOUR child."

Dear Rabbi,

Here's my name info: I had a sheet with adults listed. I selected a woman whose year of birth and death indicated she was 51 when she was murdered. That's how old I am.

Chaja Zycher was a housewife from Warszawa, Poland. This is the Polish spelling for Warsaw. I do not know if she was taken out by train, or whether she died in the ghetto, or by some other means. A relative of Chaja's knew only enough to indicate that she had been murdered, not how or where. But Yad Vashem provides this information by way of filling in missing material:

During the Shoah, Jews were murdered in a variety of ways, among them gassing, shooting, burning, drowning or burial alive, exhaustion through forced labor, starvation, epidemic diseases, deprivation of medical care and minimal hygienic conditions, and more. Some Jews took their own lives to escape arrest and further persecution, or to end their hopeless, relentless suffering.

So how to memorialize someone about whom I know so little? All I know is she was married, her mother's name was Rakhel, she lived in Warsaw, and she was murdered because she was a Jew. I assume a housewife of her age had children, and probably grandchildren. If they lived in Warsaw, it is also likely they all were murdered as well.

According to the United States Holocaust Museum web site, Warsaw's population pre-war was 1.3 million, and of those, 350,000 were Jews, about 30% of the total. Warsaw was home to the largest Jewish population in Europe, second in the world only to New York. It is estimated 77% of all of Poland's Jews were killed during the Holocaust. I don't know how many from Warsaw survived, but I found a search engine on JewishGen that a child, named Danuta Zycher, from Poland, was evacuated to England. She later left, presumably after the war, for Palestine. Looking up Danuta's information, she does not appear to be the child or grandchild of Chaja, but perhaps she was a niece.

As a way to memorialize this family, I donated to
ASAF, an organization in Israel that aids asylum seekers
there (mainly from east Africa). Just as Chaja was taken
in as a refugee in Israel, an orphan, may Israel, which has
been overwhelmed by asylum seekers from Africa, be able
to find a way to help those most desperately in need.

Dear Rabbi,
The responses you shared inspired me to stop
working and go to the Yad Vashem website.
I chose the name Beila Hoffman from your list, because
my grandmother's maiden name was Hoffman. The first
thing that shocked me was that when I searched this name
I got 96 hits. For a single name (with alternate spellings).
I found the entry for Beila Hoffman of Kruszelnica, Poland.
Beila was murdered on July 13, 1941, at the age of 10.
Her parents were Hersh David and Ettl Hoffman.
Then I went back to the hit list and selected Izabella
Hoffman from Tab, Hungary, since my grandmother's father
came from Hungary. She could be family. Izabella, also known
as Bella, was born to Julianna Kohn and Lipor Hoffman
and she was a student. Bella turned 13 in 1944. She should
have been celebrating her bat mitzvah and looking forward
to her future. Instead, she was murdered in Auschwitz.
Tomorrow, I will light Yahrzeit can-
dles to remember these girls.
This project is one of the most meaningful Holocaust Remembrances that I have experienced. For the
first time, the victims are not "the 6 million"—mere
numbers—but real people with names and stories.

Divine Images

Recalling and reading names has long been a staple of Holocaust memorial ceremonies. But the *Torah of Auschwitz* asks us to go beyond just reciting names. We need to learn their stories. But in this hyper-visual era, where a picture is worth a thousand words and an Instagram a thousand Tweets, we need to go one step beyond even that: We need to remember faces too.

Once when visiting Israel, I stopped at an absorption center for Ethiopian immigrants at Kibbutz Merhavia, near Afula. As soon as my group arrived, the children began clustering in front of us, begging *"Titzalem oti,"* "Photograph me!" The kids especially loved seeing their images instantly on the back of digital cameras, so when I took their pictures with an ancient Instamatic and told them there was nothing to see until the film was developed, they walked away.

A couple of weeks later, I visited Yad L'Kashish, an artist's workshop in Jerusalem for the elderly and infirmed. It's called "Lifeline for the Old" in English; but it's really a lifeline for the rest of us, reminding us of the light that can shine from any human face no matter what the age, when people are able to live out their years in dignity.

After a brief introduction, the guide escorted us into one of the workshops. There an elderly woman sat knitting by the door. She was demonstrating some of the secrets of her craft when I walked up to her, after having snapped a few photos of the room. Suddenly she turned to me, gestured to my camera and said, *"Titzalem oti."*

I took her picture, which is amazing, because I was in a state of utter shock. Whose voice was I hearing? Was it the old Russian woman or the tiny Ethiopian child? I could understand why the kids wanted to be photographed because it's exciting to see yourself in this magic technological mirror, because it's cool. But why this woman, who at the other end of the lifecycle would ostensibly have had little reason to want to be photographed by a stranger? But she said it again: *"Titzalem oti."*

And in that request, I heard her saying:

Remember me. Let my life be made meaningful through your camera's eye; my years of enslavement to the communists, my long journey of exodus; the miracle of my return, to a faith I never knew, to a land I'd never seen—and to a people who never forgot me.

My entire trip to Israel had been framed now, at the beginning and at its end, with the lingering mantra, at first playful and now haunting: "*Titzalem oti.*"

A highlight of the expanded Yad Vashem museum is the Hall of Names, where the visitor stands suspended between two enormous cones. Above is a display featuring 600 photographs of Holocaust victims; their faces are reflected in the waters below. It is most moving to go from there right to the brightest and most photogenic sight in the entire world, a vista of the bustling hills of modern Jerusalem. The city itself appears to be crying out "*Titzalem oti.*"

Four-and-a-half million names of victims are now on the Yad Vashem online database, many of them with pictures. You can get lost in this site—name after name, photo after photo. I once saw there a quote from a young man named David Berger, who was shot in Vilna in July 1941 at the age of 19. Two years earlier his friend Elsa had made her way safely to Palestine. Berger corresponded with her, and in his last card he wrote, "I should like someone to remember that there once lived a person named David Berger."

The word "to photograph," *l'tzalem*, contains within it the Hebrew word for image, *tzelem*. And the first chapter of Genesis informs us that all human beings are created *b'tzelem elohim*, "in God's image."

So when we are asking "*Titzalem oti,*" we're not merely asking to be photographed. We're saying, "Imbue me with *tzelem*. See my face for what it really is—a reflection of the divine image. See what is eternal in me. Love me, with a Godlike love."

Yehuda Amichai's classic poem, "Tourists," states:

Once I sat on the steps by a gate at David's Tower, I placed my two heavy baskets at my side. A group of tourists was standing around their guide and I became their target marker. "You see that man with the baskets? Just right of his head there's an arch from the Roman period. Just right of his head.

"But he's moving, he's moving!" I said to myself: redemption will come only if their guide tells them, "You see that arch from the Roman period? It's not important: but next to it, left and down a bit, there sits a man who's bought fruit and vegetables for his family."

Those Ethiopian children in Merhavia helped me to understand that that image in the tourist's lens, the one just to the right of the Roman arch, is what we've been seeking all along. And if we focus on that face, and listen closely enough, we can hear God whispering: "*Titzalem oti.*"

If we recall the victims, the names, the faces and the stories, they maintain, even in death, a spark of eternity.

To all of this, I want to add one more dimension to the summons to remember victims. Not only should we recall the names and faces of the fallen, but we should also demonstrate eternal reverence and remembrance with regard to survivors. The category of "survivor" should include not only those who survived in Nazi-occupied lands during the Holocaust, but also those who managed to escape beforehand, along with those who helped to rescue the remnant as members of the liberating armies. Too often they are overlooked as we tally the collateral damage. All of them are victims, and sometimes survival was a fate worse than death.

And so, the *Torah of Auschwitz* has given us perhaps its most seminal commandment, the one that Fackenheim and Yad Vashem helped to transform: *Zachor. Remember;* but not in the way the Torah of Sinai would have us remember. Not to remember to avenge what our enemies did to us, but to remember those who suffered—and who still do—those who are alone, those stripped of their dignity and their uniqueness, those who have no one else to remember them—whether in Auschwitz or Janus Korczac's orphanage or David Berger's Vilna.

They will be remembered.

And they will be found.

Chapter Six

THE BOOK OF DISRUPTION
The Mitzvah of Adaptation

Judaism has always been supremely adaptable. But the *Torah of Auschwitz*, which chronicles the most disruptive event in all of history, empowers us to go even beyond adaptability and make radical changes where necessary. While the Torah of Sinai states that Judaism must be flexible enough to enable a life to be saved, the *Torah of Auschwitz*, having seen six million lives needlessly lost, goes one step further, asserting that Judaism, in the face of this thundering repudiation of its own theological underpinnings, must be flexible enough to save *itself*; and in doing so, to lend a shining example of how to regenerate when the world is spinning out of control.

I used to be anxious about change, back when I thought religion's purpose was to act as a bulwark against it. I was wrong. Judaism has a bias toward change, recognizing that both the world and our bodies are continually being reinvented. Each person replenishes up to 70 billion cells daily; we're not so much human beings as human *becomings*. At the Passover Seder, the agent of stability (matzah, which you could put into a time capsule and fifty years later it would taste the same) confronts the force of fermentation (wine, which is perpetually flowing and always changing). Long after the final crumb of matzah is consumed, either by my guests or my dog, the wine—the symbol of transformation—remains on the table. We still have two cups to go, plus another round for Elijah. Change wins.

Darwin was right. Survival requires constant adaptation. I learned the hard way how we must continually grow with the flow and how each breath propels us forward; I learned that lesson in the shadow of Auschwitz.

Just a couple of hours after my first visit to Auschwitz, back in 2010 when I escorted the *March of the Living* teen tour, I nearly died of suffocation. Earlier that afternoon, I had visited the gas chambers of Auschwitz, struggling to imagine how I would have responded if crammed alongside hundreds of victims gasping, denied of air. My eyes were transfixed by the scratch marks that can still be seen on the walls.

Still shaken from that close encounter with genocidal asphyxiation, two hours later I was having dinner with the group in large hall in Krakow, when a soup crouton no bigger than a pea—about the size of a pellet of Zyklon B—somehow got lodged in my trachea.

For what seemed like an eternity, I couldn't breathe.

The world was filled with clogged air passages that week. My group's flight from New York to Krakow had been delayed because of thick fog over Poland—the same fog that took the life of Poland's president on a flight to Russia the next day. The following week we left Warsaw for Israel just as the airways of Europe were being choked by the ash cloud from an Icelandic volcano.

In that large hall filled with hundreds of *March of the Living* teens and chaperones gobbling their dinner, the adults in our group sat at a long table for an impromptu staff meeting, a fortunate thing since our staff included two physicians. I sprinkled a couple of spoonsful of soup nuts (the Israeli kind that I've always loved) into my vegetable soup. A few gulps in, I felt something not quite right in the back of my throat. When a swig of water didn't clear up the problem, I began to get concerned. A few seconds later, I could feel the crouton slide an inch or two and my air passage was nearly completely blocked.

I stood and began shaking my head. Someone near me asked me to try to breathe, but all I could do was let out a seal-like bark, loud enough to startle everyone in room. One of the doctors came up behind me, wrapped his arms around my diaphragm and pumped hard. I felt some air squeeze out, but the Heimlich didn't work.

The doctor said that some air was getting in, but I didn't believe it. Frankly, I'm not sure what I believed at that moment. I'd be lying if I said I thought about the irony of choking *there*, in Zyklon's backyard. I didn't see how people were reacting around me. All I knew was that my mouth was wide open, my face a contorted "Scream" mask, but no air was getting in.

My time was running out.

I mentally clutched every molecule of oxygen still in me and began to feel the compulsion to breathe again.

Another deathly croak.

"Some air is getting through!" I heard the doctor, but began to feel dizzy and a full panic set in. Not here. Not now. Not this way. Don't black out!

The doctor behind me attempted one more Heimlich thrust. Hard.

I felt a whoosh.

Something moved inside. It was the soup nut.

I sucked in my most significant breath since the moment I exited my mom's birth canal, the last time a doctor had slapped some air into me. I breathed in *Neshama*, the sacred breath of Life, and each act of inhaling became a prayer, a testimonial to the priceless, fragile gift of being alive.

And then we all continued with our dinner.

Analogies are dangerous and I would never claim to have nearly become victim six million and one. I was no Janusz Korczak or Anne Frank; just an unlucky swallower, one fortunate enough to have doctors around who were trying to save me rather than preparing to experiment on me with the intent of dispatching my body to a mass grave.

But I will now be able to convey the martyr's story with a unique empathy. The overwhelming drive to survive and the terror of asphyxiation are things that I can now begin to understand as I wasn't able to before.

Ten days later, our plane home from Israel took a circuitous, southern route to avoid ingesting that volcanic cloud of Icelandic ash. Somewhere over Provence, I set my iPod to shuffle and up popped John Denver's "Sunshine on My Shoulders." It's the corniest song ever written, but some combination of the lilting music and thoughts of Denver's own untimely demise led me to suddenly appreciate the crematorium and the crouton, the overwhelming beauty and fragility of life, and the enormity of what had nearly happened to me. Metaphorically, it took my breath away.

Did that incident change me? Well, I've stopped eating those croutons. I smile more. I don't sweat the small stuff. I get angry less. I feel revitalized. Rebooted. Regenerated. And I thank God every day for the chance to keep on growing and changing.

I've taken about 80 million breaths, give or take, since that April evening. My heart has thumped about 700,000 times and, maybe 100 trillion of my cells have been replaced. If it's true that the human body replaces itself every seven years, I'm a totally new me, and then some. Now, for the rest of my days, I'll be doing literally what the Jewish people have been doing for the past seven decades—measuring my life by the number of breaths taken since I was at Auschwitz.

When "New Normal" becomes normal

On September 15, 1944, in the Wolfsberg Labor Camp in Germany, Naftali Stern, a Hungarian Jewish inmate, had a dilemma. Rosh Hashanah was approaching that week and there was no *machzor* (High Holiday prayer book) from which he might be able to lead the prayers for others in the camp. Stern, who later became a renowned cantor, took some paper scraps from bags of cement that he had purchased with bread rations. Using a pencil stub he had found, he began transcribing from memory the prayers of the *Musaf* (additional) service. When he finished, he wrote down the date as well as the names of the people from his city who had died. On Rosh Hashanah, the Germans allowed the Jews to have a service, and that Rosh Hashanah was a pivotal moment for Stern and the other Jewish prisoners, who for a short while could forget about the hell that persisted around them.

For Naftali Stern, no prayer book, no pencil, no paper—no problem. He literally gave up his daily bread to write his own *machzor*. This hand-written, 25-page cement bag *machzor* is now part of the collection of Yad Vashem in Jerusalem. It is a remarkable achievement—the entire service, from memory, scribbled onto a scrap of litter. Using the only means at his disposal, he reinvented the High Holidays. "Blessed are the hearts that can bend," said Albert Camus, "They shall never be broken."

One summer when I was leading a group to Israel, we were victims of a scheduling snafu at Yad Vashem, denying us the chance to have lunch in their cafeteria. A museum representative apologized profusely and ushered us into a conference room. At that point, I wasn't hungry. It was all so annoying, and the mishap threatened to cast a shadow over our Yad Vashem experience, until something happened that made me realize how Israelis have overcome their greatest challenge—they've discovered customer service.

A distinguished man came into our room. He told us the story of Naftali Stern and his handwritten *machzor* and presented me with a facsimile to take back to the congregation. Here is the inscription:

To Temple Beth El, Stamford Connecticut. In testimony to the triumph of the spirit over the frailties of the body and an expression of spiritual steadfastness that sparks a commitment to Jewish continuity and the hope for continued growth of the Jewish People.

He signed it, *Shaya ben Yehuda, Director of International Relations, Yad*

Vashem.

At that moment, it seemed much less annoying and far more fitting to have given up my daily ration of lunch for this *machzor.*

The Maggid of Dubno (Jacob ben Wolf Kranz) in the eighteenth century was once asked how he always came up with perfect tales for every occasion. He replied with a story:

> Once I was walking in the forest, and saw tree after tree with a target drawn on it, and at the center of each target an arrow. I then came upon a little boy with a bow in his hand.
>
> *Are you the one who shot all these arrows?* I asked.
>
> *Yes!* he replied.
>
> *Then how did you always hit the center of the target?* I asked.
>
> *Simple.* said the boy. *First I shoot the arrow, then I draw the target.*

The experiences of the Holocaust can help us confront a dizzying world where everything has been turned on its head; where everything we thought was true turns out not to be; when "new normals" become what's normal. The *Torah of Auschwitz* instructs us never to stop dreaming of the destination, even as our inner GPS seems to be constantly recalculating the route. If people like Naftali Stern could adapt themselves to the most inhumane conditions ever fashioned, we can adapt today to our frightening world of exponentially accelerating change; and, as I did after my encounter with the crouton, we can pledge never to stop growing.

The People of the Rope-a-dope

In the Torah of Sinai, Leviticus 18:5 states, "You shall therefore keep my statutes and my rules; if a person does them, he shall live by them: I am the Lord."

From this injunction to "live by them," the rabbis derived the principle of *Pikuach Nefesh*, which states that almost any Jewish law can be circumvented if it will save a life. Examples given in the Talmud include Sabbath violations, such as rescuing a child from the sea, breaking down a door about to close on an infant and extinguishing a fire to save a life. In the *Mishna*, we read (*B Yoma* 83a) that someone seized with a "life threatening" hunger can break the fast on Yom Kippur. In 1848, during a cholera epidemic, Rabbi Israel Salanter ordered his community to disregard the fast in order to preserve their health. Famously, he ate in front them. So, from the start, Judaism has always been so flexible as to have a built-in GPS that allows for instant recalculation of religious obligations during times of extreme disruption.

But here's where the *Torah of Auschwitz* takes over and raises *Pikuach Nefesh* to the next level. Adaptation, once a grudging concession to reality, has now become a *mitzvah*. Once an exception to the rule, it has become the rule.

The last stop on my 2017 congregational European trip was the Olympic Stadium in Berlin, home of the 1936 Games—that grotesque pageant of Nazi propaganda thankfully punctured by Jesse Owens' heroics. At the stadium, it was positively chilling for us to sit just behind the Fuhrer's box, as close to his chair as John Wilkes Booth was to Lincoln's. The architecture of this magnificent structure screams of the power of brute force and the exaltation of the fair-haired Aryan body.

Our guide, Dennis, who was not Jewish, said, "You know, Hitler had it all wrong." He explained that the Nazis' ideology was based on social Darwinism, which emphasized the survival of the fittest. Hitler assumed that meant the strongest, and he tried to pervert the Olympic movement to use these games as a showcase for his racial theories of Aryan physical superiority.

"But that's not what Darwin was talking about at all," Dennis said, repeating something that I figure he learned in the German educational system. "Darwin was talking about *adaptation*."

Darwin, as described by Dennis, seemed to echo the words of the prophet Zechariah: "Not by might, not by power, but by my spirit, says the Lord of hosts." Jewish superheroes have never won through brute force; and those species destined to survive are not the ones who are most macho, not the ones who can run the fastest or jump the highest. The species that endure are the ones who can adjust on the fly, the ones who are pliable, the ones who can recalculate, who can figure out how best to take lemons and make them delicious. They win with courage and persistence, ingenuity and compassion. To be Jewish is, at its very essence, to be able not merely to manage change, but to flourish amidst the chaos. That's the key to surviving a 4,000-year history of expulsions, deportations and pogroms, and it's what Jews can teach the world.

At Sinai, we became the People of the Book.

At Auschwitz, we became the People of the Rope-a-dope.

We're also the people of the *dreidel*. As hectic and dizzying as life can be, we just keep on spinning until we get it right. We may drop from time to time, but we never drop out of the game.

At times of great stress, Jews have always been able to adapt, and never more so than during and following the Holocaust. And we have much expertise to share with the world.

Many have grappled with the meaning of the Holocaust, this existential earthquake that changed everything. But for the most part, for the past seventy years we've limped along, dazed, clinging to our omnipotent sky-god and age-old rituals, pretending things haven't changed. It's comforting, but so much of our tradition has become hollow and meaningless to the younger generation—which was to be expected, following the most disruptive event of all time.

Embracing Auschwitz means embracing the constant flow of change.

The God I believe in is a God of change. Our lives are governed not by stagnancy but by flow. The only constant is change, and we need to adapt to it constantly. Like nature itself, we are not perfect. We make mistakes. When we become perfect someday, we'll cease to be human. We'll be robots. Perfection is not a goal to aim for; it is an illusion to dispel.

Given the newest discoveries in DNA research, Darwin's theories on evolution have now been nearly universally accepted by the scientific community. Even Pope Benedict gave them a thumbs-up in 2014. The evidence of our evolutionary ancestry is written all over the human genome. Intelligent Design has been discredited—notably in trials in Pennsylvania and Ohio. But that doesn't mean God is out of the picture.

There are those who are very concerned that accepting Darwin's notion that humanity is an accident of nature would be a bad thing for morality. They claim that if you teach kids that they are evolved from apes they are going to behave like murderous animals. I suppose that if Darwin hadn't come around, there wouldn't have been over 1,624 American mass shootings in the 1,870 days leading up to the Parkland school massacre of February 2018.

Professor Kenneth Miller, a biologist at Brown and bestselling author, disagrees with the Creationists on evolution's role on morality. The core of the Creationists' argument is that evolution is driven by mistakes. And it's true that evolution is driven by mutation. "But imagine an organism that never made these mistakes," Miller says. "We think of mistakes as being bad, but if you have no mistakes, you have no mutation, you have no evolution. What's going to happen to an organism that replicates its DNA perfectly every time? It's not going to survive. So by what standard are we calling these mistakes?"

In Darwinian evolution, perfection is the road to extinction. The path to survival is the path of growth, of change, of shattered patterns.

Maybe evolution is not a mistake of nature, Miller suggests. Maybe it is, in effect, the "design" of nature, the way nature is supposed to work. Somehow, and we don't know how, something happened that drove that first fish to take a big gulp of air and climb ashore. Somehow, at some point, something drove that first bird to flap its wings and soar. Somehow, at some point, a pair of chromosomes melded together—we know which ones they are—marking the evolution from ape to human. Maybe it was random, maybe it wasn't. But either way, one can easily fit a model of God into this scenario; not a God who micromanages every detail of the universe, but who created a process of flow and change that we call evolution, which reflects the will of the Creator.

Evolution, therefore, is *completely compatible* with Jewish sensibilities and belief. And Genesis provides us with crucial lessons on growth, change, and how we have all evolved from day one.

One could easily make the claim that evolution is simply the Jewish notion of *teshuvah* (repentance) writ large. Just as we make mistakes and grow from them, so does DNA. So does the universe. So does God. Yes, even God has evolved, at least our conception of God; it's shifted dramatically from the warrior sky God of the Bible to the rabbis' concept of *ha-Rachaman*—the womb-like embodiment of love (which is also, by the way, a Muslim name for God). Maimonides looked to reasoned Aristotelian thought for his God; while the Kabbalists added a sense of balance, of yin and yang, to their mystical eroticism. Arthur Green writes, "The Oneness of God, for the Kabbalists, is dynamic and flowing rather than static and unmoved." God is flowing, emanating, unfolding. So is Creation.

Conservative Columnist Charles Krauthammer, who died in 2018, wrote the following after a trial where the Kansas Board of Education tried to impose anti-evolution curricula on classrooms—and lost.

> How ridiculous to make evolution the enemy of God.
> What could be more elegant, more simple, more brilliant,
> more economical, more creative, indeed more divine than a

planet with millions of life forms, distinct and yet interactive, all ultimately derived from accumulated variations in a single double-stranded molecule, pliable and fecund enough to give us mollusks and mice, Newton and Einstein? Even if it did give us the Kansas State Board of Education, too.

The *kulturkampf* between Nazism and Judaism pits force against flexibility, subjugation versus adaptation. That conflict is still going on, as fascism once again has reared its ugly head and has targeted—to no one's surprise—the Jews.

But Jews are uniquely prepared to play the rope-a-dope game; we've been doing it for a very long time. I think Einstein would agree. That Judaism, like the universe, has a bias for change.

The Most Powerful Ritual Ever

When it comes to disruptive innovation in Jewish history, there is no greater example than what happened after the Second Temple was destroyed in the year 70. As mentioned in chapter 4, the great works of the rabbis began to take shape a generation later. It was during that time frame that one of the most remarkable evenings in Jewish history took place.

Every Passover at the Seder, toward the beginning of the long section that many Jews skip—er—*abridge*—there is a section describing five rabbis in B'nai Brak. You know, the one that includes Rabbi Yossi, whom your great Aunt Sadie insists on calling Jose. They stayed up all night before their students came to tell them it was time for the morning *Sh'ma*.

What was going on at this time? It was a calamity that was unprecedented; on this fateful Passover, the emperor Hadrian was planning to build a temple to Jupiter on that very spot where the destroyed Jewish temple still lay smoldering in ruins.

So, these five rabbis in B'nai Brak sat up all night reinventing the observance of Passover. Some of them could still recall the power of the sacrifices that were held at the temple when it stood. They needed to do something or the memory of those great Passovers would fade away, and along with it, so would the Jewish people. So, they threw together this ceremony with a little plate holding a bone, bitter herbs and an egg, with some wine and matzah on the side (hear this scene meticulously described by Rabbi Irwin Kula in the podcast *Judaism Unbound*).

Just a makeshift, temporary solution. Their students weren't even in the room with them. No wives. No kids. Not even Aunt Sadie. They thought they were just applying a quick, insufficient, lousy Band-Aid over a deep, deep wound.

But here we are, two thousand years later, and that stopgap solution of five B'nai Brak rabbis has become the most powerful and meaningful ritual in all Jewish history, one that still has great power even among Jews who have long since stopped doing anything else Jewishly. And the Seder has been reinvented again and again—with over 4,000 different Haggadahs published, one to fit any occasion.

In 2020, Passover had to be reinvented once again, along with many other Jewish rituals, when the coronavirus crisis led to the practice of social distancing, a mandatory isolation of individuals from their families and communities. Such physical separation flies in the face of centuries of Jewish practice, with its focus on social and familial bonding—especially with regard to Passover. For my community, which has long championed the use of technology to cultivate community (though never at the cost of face-to-face interaction), it was natural to offer a Zoom Seder, where large numbers of people could come together in a virtual meeting room. Because of the emergency, even Ultra-Orthodox rabbis in Israel approved the use of technology on the festival to facilitate virtual gatherings at Seder tables across the land. Covid-19, perhaps the most socially disruptive event since the Holocaust, has led to a burst of innovation, in the Jewish world and beyond.

As Albert Einstein said, "The measure of intelligence is the ability to change." Disruptive innovation was defined in a seminal 1995 article in Harvard Business Review by Clayton Christensen, as a process by which a product or service takes root initially in simple applications at the bottom of a market and then relentlessly moves upmarket, eventually displacing established competitors.

The classic example of the consequences of not adapting to disruption in the business world is Kodak, which once was as synonymous with photography as Kleenex is to tissues. But Kodak's moment ended when they turned down digital photography and placed all their bets on film. Bad choice; but you can find similar examples in so many industries.

Our nation and world right now are immersed in a period of great political and economic upheaval. Disruption rules everywhere: in business, medicine and communications, in our climate and in our politics and in technology. Some adapt and thrive. Some don't and die. Extremism flourishes in such an environment of chaos, and democracy can be challenged to the limits. My synagogue's group learned about that as we stood outside the Reichstag.

But from destroyed worlds, new possibilities emerge. It took the rabbis decades to reinvent Passover. After Auschwitz, it took the Jewish people only three years to return to our ancient home in Zion and establish the State of Israel. But still, we are at a crossroads, following the most disruptive event in all of human history.

And so, the time has come to do what our GPS does all the time: recalculate.

The Torah of Sinai says, Judaism should be flexible enough to save individual lives. That's *Pikuach Nefesh*.

The *Torah of Auschwitz*, which reflects Jewish historical experience with a Darwinian twist, says that Judaism must be flexible enough to save *itself*, to remain relevant in a radically changing world—while remaining true to its core values.

The Shoah narrative includes a moral message that we have long championed: not brute force, not blood and soil; but *adaptation*: That is the true survival of the fittest. We, the People of the Rope-a-dope, float like we-never-saw-another-butterfly and sting like a bee.

There is no greater task for post-Holocaust Jews than to teach humans how to live with hope and dignity, like Naftali Stern and those who prayed with him on that fateful Rosh Hashanah in 1944. How to rise above the raging torrent, how to survive with grace and love, and how—as I learned so painfully on a cold night in Krakow—to appreciative the regenerative powers of each breath and to never stop growing.

Citius, Altius, Fortius—Faster, stronger, higher?… No!

Not by might, nor by world record speed, nor by the higher scores granted by the East German judge; but by resilience, creativity and visionary spirit, says the Lord of hosts.

For while some might be able to long jump 29 feet and pole vault to the sky, our visionary eyes can see much farther, our eyes can see from the dusty chamber of a concentration camp—clear through to Jerusalem.

And I pledge, as the *Torah of Auschwitz* instructs, never to stop growing until the moment I breathe my last.

Chapter Seven

THE BOOK OF LOVE

A Human Tapestry

In the evening liturgy of Yom Kippur, there is a poem with imagery that I find among the most evocative of anything from the High Holidays. It's based on a verse from Jeremiah 18, describing human beings as clay in the hands of a divine potter. The medieval poet expands on this to compare God with various other artisans and people to the objects created by him. One image that is particularly striking compares humanity to a tapestry, with God as the weaver:

"As cloth in the hand of the weaver, who drapes and twists it at will, so are we in Your hand, righteous God."

I was thinking of this image when I heard a lovely and popular Israeli song hauntingly sung by the musician Roni Dalumi at Israel's 2017 national Holocaust Remembrance Day ceremony at Yad Vashem. Its title is *"Rikma Enoshit Echat,"* "One Human Tapestry," and the translated lyrics go like this:

> *When I'm gone,*
> *Something inside you,*
> *Something inside you,*
> *Will die with me, will die with me.*
> *When you're gone,*
> *Something inside me,*
> *Something inside me,*
> *Will die with you, will die with you.*
> *For we all are, yes, we all are,*
> *We all are one human tapestry,*
> *and if one of us fades away, something within each of us dies*
> *But something of him remains in us.*

The beauty of the Hebrew here is that there is a double meaning for the word *Rikma*, which is translated best into English as "tapestry" or "embroidery"—but in fact also is a word for human tissue. When anyone dies, a part of us has died, not just spiritually but physically; and we are all part of the same human body. There is no real place where "I" end and "you" begin. There is no dividing line. We are all joined at the hip. The air we breathe is shared, not just with other humans but with all creatures, and we are engaged with vegetation in and act of mutual and reciprocal CPR as we barter Oxygen for CO_2. Every time I touch a doorknob, my body is welcoming in millions of your germs. Every time I sneeze, part of me is paying a visit to your immune system.

Think of the historical progression here in describing how human lives interconnect. A century ago, people were talking about the mass of immigrants coming together in America as a melting pot. It's a great image; but in a melting pot, all individuality is subsumed into the whole. So, to enhance that, in the 1980s Mario Cuomo and David Dinkins called New York a "magnificent mosaic," thereby preserving cultural diversity; but what's holding a mosaic together, except a little glue? The tiles are otherwise disconnected, like many neighborhoods in New York.

But a *Rikma*, an embroidery of cross-stitched sinew, maintains the uniqueness of each thread, each strand, while at the same time validating that we are inextricably intertwined, body and soul.

Dr. Martin Luther King, Jr. writes in his letter from the Birmingham Jail, "We are caught in an inescapable network of mutuality, tied in a single garment of destiny. Whatever affects one directly, affects all indirectly."

At the museum in Auschwitz, the overwhelming, unspeakable photos of the intertwined bodies of the victims (at peak efficiency, they gassed up to 3,000 at a time in Birkenau) give us a completely new way to understand that network of mutuality. In those photos, it is nearly impossible to detect where one body begins and another ends, and there is nothing to indicate which victim was from Germany, from Hungary or from Slovakia. There is very little to determine who was a Hasidic, Reform or secular Jew; Jewish or just Jew-*ish*, or not Jewish altogether.

After Auschwitz, a song like *Rikma Enoshit Echat*, One Human Tissue, leads ultimately to that searing image of interconnection. We go beyond the network of mutuality, the melting pot, or fabulous mosaic, or even the woven tapestry of that Yom Kippur liturgical poem, and we see *Rikma* in its most literal sense. We are one human body.

Those ineffable photographic images are so intense, and so personal to those who lost loved ones, that I cannot in good conscience display them here. But you can find prime examples of what I have in mind at http://www.auschwitz.dk/Nyiszli.htm.

A principal goal of authoritarian regimes is to forge order out of chaos; the Nazis were experts at that, efficiently categorizing things and people. Their racist theories meticulously delineated Aryan from Jew by pseudo-racial characteristics, as well as genealogy. Being Jewish had nothing to do with belief. A Jew who converted to Christianity was still a Jew, and thereby marked for death, even if he became a bishop.

It's not inherently evil to make the trains run on time, and mainstream religions also endeavor to supplant chaos with cosmic order. We need a sense of order in our lives. Two of Judaism's key rituals are even called "Order" (the Passover *Seder*) and "Separation" (*Havdalah*, which ends Shabbat). Jerusalem is considered holier than other cities and Shabbat is on a higher spiritual plane than other days. Yom Kippur, called the Sabbath of Sabbaths, is the peak moment of holiness for the year. Drawing boundaries and forging distinctions has characterized Judaism over the centuries, but the ultimate end has never been to hoist one group over another, but to lift all to greater degrees of godliness. A life of holiness is available to everyone. A rabbinic text specifically states that the righteous of *all* peoples have a share in the World to Come. No distinctions are drawn where it matters most. The ancient rabbis lived in hard times and could have easily fallen into the insularity that is so prevalent in our world today, but they rejected that.

Following the Holocaust, we've reached a different place in the evolution of Judaism and human civilization. The Torah of Sinai promoted the creation of boundaries for the purpose of distinguishing one person, and one nation, from the next, so that the "chosen" nation might take responsibility for bringing holiness to the world. But we have seen what can happen when such goals are distorted through the funhouse mirror of modern racist ideology. Well-intentioned boundaries metathesize into something they were never intended to be. Not that Nazi racism or fascist nationalism are the inevitable products of the biblical ethos when taken to the extreme—I'll leave to scholars the inquest on the ties between medieval Christianity and the rise of modern anti-Semitism. I'm just saying two things:

1) We have seen what can happen when the world of boundaries and distinctiveness is taken to its nationalist, secular extreme. And...

2) The *Torah of Auschwitz* compels us to eradicate those boundaries.

I believe we have entered a world of connection rather than separation and distinction.

We are moving, in a sense, from *Kosher to Kesher.* These nearly identical Hebrew words signify the old ways and the new. The laws of keeping Kosher are, like the rest of the Sinai laws of holiness, built on distinction, on drawing lines of separation.

Kesher, on the other hand, is the Hebrew word for connection, calling on us to dissolve distinctions.

The Kosher laws remain a worthy concept (and I'm a huge proponent of them), as does holiness in general; but holiness cannot be an end in itself. Living a holy life is just a first step leading to what's more important: the goal of tapping into that inescapable network of mutuality, rather than separating one being from another. This was true, to an extent, even in the Torah of Sinai, whose central principle, after all, is that we love our neighbor as ourselves, not that we eat pastrami at Ben's Kosher Deli.

We are not leaving Kosher behind, but now we need to look at it through the prism of *Kesher;* because in the end, we are all one human tissue, as we were at Auschwitz.

When *you* die, something dies inside of *me.* Separation is an illusion. What unites us is that, when the blinders are taken off, we are One. Not just all Jews, but all of humankind—forever linked, woven tightly into this human tapestry.

When the screams were heard by the *Sonderkommandos* waiting outside the gas chambers (these were Jews who had to do this horrible work in order to live another day), well, here's how one described it, in a testimony from the Shoah Foundation archive:

In the beginning [pause]... I was there. After they close the door I could hear the three thousand people, voices, cry and screaming...And you could hear [sings] Sh'ma Yisrael Adonai Eloheinu...[Pause] they were calling God! Nothing happened, nothing happened and these voices still in my ears. But, other transports were coming, I was hiding again. I was getting TOO FAR AWAY not to hear those voices calling God. I never went back again. But! If a soldier or German or SS was finding me hiding he could shoot. But! I could not stand those voices.

Three thousand voices became One Voice. Scores of languages became One Tongue.

So not only are we One Human Tissue—but ultimately, we are speaking as One Human Voice.

We often ask, where was God at Auschwitz? One thoughtful response would be that if God was anywhere in the vicinity, God was right there, in the cries of the martyrs. They cried out for God—and the silence of the divine response will perplex and enrage people until the end of time. But it is the last word of the prayer that they cried, the last word of the *Sh'ma*, that was their call to us: The last word on their lips was "*Echad.*"

One.

The Torah of Sinai says, "*God is One,*" referring to that ineffable name proclaimed only by the High Priest on Yom Kippur Day, as he hoped for the expiation of Israel's sin.

And the *Torah of Auschwitz* responds, "*We are One,*" with that word being the final, ineffable cry of battered bodies and intertwined souls; and still we await the expiation of *God's* sin.

The final letter of *Echad,* the *daled,* trails off into silence, opening the door—*delet,* in Hebrew—to eternity, as the doors to the gas chambers were pried open and the bodies were heaped in piles.

We are *Rikma Enoshit Echat,* "one human tapestry"—but embroidered by whom? It is far easier to believe that God was an expert embroiderer at the beginning of time, than to believe in a God who stitched together this living hell in real time. There was no semblance of order to be made out of this chaos. Order itself, like our stale understandings of God, is incompatible with what happened there, or with this Oneness.

When the *Torah of Auschwitz* cries "*Echad,*" it is far less concerned with the embroiderer than with the tapestry itself. It is not dwelling on God's essence but rather on the Oneness of humankind; and when we speak of our being "one," we're not merely speaking of a virtual oneness, a cyber community or a soulful connection, but a physical connection too, body and soul; spirit and sinew, *Rikma Enoshit Echat*—sharing our very real and very fragile earth, the same heating air, the same rising oceans, the same parched soil.

And the same invasive microbes as well. As I complete this book in 2020, the world is immersed in the Covid-19 coronavirus crisis. Despite the forced separation of social distancing, rarely has all of humanity felt—or been—so interdependent. Our fates are literally in the hands, washed or unwashed, of millions of people we will never meet. College students who defy the calls to avoid bars and beaches during Spring Break literally endanger the lives of their grandparents. Through each cough or sneeze, our bodies have become One Human Tissue. When HIV first spread, it was suggested that when a person had unprotected sex, they were having sex with every prior partner as well. Now with this pandemic, that contention has been extended to breathing and touching. Each hug is a potential dagger, not just for the person opposite you but to people on the other side of the world, no matter where you live or who you are. Front pages from all over the world are screaming the very same headlines. We've never been so lonely and fearful, sitting in our cold, quarantined rooms; but through our very separation, we've never been so inextricably interconnected.

The great Israeli novelist David Grossman penned an essay for *Ha'aretz* during the early stages of the crisis, "The Plague Is a Formative Event. When It Fades, New Possibilities Will Emerge."

He writes:

> The very act of exercising the imagination from the depths of the despair and the fear that now prevail possesses a force of its own. The imagination can not only see doom, it can also sustain freedom of the mind. In paralyzing times like these, the imagination is like an anchor that we cast from the depths of despair into the future, which we then start to pull ourselves toward. The very ability to imagine a better situation means that we have not yet allowed the plague, and the dismay it causes, to nationalize our whole being. As such, it is possible to hope that perhaps, when the plague ends and the air will be filled with feelings of healing and recuperation and health, a different spirit will pervade humanity; a spirit of easefulness and of a new freshness. Perhaps people will begin to reveal, for example, engaging signs of innocence unspoiled by even an iota of cynicism. Perhaps softness will suddenly become, for a certain time, legal tender. Maybe we will understand that the murderous plague has given us an opportunity to slice from ourselves layers of fat, of swinish greed. Of thick, undiscriminating thought. Of abundance that became excess and has already begun to suffocate us. (And why in the world did we collect

so many objects? Why did we heap up our lives until life itself was buried beneath mountains of objects that have no object?)

It may be that people will look at all manner of twisted handiwork of the society of abundance and excess and simply want to throw up. Perhaps they will suddenly be struck by the banal, naive awareness that it is absolutely terrible that there are people who are so rich and others who are so poor. That it is absolutely terrible that such a rich and sated world doesn't give every baby that's born an equal opportunity. For surely, we are all one infectious human fabric, as we are now discovering. Surely the good of every person is ultimately the good of us all. Surely the good of the planet on which we live is our good, it is our well-being and the clearness of our breathing, and the future of our children.

The legacy of the Shoah has been amplified by a global pandemic that will define this century just as World War II defined the last. The message could not be any clearer: We are all inextricably connected.

And so, you may ask, if we are all One, what of all the horrible people who murdered us or who ignored the crime? How could we be one with *them?* For that matter, how can we be one with our personal rival, with those who troll us on the internet or bully us, or vote differently? Or our ex? How can we be one with the Other?

And to a point, you would *have* a point. Those who harm others need to be brought to justice, but not because they are any less human. To render them subhuman or to enact bloodthirsty vengeance would be to act like them.

Martin Buber told this story in his *Tales of the Hasidim*. A disciple asked Rabbi Shmelke: "We are commanded to love our neighbor as oneself. How can I do this, if my neighbor has wronged me?" The rabbi answered: "You must understand these words aright. Love your neighbor like something which you yourself are. For all souls are one. Each is a spark from the original soul, and this soul is wholly inherent in all souls, just as your soul is in all the members of your body."

We've talked before about the Amalek within each of us, and that internal, eternal dance between us and our *sitra achra*. But there's another reason to include our enemies in this tapestry.

Back in the Torah of Sinai, it says we should love and embrace the stranger—care for the stranger—help the stranger. It says so in some form or another *thirty-six* times. And why? The constant refrain: *because we were strangers in the land of Egypt.* We know what it is like to be enslaved, to be persecuted, to be killed simply because of our different background or beliefs. We experienced it in Egypt.

Well, we experienced it at Auschwitz too; and because of that, we should love the stranger all the more. We suffered more there. The *Torah of Auschwitz* has bolstered that pronouncement from Sinai.

But there is a difference.

Both Torahs instruct us to love the stranger because we were persecuted, because we were strangers "there." But only the *Torah of Auschwitz* tells us to love the stranger for precisely the opposite reason—*because the stranger loved us.*

In Egypt, no one helped us, save for a cameo appearance by Pharaoh's daughter by the river, when baby Moses came floating by. That was a big deal (and some traditional commentators do calisthenics to show that she was actually a closeted Hebrew named Batya, "Daughter of God"). But that was it.

The classical commentators go out of their way to say that *all* the people of Egypt were willing co-conspirators in Pharaoh's genocide. There is some dispute about the midwives who helped save some babies, whose national origin is in question. But clearly, in Exodus chapter 1, Pharaoh enlists the entire population, saying "Get ready, let *us* deal shrewdly with them, lest they increase, and a war befall us, and they join our enemies and wage war against us and depart from the land." And so (in verse 13) it states, "The Egyptians enslaved the children of Israel with back breaking labor." Not just Pharaoh—*all* the people. The medieval commentator Ramban suggests that since the original decree of forced labor hadn't done the trick, it was then decreed that all Egyptians had the power to seize an Israelite to do any work they needed done. Everyone in Egypt who needed work done. Mow the lawn? Get Yossi to do it.

There is not one instance of an Egyptian harboring an Israelite fugitive. For the rabbis, this narrative justifies the collective punishment of the ten plagues and the despoiling of the country by the freed slaves. But neither in the Torah nor the traditional commentaries are there any who help; there is no underground railroad in Pittom or Rameses, no Oskar Schindler to save his thousands (1,200 plus their descendants) or Raoul Wallenberg to save his tens of thousands.

The Holocaust was different from Egypt, or anything in the Bible. As of January 2019, Yad Vashem has honored 27,362 Righteous Among the Nations from 47 countries.

So, the *Torah of Auschwitz* states, "Love the stranger, because not only do you know how it feels to be a stranger who is hated, but you also know how it feels to be a stranger who is loved—by someone who was a stranger to you." And it says, "Don't merely love your neighbor as yourself, cultivate kindness in yourself and accept grace from others. Love your neighbor, because you have been loved **by** your neighbor. And through that love, your faith in humankind has been restored. As Primo Levi wrote in *If This Is A Man*, describing his rescuer, Lorenzo Perrone, "*I believe that it was really due to Lorenzo that I am alive today; and not so much for his material aid, as for his having constantly reminded me by his presence… that there still existed a just world outside our own, something and someone still pure and whole… for which it was worth surviving.*"

Enter, Mirosława (Meer-o-SWA-va) Gruszczyńska (GRUSH-chin-ska) a righteous gentile whom my 2017 group met in Krakow. Her family saved a teenage Jewish girl fleeing the destruction of the ghetto. She told her story in a manner that was so mesmerizing because it was so matter of fact. There was a knock at the door to her apartment and her mother answered—and they let someone in.

A knock. A plea. A response.

God? Are you listening? That's how you do it! That's how you answer a prayer.

Or maybe, just maybe, Mirosława *was* God's answer to the prayer of young Jewish girl.

Mirosława's aunt approached her mother Helena with the question of whether the family would be able to temporarily shelter a Jewish girl. The family said yes, and Anna Allerhand came into their lives, but when she stayed with the Przebindowskas (Prej-bin-DOV-skas) she went by "Marysia." They initially thought the hiding would last for just a few days; it turned out to be a couple of years. When Anna arrived, she expressed her gratitude immediately that the Przebindowskas had agreed to help her. Mirosława recalls that Anna immediately ran up and hugged her and kissed her on both cheeks. They quickly became close friends.

When Anna became very sick the family was able to nurse her back to health, and by that time there was no distinguishing her from the rest of the family. She was family—and the love was mutual. The Polish family couldn't imagine sending the Jewish girl back out into the dangerous world where surely, she'd be caught by the Nazis and sent to the camps.

When we asked if she ever thought twice about insisting Anna stay, Mirosława said she never for a moment regretted her decision. She said that she had to do it because it was the right thing to do.

Anna is still alive, living in Israel, and she and Mirosława continue to stay in touch.

Professor Nechama Tec, author of *When Light Pierced the Darkness: Christian Rescue of Jews in Nazi-Occupied Poland* (Oxford University Press, 1987), has researched why two percent of the Polish gentile population acted so selflessly, choosing to rescue strangers at supreme risk to their families and themselves. What these heroes have in common has almost nothing to do with their religion, nationality or education. They tend to be non-conformists with a proclivity for virtuous acts.

Hannah Arendt wrote of the banality of evil. Mirosława is an example of the banality of goodness. On the surface, there is nothing particularly heroic about her. There was nothing particularly herculean about what she did. She just instinctively understood that we are *Rikma Enoshit Echat*—a single human tissue; and our group responded by giving her a standing ovation, and wondering whether we would have been so heroic.

For former NBA star Ray Allen, his first visit to Auschwitz, which occurred almost exactly at the same time as my group's, put him in touch with a similar hero.

For Allen, the Holocaust was about how human beings—real, normal people like you and me—treat each other. In a deeply moving essay, he wrote about a family that hid Jews under the floorboards in a small brick house in the Polish town of Ciepielów, which when they were found out, resulted in most of the Polish family being shot by the SS.

He writes, "When the Skoczylas (SCOTCH-less) family was risking their own lives to hide people they barely knew, they weren't doing it because they practiced the same religion or were the same race. They did it because they were decent, courageous human beings. They were the same as those people crouched in a hole. And they knew that those people didn't deserve what was being done to them. I asked myself a really tough question: Would I have done the same?"

Many people bemoan the fact that more gentiles, in Poland and Hungary especially, didn't do more to save Jews. There is some validity to that, but I am amazed that anyone would have risked their lives to help a people who, since early childhood, they had been taught to despise, who, they had been taught for many centuries, had killed their god. Anti-Semitism was thoroughly ingrained in their culture and especially in the church. But still, some were able to bypass centuries of prejudice and get right back to the core values that spawned Christianity in the first place. Something was able to cut through it all, something innate and good, and it led thousands of people to acts of incomprehensible risk and selflessness.

Take the "Zookeeper's Wife," a book amplified by a recent film. In it, Antonina Zabinski, the hero, states, simply, "I don't understand all the fuss. If any creature is in danger, you save it, human or animal."

The banality of goodness.

Ray Allen writes this about the Jews of the Shoah: "The people of these Jewish communities were pushed to the absolute limit of their human instincts. They just wanted to survive. And from that, the tales of brotherhood and camaraderie are so awe-inspiring. It was a reminder of what the human spirit is capable of—both for good and evil."

I read these ineffably heroic stories and shudder in embarrassment when someone calls *me* courageous for going to a local park to support Dreamers who face deportation from the country they've always called home, or when I invite Muslim clergy colleagues to address the congregation. Compared to people like Mirosława and Antonina, I'm a coward. If I were truly courageous, I would do much, much more in the face of current challenges to democracy—and I would call upon my congregants to do much, much more too.

It's like the way I instruct mourners not to thank those who come to visit them during the mourning period following a death. Of course, gratitude is natural. But when I visit your *shiva*, I'm not doing it out of pity or professional obligation. When I come to comfort you, I'm binding my *own* wounds. We are all woven into the same human tapestry—if you scrape, I bleed. If you mourn, we all mourn.

Victor Frankl was a prominent Viennese Jewish psychiatrist who was transported to a concentration camp in 1942, who survived to write the 1946 bestseller, *Man's Search for Meaning*, a book chosen by the Library of Congress in 1991 as one of the top ten most influential books in the United States. He calls the search for meaning "the last of the human freedoms," one that not even the Nazis could take away. And for him, survival in those extreme circumstances was dependent on the ability to understand "that life was still expecting something from them; something in the future was expected of them." Frankl adds:

> A man who becomes conscious of the responsibility
> he bears toward a human being who affectionately
> waits for him, or to an unfinished work, will never be
> able to throw away his life. He knows the "why" for his
> existence, and will be able to bear almost any "how."

The key to a meaningful life, then, is not distinctiveness but mutuality, not holiness but wholeness, not *Kosher* but *Kesher*.

In Berlin, a new home for interfaith fellowship is being built. It's called the "House of One," and my group passed it on our way back from the Berlin Wall, the past century's definitive symbol of division. This House of One will be a beautiful construction, one that will bring a synagogue, church, and mosque together under one roof. The three distinct sanctuaries will be linked by a community room in the center of the building. I couldn't stop thinking about how that building belongs in Jerusalem.

But no, it's in Berlin, the city where nearly every synagogue window was smashed in 1938, and where a wall split the world in two. In one of history's great ironies, Berlin is the place where Jews are flocking, especially now, when so many other countries seem to be succumbing to the worst nativist and nationalist impulses. Since Brexit, there has been a stunning migration from England back to Germany by a number of Jewish families who had fled Germany in the 30s. They are now returning to Germany.

And so, what does it mean to be one human tapestry?

In April of 2010, as I escorted that group of teens to Poland, when we arrived, we had every reason to be suspicious of the Poles. With all that history of anti-Semitism, it's hard to wipe the slate clean. I was astonished to see anti-Semitic figurines of Jews with moneybags for sale at the airport gift shop (they are still found throughout the country). But when the Polish president was killed in a tragic plane crash on the day after we arrived, suddenly we became the emissaries of the Jewish world at the Polish national *shiva*. Suddenly the fact that we were in Poland was not simply a coincidence of geography, but a summons to responsibility. And our responsibility was to love.

We asked our hotel to secure for us 80 black ribbons, so that we could wear them on the March. We asked our Polish guide to teach us how to say *I'm sorry*, and we said it to every Pole we passed. The word we used was *Solidarnosc*—meaning "we feel Solidarity with you," a term evoking positive memories of our relationship with Poland, including the epic partnership that laid the groundwork for the total collapse of the Soviet empire.

But these are Poles. They're supposed to hate us. And we're supposed to hate them. Aren't we?

Two quick stories:

First from the Zohar (Vol.1:201): A man traveling on a hot day grew weary and sat down to rest on a rock. A snake slipped toward him but a gust of wind came, snapped a branch from a tree and it killed the snake. When the man awoke and stepped away from the rock, the rock suddenly slipped off the cliff.

Rabbi Abba sees what had happened and asks, "What is your merit that you have been saved from death twice?"

The man answers, "I never fail to make peace with those who harm me. I become their friend and repay good for evil. And before I go to sleep, I forgive all who require forgiveness.

Rabbi Abba replies, "You are greater than Joseph. He forgave his brothers, but you forgive strangers as well."

And second, from the Talmud, tractate Ta'anit 25b:

During a drought, Rabbi Eliezer prayed long for rain, but nothing happened. Rabbi Akiva offered a short prayer and the rains fell.

A Voice from Heaven calls out, "Not that Akiva is any better than Eliezer, but Eliezer carries a grudge against those who slight him, while Akiva forgets it and moves on."

Sometimes it is better to have a short memory, as Akiva did; and sometimes it is not. As our Polish guide, Ziggy, suddenly broke down in tears when he realized that he now had to speak of his leader in the past tense, I connected with him on a most human level. We can all recall the shock of first saying a loved one's name in the past tense. I've sat in hundreds of homes and hospital rooms where that has happened. It usually takes a few days, or even weeks, to adapt, as we switch back and forth.

And at that same moment that Ziggy began to cry, I recalled those wintry days in 1980, when Lech Wałęsa's *Solidarnosc* party courageously broke the Soviet stranglehold of Eastern Europe, working in perfect synchronicity with Russian Jewish *refuseniks* who were destroying the Evil Empire from within. Together, working as One Tapestry, the Jews and Poles broke the back of the Soviet Union.

And I remembered March 26, 2000, when a Polish pope wrote a note at the Western Wall and cried at Yad Vashem and prayed for God's forgiveness for "the behavior of those who in the course of history have caused these children of yours to suffer." Rabbi Michael Melchior described the moment as being "Beyond history. Beyond memory."

We felt loved by an unbounded love.

I said to myself as I sat with our guide on that rainy, cold night in John Paul's hometown of Krakow, "How could I possibly hate this man—and these people?"

The Yad Vashem website is overflowing with stories of unfathomable acts of kindness perpetrated by the righteous of all nations—see them at https://www.yadvashem.org/righteous/stories.html

Here's another story from the *Torah of Auschwitz*. In September 1943, as the German military commanders took control of Rhodes, British aerial bombings caused much damage in the Jewish quarter. The Jews wished to protect their Torahs, among them an 800-year-old scroll. In secret, the Torahs were given to the Turkish Muslim leader, the grand mufti of Rhodes, who agreed to house them in, of all places, the pulpit of his mosque! The following July, the Jews of Rhodes were deported to Auschwitz. Of the 1,676 who were deported, only 151 survived. After the war, the Torahs were returned to the few who came back.

But that's not the end of the story. In 1971, the grand mufti confided to a longtime Jewish friend, "One of the greatest moments of my life was when I was able to embrace the Torah, carry it and put it in the pulpit of the mosque—because we knew that no German would ever think that the Torahs were preserved in the pulpit of a mosque."

After all, the Nazis based their worldview on hatred of those who are different. They had perfected the art of turning good people into paranoid haters through the use of demagoguery, by transforming the Other into a subhuman life form: easy to destroy, like a roach. How could the Nazis, of all people, imagine a scenario so filled with the love of one's neighbor? Theirs was a world of black and white, of us and them. It was beyond their capacity to imagine a Muslim leader actually helping Jews.

And that's still not the end of the story. In 2004, a journalist interviewed the daughter of the grand mufti, expressing how much the Jewish community had appreciated her father's gesture. She acknowledged the recognition and then stated, "I have Jewish blood." Not quite sure what she was trying to explain, the journalist asked the translator what she meant by that. She replied, "My grandfather was Jewish, on my mother's side."

That meant that the grand mufti's father-in-law was *Jewish*. Who knew!

Seventy percent of Albanians are Muslims. According to Yad Vashem, there is no evidence of a single Albanian Jew being turned over to a Nazi. Norman Gershman, a Jew who researched this subject, adds that "In many cases, Jews were arrested or were refugees, and those (Albanians) living there would give them false passports and dress them in Islamic garb. In many cases, the Albanian rescuers never even knew their real names."

One Human Tapestry.

After the Holocaust, a new generation of Jews is asking, now more than ever, *why be Jewish?* It no longer suffices to respond to that query, "so that the Jewish people will survive." A religion whose sole purpose is simply to perpetuate itself is already bankrupt. And this new generation has already rejected the arbitrary divisions between groups that marked the old thinking.

In fact, Jews do have a purpose; it is to love. It is to promote dignity and mutual responsibility and to cultivate kindness. It is to channel lives of holiness into lives of utter interdependence—to channel *Kosher* into *Kesher*. We've got to get away from drawing lines in the sand that will be washed away with the next tide. Instead, we must look toward finding that common ground between ocean and shore. It is time to stop building fences and to begin climbing down from them.

If there is a God following Auschwitz, it is the God of *Kesher*—the God of interconnection. It's the God of Abraham and Sarah, whose tent was open on all four sides. And the God of Isaac and Rebecca, who loved both of their sons, as different as they were. And the God of Jacob and Esau, who reconciled with the one to whom he was joined in the womb, as one single human tissue. And it is the God of Moses, who taught us to love the stranger as ourselves.

We should love the stranger, because the stranger loved us, in Krakow, in Ciepielów and at the Warsaw Zoo, even though none did in Egypt. Love the stranger, because we are one human tissue, *Rikma Enoshit Echat*, each of us a single strand in a vast, lovely tableau.

We are caught in an inescapable network of mutuality, tied in a single garment of destiny. Those words of Martin Luther King capture perfectly the essence of the *Torah of Auschwitz*. And that garment is being woven—by us.

Chapter Eight

THE BOOK OF CRUSHED BONES AND SACRED SOIL
The Garden in the East

How can the *Torah of Auschwitz* help to save our planet?

By a pure coincidence of the calendar, the Jewish observance of Holocaust Memorial Day (Yom Hashoah) often coincides with Earth Day, which on April 22, 1970 marked the birth of the environmental movement. Theological arguments abound for aligning the Torah of Sinai with a deep concern for the environment. Jews and Christians both cling to the religious concept of custodianship of the planet, a role that Adam and Eve were assigned in the Garden of Eden.

And it is back at the Garden of Eden where we find the point of intersection of the two Torahs.

According to a rabbinic legend, Adam, on the day of his creation, saw the setting of the sun and was terrified. He said, and I paraphrase, "*Oy Vey!* It's because I have sinned that the world around me is becoming dark; the universe will now become again void and without form—this then is the death to which I have been sentenced from Heaven!"

So, he sat up all night fasting and weeping and Eve was weeping opposite him. When dawn broke, however, he breathed a sigh of relief and said: "This is the usual course of the world."

From the very first sunset, as darkness enveloped them and Adam and Eve were only a few hours old, they experienced the first pangs of Jewish guilt in recorded history. They sensed that they had somehow let God down, that this darkness thing was somehow *their* fault, that they had already messed up the marvelous gift that they had been given.

The *Midrash* continues. God leads Adam around the Garden of Eden, and God says, "Look at My works. See how beautiful they are, how excellent! For your sake, I created them all. See to it that you do not spoil or destroy My world, for if you do, there will be no one to repair it after you."

That's what God tells Adam and Eve. When giving the world's first garden tour, they are warned: This is a beautiful world; but this is it. Don't mess this up. Because if you do, there could come a time when that sun will not rise at the end of a cold, dark night. And if that happens, it will not be *my* fault, God says; it will be *yours.*

As if to underscore that point, God creates a sign a few generations later, following the great flood of Noah. The rainbow is the symbol of the covenant that God made with humanity, signifying that God will never again bring about the kind of massive natural disaster that could destroy humanity. The implied message is that not only are we the earth's custodians, but if we break it, we own it. If we can't make things work on this beautiful planet, we have only ourselves to blame.

The narrative is a folktale, of course. It tells us less about actual goings-on in the long-ago Garden as it teaches us deep-seated Jewish values for our time. And the punch line is that we have messed it up.

The Torah of Sinai doesn't end its eco-advocacy in Genesis. In the words of environmental activist Nigel Savage, "You could argue that the Jewish people have been thinking about sustainable energy ever since God spoke to Moses out of a bush that burned but was never consumed. Moses was perhaps the first environmentalist: He recycled his staff into a snake, got Egypt to turn off all its lights for three days, and convinced an entire nation to go on a 40-year nature hike. The Maccabees took a small cruse of oil and stretched it out for eight miraculous nights."

That climate change is real and a product of human action is now incontrovertible, undeniable, unquestionable, categorical, absolute, incontestable and conclusive; people all over the world have experienced its increasingly untenable consequences. For people in my home region, there was nothing scarier than Superstorm Sandy in 2012. Sandy felt like a return to primordial chaos. But as with Elijah at Mt. Sinai, God was not sensed in the howling winds or crashing waves but rather in the still small voice of compassion that beats in each of our hearts, which led to immeasurable acts of kindness: of people sharing their homes, their showers, their Wi-Fi, of neighbors loving neighbors. At my synagogue, which was fortunate to have power throughout the ordeal, we fed and warmed and powered-up about 100 people. At one point, one congregant turned to me and said, "This feels so right. This is what a congregation is all about. Can we do this more often?"

I turned to her and said, "Unfortunately, I think we'll have to."

When we are routinely talking about one-in-1,000-year events, as we are, we know that something scary is happening to our planet. Recent storms, droughts and heat waves signal that much more needs to be done in the face of a truth that is not merely inconvenient—it is incontrovertible.

So how does the *Torah of Auschwitz* promote the cause of environmental sustainability?

First, by bringing us back to the Garden. In the Torah of Sinai, Genesis reports that the Garden of Eden was "in the east," and when the humans were driven out, angels (*cherubim*) were placed at the east entrance with "a flaming sword" to guard the tree of life. Throughout biblical literature, the journey eastward is the journey toward exile and danger (e.g., Babylon), while the journey westward is one that draws you back toward the Garden, toward safety and home, back to where humanity's sole responsibility was to be curator of wondrous flora, to name the animals and care for the land—and to avoid eating from just two *meshuggenah* trees.

During the Holocaust, the journey east was, just as in Genesis, a journey from the safety of home toward exile, danger, and death. As the Final Solution unfolded, the Germans tried to cover up the mass murder that was taking place, calling the mass deportations of Jews "resettlement to the east." While some technically traveled from other directions to meet their demise, east became the default direction of doom. For France, Germany, Holland and the rest of Western Europe, the death camps were clearly located to the east. From Budapest, Auschwitz was northeast. From Warsaw, Treblinka was eastward. Everywhere Jews went, they were headed east of Eden, and as with Cain in Genesis 4:16, the journey "east of Eden" took them "away from the presence of the Lord."

After Auschwitz, it is hard not to intertwine the two eastward journeys, and imagine the horror of Adam, Eve and their progeny, who could not yet even imagine the concept of exile, riding in a boxcar, destination unknown. No food, no hope, no God.

And from within one of those cars, we find this well-known poem by Dan Pagis:

> **Written in Pencil in the Sealed Railway-Car**
> *here in this carload*
> *I am eve*
> *with abel my son*
> *if you see my other son*

cain son of man
tell him I

Adam's family was resettled to the east. Unlike the Torah of Sinai, the *Torah of Auschwitz* begins not in paradise, but way, way east of Eden; with hell, not paradise, as its starting point, and it traces the journey back home, back to the Garden—a journey that in 1945 took the survivors through fire and water and scorched earth, far more lethal than the flaming swords of the *cherubim*. In the Zionist narrative, one might call those flaming guards British soldiers looking to deport the refugees from Haifa Harbor over to Cyprus. Others might see those guards as unrepentant Poles taking malicious action in the pogroms in Kielce or Arrow Cross Hungarians perpetrating the drownings in Budapest, or in the unending torture of those languishing stateless in DP Camps.

Wherever they journeyed, Europe was a wasteland, and a return to the Garden remained the goal, and that would mean a return to custodianship. We never really gave up our vision of caring for the earth. In Jewish tradition, respect for the health of the environment and concern for the dignity of human beings are two values that go hand in hand. The Nazis were notorious for their pillage of both the land and its inhabitants, and Eastern Europe is paying the price for that to this day. Hitler, who had no problem at all with the decimation of Europe's timeless landscape, carried the scorched earth policy to new lows with his bombing of Britain; his planned destruction of Parisian landmarks; and the 1945 Nero Decree, which called for the decimation of Germany's entire infrastructure in the face of the advancing Allies. The Paris and Nero plans were fortunately never carried out.

The *Torah of Auschwitz* goes deeper than merely confirming that war is not healthy for Jews and other living people. It's not healthy for other vegetation as well.

I once visited the site of Dachau, the concentration camp just outside Munich. I say that I visited the "site" of Dachau, because it wasn't Dachau. Yes, the name was there, right next to the infamous inscription, *Arbeit Macht Frei*. Yes, the barbed wire was there, and the barracks, remarkably well preserved, and the ovens. Yes, there were memorials to the dead, marking mass graves of nameless victims. But it wasn't Dachau.

Dachau was hell and this wasn't it. There were flowers at this place, surrounded by fresh-cut grass. I could hear birds. I even saw a butterfly, which confirmed for me that this was not Dachau, for the famous children's poem from Terezin tells us that there were no butterflies in the ghetto.

If this was not hell, then what was it, and why did it suddenly look so lovely, so natural? This image was burned into my psyche again on subsequent visits to Europe, including the one in 2017 with my congregation. Places once marked for complete devastation now look idyllic. Death camps, ghettos, even decimated cities, now look gorgeous and green and renewed. We visited Dresden on that recent tour, a name that is synonymous with carpet bombing—albeit by our side—and you would never know it had once been reduced to rubble. The countryside of Poland, where hundreds of Jewish shtetls once stood, now is as pristine and bucolic as it is *judenrein*.

Even Auschwitz itself is grassy, green and, in its own way, lovely.

What are we to make of this loveliness?

Is this a cruel trick by God, a vain attempt to reclaim that which God had ceded to the beast in humanity in 1933? Or is this God's apology, this smattering of forget-me-nots and daisies embedded in cemetery sod, a plea for forgiveness, too little and too late?

Or maybe God is hoping, beyond hope, to give Jews and others one last chance to regain the illusion of an attainable paradise on earth, a thin veneer of April hope covering the reality of August hell.

"Here," God is telling us, "I can't give you redemption. All I can give you is this spring-like illusion. Let it ease the pain of your wanderings. Take it."

So, the connection between Yom Hashoah and Earth Day is this: On Yom Hashoah we say to God that this plan, however comforting and kind, can't possibly work. We reject the illusion. We have seen hell firsthand; it won't be forgotten. Time will not heal this wound. If renewal is possible following the Holocaust, a God who was absent during it cannot bring it about. God, who could not save the Jews, will also not redeem the earth. If renewal and hope are at all possible, only human beings can facilitate it.

There are two seemingly contradictory verses in Psalms. Psalm 24 tells us, "The earth is the Lord's and the fullness thereof," while we read in Psalm 115, "The heavens are the Lord's heavens, but the earth has been given to humankind."

This discrepancy can be resolved by drawing from it this lesson:

Once upon a time, the earth was the Lord's, but since the Holocaust, it is ours and ours alone.

Anyone can grow a few forget-me-nots.

Before the Shoah, when the earth still belonged to God, we, who had once experienced Paradise firsthand, could only imagine Eden's opposite. As David Grossman writes in his masterful novel, *See Under: Love*—

"We always pictured hell with boiling lava and pitch bubbling in barrels," until the Nazis came along, "showing us how paltry our pictures were."

Now, nothing is left to the imagination. The earth is ours and we are utterly responsible for all that happens to it; all of it—the people, and the flowers, too. Those flowers at Dachau have become a symbol of God's ultimate helplessness and our ultimate responsibility. We still pray, though no longer for divine intervention, but in gratitude for the basic tools provided us: warm summer days, rain in its season, the miraculous ecosystem. We look to heaven for resolve but for little else, for "the earth has been given to humankind."

That is the environmental message of the *Torah of Auschwitz*.

And this:

The blood of our brother Abel is screaming from that very earth. We must care for the earth because our ancestors and martyrs are buried within it. The earth is not only their legacy to us; it **is** them—their bones, their blood, their illusions, their dreams, and their follies. Their cries seep through the thinning atmosphere. Their tears fall as acid rain. Defoliated rainforests uncover their nakedness. We cannot go anywhere without walking on their bones. We must tend to their graves.

The earth is not only ours, it **is** us. Chief Seattle, a Native American leader of the nineteenth century, wrote, "This we know, the earth does not belong to us; we belong to the earth."

In time my bones will rest there too, serving as a firm platform upon which a new generation will walk.

In caring for our planet, we sanctify those who died and affirm life for those not yet born. We do it not out of the illusory hope that the world can be as it was, for we shall never return to Eden. We do it because we must, because it is our responsibility. No one else will do it for us. And if we succeed, if the world becomes a more habitable place for our grandchildren, then we'll have taken a small step toward resuscitating a measure of hope.

The Hebrew word for wind is *ruach*, which also means "spirit." In Judaism, the meteorological and spiritual are deeply intertwined. The experience of a storm like Sandy—or of devastating wildfires in the tinder of California, or catastrophic famine in South Asia or cataclysmic floods in Texas or Puerto Rico or along the Mississippi River—is a profoundly spiritual one, even in our day. Perhaps *especially* in our day, since, we can pinpoint well in advance what will happen, yet we are completely powerless to stop it. The weather is one of the few things left that reduces us to mush in the face of its power. It makes us realize how insignificant we really are.

Except that we're not.

We're not insignificant here, because we can make a difference. Some of the damage of climate change can be reversed, or at least slowed. And from a Jewish perspective, what is most important is that we can fulfill God's call to Adam and Eve by preserving our planet, and we could save lives.

We are all woven into a single tapestry of human and humus, of the living and those who once were alive, whose nutrients continue to sustain life. The skies of Poland, once filled with the smoke of human flesh killed industrially, remind us that human life is unsustainable when it the air around us is filled with any manner of industrial smoke.

This is the best we can hope to accomplish in the age of scorched flesh and earth. This is the environmental message of the *Torah of Auschwitz*: We've got to get ourselves back to the Garden.

But as I write these words, Paradise has already been lost. Paradise, California was home to about 26,800 people, before the most devastating forest fire in California's history destroyed the peaceful community. After the fire did its total damage, 90 percent of the people were gone. Nine of every 10 homes were destroyed.

Hear Tamra Fisher, fleeing her home in her car, frantically texting her sister, Cindy. "Answer me!!" Tamra texted again. "It's raining ash and bark." But the power is out. The cell towers too. Her sister can't be reached. Later, Cindy spotted her home in aerial footage of Paradise on the local news. Her above ground swimming pool was unmistakable. Nearly everything else had burned into a ghostly black smudge.

Paradise is burning.

"*Es brent…It is Burning*" is a Yiddish poem-song written in 1936 by Mordechai Gebirtig. The Yad Vashem website states, "The song became a prophetic song of the impending Holocaust, describing the burning of the Jewish shtetl. The poet calls upon the Jews not to stand idly by, but to be proactive and put out the fire that is consuming their precious town. They should extinguish the fire and demonstrate to the world that they can take care of themselves."

It is burning, brothers, it is burning
Our poor little town, a pity, burns;
The tongues of fire have already
Swallowed the entire town.
Everything surrounding it is burning,
And you stand around
While our town burns.

Es brent! The shtetl is burning. Paradise is burning. The Amazon is burning. The bush is burning. The world is burning—and we are being consumed.

So what can we do? We can't stand around. Had people heeded the warning of the song *Es Brent* in 1936, who knows how many lives could have been saved. The *Torah of Auschwitz* cries out *Es brent* as a clarion call to save what can still be saved.

The burning bush is the only place in the Torah of Sinai that is specifically called holy ground, according to commentaries, precisely because it is *not* in the land of Israel and because the fire did not consume it. God evidently prefers bushes that *aren't* consumed, and holiness extends way beyond the boundaries of our holy city and holy land. It's a message to us, to hear and to heed—to hear the flames, and to feel the scorched earth. Moses took off his shoes to sense the holiness of that ground. With our shoes off, we can focus more on the impact of our footprint, our *carbon* footprint, and get to our God-given task of healing the planet.

And that work is starting. Israel, which led the way in drip irrigation decades ago to make the desert bloom, is now the world leader in the desalination of water. We've been planting trees there religiously, and tree planting is one way to save the earth. China has just undergone a project to plant 200 million trees over the next 40 years. That will help. It is so fitting that our holy land has become a focus for the salvation of our holy planet.

The *Torah of Auschwitz* shifts our attention back to Eden in one other significant way: We must care for the earth because our ancestors and martyrs are buried within it. The blood of our brother Abel is screaming from that very earth. The earth is not only their legacy to us; **it is them**—their bones, their blood, their illusions, their dreams, and their follies. Their cries seep through the thinning atmosphere. Their tears fall as acid rain. Defoliated rainforests uncover their nakedness. We cannot go anywhere without walking on their bones. We must tend to their graves.

Chapter Nine

THE BOOK OF UNRELENTING QUESTIONS
Winding Paths to a Wounded God

The experience of the Holocaust stands alone in history, a godless coun-
terpoint to all things sacred. Alongside the majestic peaks of Sinai and Zion,
our view now includes this man-made mountain of children's shoes, empty
luggage and echoing shrieks, a clump of human refuse that dwarfs everything
around it, taller than Sinai, more imposing than Zion, more insurmountable
than Everest.

Throughout this book, I've addressed the issue of God somewhat pe-
ripherally, offering a few possibilities for understanding the divine in light
of the most ungodly event of all time. I've suggested equating God with the
life force within all living creatures (chapter 1), as a source of vision (chapter
4), and as a purveyor of unity (chapter 7). But the *Torah of Auschwitz* is a
human-centric document. It is a fool's errand to attempt to explain God's
ways in a Holocaust setting. As Rabbi Irving (Yitz) Greenberg has explained,
any theological explanation for the Shoah must consider the specter of living
babies being thrown into flames. If your understanding of God can survive
that and still be coherent, all power to you.

The great Israeli poet Yehuda Amichai presented the matter succinctly in
his 1999 poem, "After Auschwitz."

> *After Auschwitz, no theology:*
> *From the chimneys of the Vatican, white smoke rises—*
> *a sign the cardinals have chosen themselves a Pope.*
> *From the crematoria of Auschwitz, black smoke rises—*
> *a sign the conclave of Gods hasn't yet chosen*
> *the Chosen People.*
> *After Auschwitz, no theology:*
> *the inmates of extermination bear on their forearms*
> *the telephone numbers of God,*
> *numbers that do not answer*
> *and now are disconnected, one by one.*

After Auschwitz, a new theology:
the Jews who died in the Shoah
have now come to be like their God,
who has no likeness of a body and has no body.
They have no likeness of a body and they have no body.

Even Amichai, the inveterate skeptic, seeks a theological basis for a world that can include both God and the Holocaust. We are drawn to theological speculation as moths to a flame. Some say we have a "religious instinct," asserting that if there were no God we would be compelled to invent one. Whether or not that's true, it's worthwhile to explore new ways to imagine God, ones that do no shame to the memory of the abandoned martyrs.

While humbly acknowledging that post-Holocaust God-talk is often a fool's errand, allow me to offer some theological saplings from which a post-Auschwitz theology might germinate (somehow that word seems inappropriate), with the understanding that these are not intended to be comprehensive treatises, but simply kernels to provoke thought:

The God of Toyota and the God of Chelm

In the spring of 2010, as I prepared to face the enormity of Auschwitz for the first time on the March of the Living, that annual gathering of thousands of Jewish teenagers in Poland, it occurred to me that since the Shoah, rabbis have become like Toyota salesmen.

At that time Toyota was going through an existential crisis, having had to recall 7.5 million vehicles because gas pedals were getting stuck and people were dying as result. The company was faced with a branding catastrophe.

Let's play this analogy out. What, after all, is religion selling but a product once universally revered but now questioned. The myth has been detonated, the brand exposed. Just as the 2010 Toyota crisis evoked memories of a time when "Made in Japan" was considered derogatory (meaning cheap, fake, laughable), after the Holocaust, the "Made at Sinai" Torah suddenly feels too fragile and cheaply designed, like the postwar version of "Made in Japan."

To be frank, we clergy have been trained too well to contain the damage, having been taught numerous diversionary strategies when the Holocaust comes up, enabling us to refocus the question ("Where was God? Well, where was **Man?**") or simply foster a perpetual state of denial ("We can't know God's ways"). Some have chosen to relinquish some of God's omnipotence; others go much farther. But for the most part, we hammer home the message that religion still has an important function to serve, even if there's a gaping hole under the hood. Some deny that the hole exists, clinging naively to pre-Auschwitz fantasies. It is astonishing how many otherwise intelligent, modern, skeptical Jews still adhere to the old, omnipotent "what-me-worry" patriarchal Santa-God in the sky, slickly packaged by various groups, as if the Holocaust had never happened. But most rabbis, while not denying the seriousness of the challenge, prefer to set the questions aside and punt, suggesting that maybe the next generation will gain the insight to solve the problem. I, for one, have become an expert punter.

Over the decades, there have been noteworthy attempts to deal with this dilemma. Some, like Richard Rubenstein, writer of the existentialist treatise, *After Auschwitz*, have been powerfully honest. Radical theologies like his proliferated in the 60s, during the so-called "Death of God" era. Since then, God has managed to survive quite nicely, thank you, while those bold theologies have yellowed with age.

Reinhold Niebuhr (1892-1971) offered that "God" is simply a metaphor for God; in other words, we shouldn't get too hung up on any name or particular image of what God looks like or does. Harold Kushner, in *When Bad Things Happen to Good People*, offered a post-Holocaust notion that God can no longer be seen as omnipotent, but that God is found in the love that enables us to recover from tragedy. I lean in that direction, but it sounds a bit too convenient for us to be able to mold God in our image, according to our current theological needs, while divorcing God from the responsibility of evil. It makes God sound too clever by half, parsing responsibility onto some other god over there. Many Jews are choosing more Kabbalistic imagery, which imagines God more as a system of forces, or emanations, in a carefully balanced yin-yang type of universe. Many are groping for a metaphor that allows for a more complicated, wounded deity; or at the very least a not-so-omniscient one; or perhaps a preoccupied one; or one who was simply asleep on the job. The question of Auschwitz remains as vivid as ever, but after seven decades, many seem to be tiring of asking why and have given up on God altogether.

The *Torah of Auschwitz* compels us to continue that unrelenting questioning and not to give up on God so easily, whether or not God has given up on us.

Toyota eventually solved their branding problem; but if they hadn't, one wonders whether the marketers would have eventually worn us down by constantly repeating old canards. Would we all have started believing in their product again, even without discernable evidence of improvement? Would we have eventually tired of asking the questions?

Is the same true of God? Would we go back to clinging to naïve superstitions, simply because they are more comfortable than the yawning, hopeless abyss that awaits those who dabble in a godless universe? Would we eventually accept intellectually comatose rationalizations like the one made by an Ultra-Orthodox rabbi in Israel, who claimed that God caused a bus accident to occur because a mezuzah hanging on a passenger's door at home was not kosher?

Perhaps the antidote to such spurious speculation is to leave the realm of logic altogether—though without abandoning our skeptic's scalpel. Perhaps the answer is to accept a dash of madness with our theology.

In 2010, the day after I marched at Auschwitz with the teens, my group stopped off on the way to Warsaw in a quaint town called Chelm, which for Jews is the eternal capital of absurdity. Chelmites are mythical Jews from a real town, known for their propensity to take logic to its bizarre extreme.

Two men of Chelm went out for a walk, when suddenly it began to rain. "Quick," said one. "Open your umbrella."

"It won't help," said his friend. "My umbrella is full of holes."

"Then why did you bring it?"

"I didn't think it would rain!"

A New York-based Klezmer group named Golem wrote a song about a Chelmite who leaves on a journey to Warsaw, gets lost and ends up back in Chelm. "He's so stupid that he thinks he's actually in Warsaw," bandleader Annette Ezekiel told SPIN.com. "The moral is, any place can be any place else—it doesn't matter where you are."

But for me it mattered a lot; that this journey from Auschwitz, the darkest place in Jewish history, led directly to Chelm, the most absurd. Chelm was the place where I could wash and purify my hands after visiting the countrywide graveyard that is Poland, a waystation before heading to Jerusalem for the second part of the March.

Two points about Chelm: First, for the storytellers, laughter provided a great outlet from hunger, poverty and hatred, of which the Jews of Poland had no shortage. But rather than laugh at real people, the genius of these storytellers was that they invented a mythical community to laugh at. Yes, the people of Chelm were not *really* bumbling idiots. Not only is that practical (as opposed to laughing at Poles, who might have responded by killing them), it is far more ethical to make fun of fake people than real people. So instead of telling Polish jokes, Jews told Chelm jokes.

Second, Chelm might hold the key to our getting beyond the theological quandaries of our age. If the commanding voice of Auschwitz has muffled the God of Sinai for the time being, maybe we need to pay more attention to the God of Chelm. The Yiddish aphorism, "Man plans, God laughs," just might be the most apt theological response to an age of absurdity. It's not that God is laughing at us, simply that God has taught us that laughter is the only way one can respond to a world of unfathomable evil and unspeakable tragedy, while clinging to life and dignity.

Maintaining some semblance of sanity requires a modicum of insanity; it's an art we've been perfecting for centuries, ever since we figured out how a poor peasant living in rags could be transformed into royalty through the simple act of lighting candles, drinking wine and blessing bread on a Friday night. If that isn't a little taste of madness, what is? The first Jewish kid, whose life was replete with tragedy, was nonetheless named laughter (Isaac). We've been reliving Isaac's story ever since.

Whatever enables us to escape from a bitter and unjust reality can help to preserve our essential humanness. Jews were quixotic long before Quixote, waving at windmills and looking perfectly ridiculous while clinging to their dignity in the most undignified of settings.

Elie Wiesel often told this Holocaust-based modern midrash about the significance of flailing at windmills in the ancient, corrupt city of Sodom:

"One day a *Tzadik* (righteous person) came to Sodom. He knew what Sodom was, so he came to save it from sin, from destruction. He preached to the people. "Please do not be murderers, do not be thieves. Do not be silent and do not be indifferent."

He went on preaching day after day, maybe even picketing. But no one listened. He was not discouraged. He went on preaching for years. Finally, someone asked him, "Rabbi, why do you do that? Don't you see it is no use?"

He said, "I know it is of no use, but I must. And I will tell you why: in the beginning, I thought I had to protest and to shout in order to change them. I have given up this hope. Now I know I must picket and scream and shout so that they should not change me."

And picking up on this theme of absurdity, Woody Allen ends his classic film, *Annie Hall*, with a similar story containing a perfect message for the *Torah of Auschwitz*:

"A guy walks into a psychiatrist's office and says, 'Hey doc, my brother's crazy! He thinks he's a chicken.' Then the doc says, 'Why don't you turn him in?' Then the guy says, 'I would, but I need the eggs.' I guess that's how I feel about relationships. They're totally crazy, irrational, and absurd, but we keep going through it because we need the eggs."

Despite the near impossibility of accepting theological explanations for God's silence during the Holocaust, we still need the eggs—we still need to struggle with a notion of God, and the possibility of a just universe and a hopeful existence. And who says we can't struggle and giggle at the same time?

The God Particle

Here's another God-option from the *Torah of Auschwitz*.

In October of 2012, on the night that Hurricane Sandy roared in, two giant trees sandwiched my house and pierced the garage roof. It felt like the world itself was crashing down, as if I was witnessing before my eyes an undoing of Creation's primal act. In Genesis, a wind brought about a separation of earthly and heavenly waters, and then a separation of water from dry land. But with Sandy, the waters of the deep appeared to be reclaiming that coastline and undoing that initial act of separation. It felt apocalyptic.

During that season of Sandy, I did some exhaustive research on the Mayan Apocalypse—which was subject to immense speculation late that year. According to an ancient Mayan prophecy, the world was scheduled to come to an end on December 21. On the plus side, had that prophecy come true, Jews would have been able to squeeze in all eight days of Chanukah (sorry, no Christmas). On the minus side, the world would have ceased to exist.

But my research turned up a different vision. According to Guatemalan author Carlos Barrios, that fated date of December 21, 2012 marked not the end of time as Hollywood would imagine it, but the beginning of a change in consciousness, when "a new socioeconomic order will arise in harmony with Mother Earth." These beliefs all revolve around the winter solstice coinciding with the Earth's being located at a point of particular balance, midway through the Milky Way.

What we have with the Mayans, then, at least in some people's estimation, are cycles of creation and destruction, leading not to an apocalypse, but rather to a time of eternal peace and bliss—a *better* time, not an end time at all.

It all sounds very, well, Jewish. Midrash Genesis Rabbah cites Rabbi Abahu's claim that God created numerous universes prior to the creation of this one. Each time that God created a universe, something went wrong and the experiment was discarded. But when this one was created, God looked around and saw that it was very good. Our version of the cosmos was a keeper. This one God could work with.

What a great story. It teaches us that for the ancient rabbis, not even God could determine in advance whether a given world would work out. There were apocalypses aplenty. But this teaching leads inevitably to the question, why has *this* world not been destroyed? And the answer is either 1) it hasn't been destroyed *yet*; or 2) because this time, for this cosmos, creatures called human beings have entered into the picture, and they've demonstrated a capacity to grow and adapt. This midrash adds that the entire cosmos possesses the same innate ability to regenerate.

A few years ago, scientists reveled in the discovery of the Higgs Boson, or so called "God particle." In my layman's understanding, this subatomic particle somehow takes mass and propels it into energy. It drives everything forward, and in doing so, it enables existence to happen.

Maybe this little particle, seen from a more theological standpoint, is also that microscopic spark of divinity that pushes us to get up when we've fallen, like that panic button seniors wear. Even if we are physically unable to rise from the floor, there is something pushing us to live on. We've got the God particle. And we've learned that not only is it in our DNA, it's in our every atom. It's implanted into the workings of the universe.

So despite the Holocaust and all the inexplicable evil around us, God imbedded within us a gift that no prior creation received, the gift of a second chance…and a third, and as many chances as we need, to rise from the ashes.

There is something in our makeup that keeps pushing us forward.

In chapter 2 I spoke about that inner drive to "choose life" that propelled the Candy Man and Elijah Girl, the same one that lends sweetness to the freezing carrot and has boosted the against-all-odds revival of the Jews of Budapest. Here I'm going one step beyond that conscious will to live; I'm suggesting that the drive is not a choice at all, but something embedded within us, and I give that life-force a name. For lack of a better one, I call it "God."

The survival instinct goes beyond free will. We recognize that when we try to hold our breath until our bodies force us to submit and breathe. Even after Auschwitz, there is something pushing life forward. It is the God particle, and it is in us all.

The Shadow of God

In the *Torah of Auschwitz*, the path back to God is littered with shattered dreams, flavored with a strong sense of the absurd mixed with a pinch of wonder. We remain attuned to the possibility of an orderly universe, despite all that we have witnessed.

Borrowing from a term used by physicist and philosopher Thomas Kuhn, Reb Zalman Schachter-Shalomi sees our new era as a "Paradigm Shift," post-monotheistic, post-patriarchal, more universal and syncretistic. One might quibble with the details, but it's clear that we have entered a time of theological creativity, equaled perhaps only by the Axial Age 25 centuries ago, when theological giants from Buddha and Jeremiah to Confucius and Homer changed everything.

If we allow ourselves to be swept up by these new winds, maybe the scent of sanctity might be sniffed through the swaying treetops. Maybe God can appear to us again—and if not God, or even a crescent of the eclipsed God, perhaps the shadow of God.

Betzalel was the leading artist of the Torah of Sinai and designer of the tabernacle in the wilderness, mentioned first in Exodus. His name means "in the shadow of God." It is through the mind of the artist that a new sanctuary will be designed, allowing us, if we are fortunate, brief glimpses of the divine silhouette.

It says in the Talmud (Avot), "In a place where there is no humanity, try to be human." And how do we do that? We don our smock, we pick up the brush, and we begin to paint a picture of such beauty and goodness that it could survive even its own destruction. Even if we succumb to the evil around us, as Anne Frank did, the art remains, her words remain, rising above even the smoky pyres of Bergen-Belsen—much as occurred during the Hadrianic persecutions of the second century, when Rabbi Haninah ben Teradion, wrapped in a Torah scroll while being burned at the stake, exclaimed, "The parchment is being burned but the letters are flying free!"

The art becomes the affirmation, and within that affirmation glows the penumbra of God's shadow.

Numerous stories of transcendent artistry have emerged from the Holocaust.

In March of 2018 in the southern development town of Yeruham, Israeli schoolchildren performed lost music written by Jews during the Shoah. An article in *Ha'aretz* describes how conductor Francesco Lotoro chastened his musicians, consisting of 20 teenagers dressed in jeans, sneakers and T-shirts, "to convey the desperate passion and dramatic tension of a tango written in the Nazi death camp of Auschwitz-Birkenau."

"*Der Tango fun Oshwientschim*"—as the anonymous Yiddish song is titled—is part of the core repertoire of this orchestra, which is dedicated to playing music composed during the Holocaust.

The article describes how Lotoro "has made it his life's mission to find, preserve and popularize music *that was composed by Jews and other prisoners during World War II*—from entire operas written on toilet paper in Nazi camps to love songs created by POWs from all sides of the conflict." He's salvaged 8,000 musical compositions created by Jews during that darkest of times in the darkest of places.

Lotoro cites the example of the imprisoned Czech composer Rudolf Karel, who wrote down a nonet (composition for nine instruments) and a five-act opera on toilet paper using medical charcoal, which he received because he was suffering from dysentery. His works were smuggled out by a friendly guard, but Karel ultimately succumbed to exposure and dysentery in Terezin just two months before the end of the war in Europe.

"The paradox is that we have more music created in Birkenau, where there was extermination by gas, than in Auschwitz I, where there were also Poles, Soviets and it was a different kind of captivity," Lotoro told Haaretz. "Where there is more danger of death, you create more music," he says.

Robert Mapplethorpe once said, "When I work, and in my art, I hold hands with God."

The *Torah of Auschwitz* sees art as a path toward a restoration of the Sacred, as we join Betzalel in continuing to defy the darkness by designing sanctuaries, making music, writing poetry and dancing.

The great Isaac Stern, of blessed memory, was performing a concert in Jerusalem during the Gulf War in 1991, and he was interrupted by a siren warning of an Iraqi Scud missile attack. After the audience put on gas masks, Stern returned to the stage and played a selection from Bach. He refused to wear a gas mask, in effect daring Saddam Hussein to silence the music.

Artists in extremis live in the shadow of God. But of all the artistic responses to catastrophe, none can match what I saw in Washington State. The canvas was Mount St. Helens and the artist—the artist in the shadow of God—was God.

On May 18th, 1980, the eruption of Mount. St. Helens in southwest Washington changed more than 200 square miles of rich forest into a gray, lifeless landscape. The lateral blast swept out of the north side at 300 miles per hour creating a 230-square-mile fan-shaped area of devastation reaching 17 miles from the crater. With temperatures as high as 660 degrees and the power of 24 megatons of thermal energy, it snapped 100-year-old trees like toothpicks and stripped them of their bark. The largest landslide in recorded history swept down the mountain at speeds of 70 to 150 miles per hour and buried the North Fork of the Toutle River under an average of 150 feet of debris. The massive ash cloud grew to 80,000 feet in 15 minutes and reached the East Coast in 3 days, circling the earth in 15 days. Death came in the wake of the eruption: 7,000 big game animals, 12 million salmon, millions of birds and small mammals and 57 humans died in the eruption. Before the blast, the mountain stood 9,677 feet tall. It now stands at 8,363 feet. A thousand feet of mountain is no more. Talk about destruction!

So, when I went there with my family in 2003, I expected to find an eerie moonscape, but I saw something absolutely amazing instead. The land around the mountain is slowly healing. There is new growth everywhere—trees and moss and animal life. What in Auschwitz and Dachau had looked grotesque and manipulative (see chapter 8), like tampering with evidence at a crime scene, here looked astonishing and perfectly natural.

In fact, life returned to Mount St. Helens even before the search for the dead had ended. National Guard rescue crews looking for human casualties during the week after the 1980 eruption found that flies and yellow jackets had arrived before them. Curious deer and elk trotted into the blast zone just days after the dust settled. Helicopter pilots who landed inside the crater that first summer reported being dive-bombed by hummingbirds, which mistook their orange jumpsuits for something to eat. A whole new ecosystem began to emerge. Peter Frenzen, the chief scientist at Mount St. Helens, put it best, "Volcanoes do not destroy," he said, "they create."

As I looked out on all this creative destruction, I finally understand how Jews developed their proclivity for confronting madness with lightness, and absurdity with artistry. We inherited it from the God who renews Creation each day. Never was that more evident to me than at Mount St. Helens.

So, to ask whether God's brand has been permanently dented by the Holocaust is to ask the wrong question. Would you buy a used Toyota from this deity? Perhaps not. But the gift of artistry, which is a shadowy reflection of divine inspiration, has granted us the courage to stare directly into that gaping hole in the chassis and chuckle at the absurdity of it all, while gasping in amazement that, despite everything, we are alive. And if we are alive, there, in some manner, must be miracles, after all.

The Eclipse of "The Eclipse of God"

On the last Sunday of August, 2005, while Hurricane Katrina was battering the southern coast, I set out from Westchester airport on a flight to Chicago for the wedding of a close friend, which I would have the double pleasure of attending and performing. The plane pulled out to the runway about 15 minutes late. No problem. We waited there another 15 minutes or so. That seemed a little strange, considering no other planes were landing or taking off. Finally the pilot got on the speaker and let us know that there had been some alarm lights blinking. It was probably a false alarm; he had seen this a few times before, but they needed to get a mechanic on board just to make sure.

An hour later, with passengers beginning to get restless, the pilot came on again. He told us it looked bad—that he was going to have to set the wheels in motion to have the flight cancelled. Mass hysteria followed as the cell phones came out and people frantically began making alternative arrangements. I just sat there. I felt terribly about the wedding but knew I was powerless to do anything about it. My friend is a rabbi—I wondered if Illinois law would allow him to perform his own wedding. But there was something in me that just wouldn't let me panic, something reassuring me that things would turn out all right in the end.

A few minutes later, the pilot came on again. "Someone must really want you to get to Chicago. The problem has been solved and we'll be departing in just a few minutes."

Now I faced another dilemma—do I really want to take off for Chicago in this plane? Again, I was calmed by an inner sense that things would be OK. We took off over two hours late and I made it to the wedding just in time.

As we were flying, I was speaking with the woman in the row behind me and we talked about the pilot's line that someone wanted us to get to Chicago, and how surreal the whole experience had been. Was it all just coincidence or part of some master plan? Did someone really want me to be at that wedding? Or was there another person on that plane with an even more important task, perhaps a task that that person was not even aware of? "It seems so odd," I said.

The woman looked at me and replied, "You know the old saying, 'Is it odd or is it God?'"

I did not reveal my secret identity. But I thought about the simplicity of the catchphrase— one that has been popularized by Twelve Step groups— and how it leaves so little room for a middle ground. And although I'm usually a bonified shades-of-grey kind of guy, when I thought about it, she was right. Either everything is completely random, or it's all part of some divine scheme.

For a Boston Red Sox fan like me, October 2004 was redemptive. Side by side in my office hang photos of Boston and Jerusalem. My exilic existence has been marked by a constant yearning for redemption in both of my ancestral homes. For one that meant a thriving Israel, freed from fear. For the other, for most of my life, it meant a Red Sox World Series championship.

Through the misty sky on Wednesday night, October 27, 2004, a ruddy moon glowed from behind the earth's shadow. At the precise time of the lunar eclipse, the Red Sox won the World Series. Some called this definitive proof that there is a God.

Too many things broke right for the Sox that year, too many of their prior indignities were undone in uncanny ways, for their improbable victory not to have somehow been written in the stars. Even before that season began, the

Sox had couched this campaign in religious terms, unfurling a huge "Keep the Faith" banner above the Western Wall—I mean the Green Monster. This would at last be the season when their 86-year-old "Curse of the Bambino" would be lifted. Their epic, seven-game series with the Yankees played out these redemptive themes, carrying the Sox and their fandom from the brink of disaster to the greatest comeback seen since the Exodus, climaxing with the parting of the Red Sea, which is what Cardinal fans called their packed stadium. It all seemed so biblical.

True to my fatalistic Red Sox roots, I had expected yet another loss, a continuation of what Martin Buber called, in his classic 1952 essay, *The Eclipse of God*, "the still unredeemed concreteness of the human world in all its horror." Buber's paper, written shortly after the Holocaust, was an effort to rummage through the ashes for some way of understanding the incomprehensible and reconciling himself to a world without an operational deity.

But a half century after Buber, I witnessed the eclipse of Buber's eclipse, and it was happening on my TV screen in real time. There was an actual lunar eclipse going on during the fourth and final World Series game, and the cameras kept focusing on that disappearing and reappearing moon over and over again. It was simply too *God* to be odd.

Among the dozens of congratulatory e-mails and calls I received the day after the Eclipse of the Curse, this message stood out: "In this world of so much discouraging news, how wonderful to have something to cheer about! The eclipse underscored this night of sports history and affirmed the importance and joy of believing in your dreams against all odds."

So against all odds, was it God?

And so, you might ask, how can we believe in a God so capricious as to allow millions to die in gas chambers and yet align stars to help a baseball team? Wasn't this concept of "believing in your dreams against all odds" now officially dead, having been incinerated at the same place as one third of my people?

The *Torah of Auschwitz* leaves that question unanswered, but offers as consolation the absurdity of Chelm, the embedded God particle to propel us forward from the inside, the silhouette of Betzalel's divine artistry and the capriciousness of an occasional sublime breakthrough—what we in the religion biz call a hierophany. Maybe a slivered corona of an eclipsed orb can peek through from time to time, and maybe a dormant deity can somehow awaken too. We've got God the artist and the standup comic. God laughs, God creates, God peeks through randomly.

But can any of these Gods save? Can any of these theologies account for babies being tossed into the flames?

In a word, no.

As we continue to call out into the void, from time to time we can hear something faint coming back. Sometimes the Joban call is answered. Sometimes, inexplicably, the Universe listens.

In the end, we are left with unrelenting questions and no true answers. While the *Torah of Auschwitz* might give us glimpses of the artist-formally-known-as-God, the focus always returns to us. We can never prove whether God is best understood as a shadowy artist, a stand-up comic, a life force within us or the corona of an eclipsed heavenly orb.

But despite all evidence to the contrary, Elie Wiesel, the great prophet of the *Torah of Auschwitz*, the one who will be recalled as long as Jeremiah and who had every reason to succumb to despair, said this in a 2006 interview with *Time*:

"(Albert) Camus said, 'Where there is no hope, one must invent hope.' It is only pessimistic if you stop with the first half of the sentence and just say, There is no hope. Like Camus, even when it seems hopeless, I invent reasons to hope."

We cling to hope and invent reasons to hope, if not for some manifestation of a traditional God, then at least for a notion of Ultimate Justice; because we desperately need the moral foundation laid out at Sinai. In that sense, we need God because no human being should ever be allowed to usurp that divine role. We need God to prevent extremists from perverting religious imagery to horrific ends. But should God tarry, we need the courage to take matters into our own hands and bring justice to our world.

Chapter Ten

THE BOOK OF THE GRAY ZONES AND BIG LIES
Thou Shalt (Not) Kill Baby Hitler

In the spring of 2015, I received a message from a journalist friend of mine. He wanted my take on an ethical dilemma that was making the rounds.

Suppose you could go back in time and you see Hitler as a two-year-old playing in the sandbox. You have two minutes to decide what to do. You could go up to him and kill him by any means. If you do kill him, all of history will be changed. There will be no World War II, no Holocaust, 50 million people and six million Jews will have been saved. The question is: is it morally right to kill him?

The question had been the subject of an academic study that spring demonstrating that, when it comes to ethical dilemmas, men are typically more willing to accept harmful actions for the sake of the greater good than women.

I thought about it and, well, the first thing I thought was, naturally (I'm a rabbi, after all), "I just got a great sermon!" But nah, that was too easy. So, I wrote a series of articles and sermons, responding to this ethical quandary in dramatically diverse ways; and in doing so, I delved into the realm of ethics, which is and must be a major component of the *Torah of Auschwitz*. While moral dilemmas are hardly new and predate the Holocaust by many centuries, since Auschwitz we've entered a brave new world of complex choices. The ethical tenets of the Torah of Sinai, highlighted by the Golden Rule, need now to be retrofitted to reflect the impossible "Sophie's Choice" scenarios described by Elie Wiesel, Primo Levi, the partisans, the *Sonderkommandos*, those who gave up their children, and those who ran away from their elderly parents to save themselves. Even the actions of the notorious *Judenrat*, who betrayed their fellow Jews hoping simply to survive, only to find themselves meeting the same fate, deserve to be addressed from an ethical standpoint. Primo Levi spoke of the Holocaust yielding a complex set of ethical dilemmas that he called the "Gray Zone," because rarely are the solutions black and white.

Given that world of complexity, just one response to this viral question about whether to kill baby Hitler would not suffice. So, I present you with four of my own, followed by some others that I've discovered.

1) I'd hug him.

I truly believe that every act of unconditional love has redemptive power. All we need to do to set the world on a course toward salvation is to hug more children more often. But instead, we're sacrificing them on the altar of our ambitions. We're humiliating them, overindulging them, ignoring them, racing them to nowhere, over-programming them and infecting them with hate. We're allowing them to wallow in loneliness. We are casting them off and burdening them with excessive educational debt. We are poisoning their earth. We're filling their bellies with sugary soft drinks and numbing their minds with electronic distractions. We are failing to show them the importance of service and seeing a world that is much larger than themselves.

The "Kill Baby Hitler" dilemma is really not about the mustachioed child we didn't hug in 1891, but the cherubic, innocent child we could hug today—and don't. Who knows where that child will turn for acceptance. That hug could save a life, or ten, or, who knows… millions. That hug could redeem us all.

2) I'd kill him, and in doing so wipe out the "Amalek within."

In prior chapters of this book, I've referred extensively to Amalek—that rogue nation that attacked the Israelites in the Wilderness—and to different ways Jews have interpreted the Torah of Sinai's commandment both to remember what Amalek did and to blot out their memory. Tradition has it that all enemies of the Jewish people can trace their lineage back to Amalek; and the command to wipe out Amalek is seen as a commandment to defeat all who seek to destroy the Jews in every generation.

One way of looking at that commandment, discussed in chapter 5, was preferred especially by the early Hasidic commentators. Rabbi Levi Yitzchak of Berdichev wrote: "Not only are Jews commanded to wipe out Amalek, who is the descendant of Esau, but each Jew has to wipe out that negative part that is called Amalek hidden in his or her heart. When the power of evil in each of us arises, Amalek is present in the world."

What is our inner Amalek?

It is that part us that succumbs to the impulse to take advantage of people's weaknesses; that is cruel and hateful and angry and derisive and out of control; that force within us that sees every encounter as a means to an end; that objectifies other human beings as if they were pieces on a game board—instead of fellow living, breathing souls created in God's image.

We've got to wipe out *that* Amalek, while it is still playing in the sandbox, before it gets so strong that it takes control of our souls. For as the most villainous embodiment of Amalek himself is said to have written, long after he outgrew the sandbox, "Conscience is a Jewish invention. It is a blemish, like circumcision…I am freeing men from the restraints of an intelligence that has taken charge; from the dirty and degrading modifications of a falsehood called conscience and morality."

Since it was Hitler's struggle to release the world from the "burdens" of morality and restraint, even more so is it our crusade to reinforce those so-called burdens. It is our task to champion conscience. Our struggle—our *Kampf*—is to subdue that inclination to follow the crowd, to succumb to our first whim and mindlessly obey the orders of impulse. In that way, we can vanquish *Amalek*—and its modern incarnation, Hitler—forever from within our hearts. That's what it means, metaphorically, to kill baby Hitler.

3) I'd spare the toddler. We cannot change history, nor should we want to.

No, I would not change history and kill two-year-old Hitler to prevent the Holocaust. Nor would I go back and change a single choice that I've made, even ones that I regret. Life is not lived backward; it is lived forward. In fact, it is lived Fast Forward. And it is lived *Far* Forward. For while we humbly accept that we can't change history, we need to boldly affirm that we can make history.

Interestingly, David Brooks began a 2015 *New York Times* column with that viral baby Hitler analogy, and then asked us to imagine a world with no Holocaust—a world where the deed of killing the young Hitler had taken place. How different would it be? A third of the Jewish people would not have been killed. They would have survived to write great novels, make fantastic scientific discoveries and bring Judaism to new heights.

But Brooks asserts that the world we *have* would *never have come to be* without World War II. The Hitler question is really about changing all of the past. To erase mistakes from the past is to obliterate your world now, he says. You can't go back and know then what you know now.

If we were to change any event in history, especially a massive event such as the Holocaust, everything taking place after that event would now be different. This means, if you want to get technical about it, that anyone born after the Holocaust would most likely not have been born. Think "Back to the Future." If Marty McFly's parents nearly don't fall in love at the high school dance, his existence dissolves into oblivion. If six million Jews had not been killed and the world had not been decimated by a cataclysmic war, would our existence have been nullified too?

So here's the tradeoff—and *this* is the *real* ethical dilemma: It's not whether or not to kill Hitler, sacrificing one life to save millions. What if the quandary is whether to kill two-year old Adolf and save the six million, with the cost being to give up *our own existence*. Six million survive—but most of us are never born. Not even Sophie faced such a choice!

Would you choose to have the world exactly as it is right now, with a Holocaust; or one without a Holocaust, but without *you*…a completely different world with a completely different set of people? Who knows, quite probably no State of Israel. On the bright side, no Edsel, no New Coke or Pol Pot—but if you are under the age of 70, no *you*.

So that question about changing the past teaches us that it is pointless to dwell on the could-have-beens, and points us toward the might-yet-bes. Can we take the long view? Taking the long view and getting beyond ourselves has been the secret to Jewish survival for 3,000 years.

One rabbi who survived a Siberian gulag spoke of how he learned the secret to survival from a tightrope walker who was also imprisoned there. The rabbi asked the tightrope walker the secret of his art. Is it balance? Concentration? Stamina?

"No," the tightrope walker said. "The secret is always keeping the destination in focus. Because, when you lose sight of your destination, even if just for a second, that's when you will fall."

The whole world is a very narrow bridge; so the key is not to fear—and not to look down. Or back. So we spare baby H, come what may.

4) I'd kill him, and in doing so cut off at the roots, at long last, the nightmares that continue to haunt us.

Google "Hitler" and you will find 101 *million*. The guy's been dead over seven decades. We are giving him a shelf life he doesn't deserve. It's time to slay the demon. It's time to put little Adolf to his bed, once and for all.

By killing the demon, I am not suggesting that we forget. Heaven forbid we should forget the Holocaust. As I said at the outset of this book, any Judaism to emerge out of this new era must place the Holocaust experience directly at its core, or it will not be authentic; it will fail to speak to our need to confront this black hole in our history. But just as the new Judaism we are forging cannot ignore or deny the abyss, it must also speak to our religious need to affirm joy, beauty, renewed life and at least the possibility of a responsive divinity, or it will not be sustainable. There needs to be a new balance between Auschwitz and Sinai that considers the lessons of both. Our goal should be nothing less than for the next generation to see bearing witness not as a burden, but as a privilege, an honor, and yet another source of pride in who they are.

You can now see how the idea of this book originated from the baby Hitler dilemma, which I explored in a series of sermons and columns in 2015.

Soon after I delivered those sermons that fall (and I presume with no causal connection), Baby Hitler suddenly was everywhere. The little rug rat was featured in the *Atlantic* and then in a *New York Times* poll, where 42% of respondents said they would do the deed. Among the candidates running at that time, Ben Carson chimed in (saying that he wouldn't kill him if he's a fetus—and that he would have given Jews guns) and Jeb Bush responded enthusiastically ("Hell, yeah!").

On his show, Stephen Colbert gave his take:

"I wouldn't let him join anything where they have to wear a uniform—no Cub Scouts, no Little League, definitely no marching band," Colbert said. "Most importantly, I would teach Baby Hitler that we do not solve our problems with violence, and then—if he starts getting mouthy as a teenager, I stick a knife in his ribs and snap off the handle. If that attack fails, and the horror of being stabbed by a person that he thinks is his father turns him into a monstrous dictator, it's easily fixable," Colbert added. "I just go back in time and kill Baby Me."

The *Washington Post* speculated on what a world without Baby Hitler would look like. Social media outlets piled on the satiric memes and tweets ("Maybe you'd grow up to be history's greatest monster too if 42% of @NYTmag's readers were always trying to kill you"); and yes, there were tasteless Halloween baby Hitler costumes galore.

Australia's Ethics Centre website presented a series of thought-provoking responses, by Matthew Beard:

Baby Hitler is Innocent

Most ethical justifications for killing start with the presumption that people don't deserve to be killed unless they've done something to forfeit their right to life. Depending on who you speak to, this might include being involved in an attack against somebody else, being in the military or even trafficking drugs.

But unless baby Hitler is running a Walter White-esque meth operation out of his preschool, he's probably done nothing to forfeit his right to life. Until he does—say, by orchestrating genocide—Hitler retains it. Killing him as a baby would therefore be wrong.

Acts of Evil Have Personal Costs

Knowingly doing the wrong thing—like killing an innocent baby—carries a personal cost. When we transgress against deep moral beliefs we can experience debilitating guilt, shame, anxiety and depression. Such actions can even come to define us permanently.

Some academics are now using the term "moral injury" to describe the personal costs of acting against our moral beliefs. "Don't kill innocent children" is arguably the most deeply-held moral belief any of us have. Violating that norm comes at a severe price.

Doing Something Wrong for the Greater Good Doesn't Always Work

German philosopher Immanuel Kant rejected the idea that ethics was just about "the greatest good for the greatest number" (a view known as consequentialism). Instead he argued that ethics was about doing what you are duty-bound to do—such as tell the truth and don't kill.

He once considered the question of whether you could lie to save someone's life. A murderer asks you for the location of a certain baby because he wants to murder him. Can you lie to save the baby's life? Kant argued that you couldn't—because you can't guarantee that your lie will save the baby.

If you send the murderer to the bowling alley knowing the baby is upstairs, who's to say the babysitter hasn't taken the baby to the bowling alley without your knowledge? Suddenly you've told a lie and the baby is still dead, so you've made the situation worse overall.

In the case of Hitler, you would need to be *certain* his death would prevent the rise of Nazism and the Holocaust. If—as many historians contend—the rise of Nazism was a product of a range of social factors in Germany at the time, then killing a baby isn't going to reverse those social factors. Butchering the babe might even allow for the rise of another power—equal to or worse than Hitler.

And you've still killed a baby.

Killing Isn't Necessary

Some people argue that killing the innocent might be justified when it is the lesser evil. But even in that case it has to be absolutely necessary. If time travel is possible it seems unlikely to be necessary to *kill* baby Hitler as opposed to, say, kidnapping him, adopting him out to a Jewish family or offering him a scholarship to the Vienna School of Fine Arts.

Human lives are of immense, perhaps even infinite value. To take one life—especially an innocent one—when it isn't absolutely necessary is a serious ethical issue.

Dangerous Precedent

Where do we draw the line? Once we're done with Hitler which baby is on the block next? Pol Pot? Stalin? The guy who spoiled the end of *Harry Potter and the Order of the Phoenix* for me in high school? We would require a set of consistent, universal ethical principles by which to determine which babies deserve death and which don't.

Giving baby Hitler all of our murderous attention betrays our cognitive and personal bias—surely there are other worthy candidates? How many lives must a person take before their infant self is a legitimate target for killing? What standard will be applied?

For me, I wouldn't do it.

The Baby Hitler craze resolved little, but it reminded us just how relevant, how current, how alive the Holocaust remains in our day-to-day conversations. And the fact that these conversations could include more than a smattering of humor indicated that we've passed a threshold where it is no longer "too soon" to speak in hypotheticals about a previously unspeakable catastrophe that was all too real.

Moral Quandaries Beyond Baby Hitler

I used to write a column for the *New York Jewish Week* called "Hammerman on Ethics," and the Holocaust seeped into a number of my responses—not simply because it had become a preoccupation of mine, but because of the nature of the questions themselves. So many ethical issues lend themselves to reconsideration after Auschwitz. Two cases in point: tattoos and cremation.

Here are the questions, and my (updated) responses:

Q—*I recall reading several years ago about a survivor's son who had engraved a tattoo on his arm to match the one borne by his father at Auschwitz. I understand that he meant it as a gesture of solidarity, but doesn't Jewish law prohibit tattoos?*

A—You recall correctly and the concerns are justified, but not simply on halachic terms. Yes, tattooing is explicitly banned in the Torah primarily, according to Maimonides, because it was seen as a form of idolatry. One professor suggests that non-idolatrous tattooing may have been permitted and certain types of tattoos used for medical procedures today are totally OK. There is also no truth to the rumor that those with tattoos can't be buried in Jewish cemeteries. And of course, Holocaust survivors bearing tattoos are exempt from this prohibition because the engravings were forcibly administered.

The case you speak of involves Dr. Ron Folman, whose father was initially appalled at the idea but eventually relented. Yeshayahu Folman actually went to the tattoo studio with his son and rolled up his sleeve so that an exact duplicate could be made. The father called it "an act of solidarity," but a painful one that would burden his son for the rest of his life. No doubt it has added to the father's burden as well.

As if there weren't enough to burden him. In fact, to a degree, we all carry that burden—and we should. Just not on our arms.

At a time when so few survivors remain, I can sympathize with the Folmans' thinking. A generation from now, we'll need all the physical reminders we can find in order to convey the message "Never forget" in as powerful a manner as possible, and no visual is as powerful as that. In a strange twist of irony, this sign ("*ot*" in Hebrew) parallels the phylacteries that Jews wear daily, wrapping leather straps around their arms as a symbol of the binding nature of the covenant. When you take off *tefillin* (phylacteries), it leaves a mark, almost like a temporary tattoo. I call it "*tefillin* arm" and it is a physical reminder that I have communed with God that day (but don't wrap so tightly that you cut off circulation!).

Here's a case where the Torah of Sinai and the *Torah of Auschwitz* come into direct conflict. One form of tattoo commands us to aspire to the triumph of life; the other marks humankind's deep descent to the realm of death.

One reason to forgo tattoos is that our bodies are divine gifts fashioned in the image of God. What right do we have to abuse that gift? Doesn't that diminish our humanity? Since God is ever evolving, so are we—we are more human "becomings" than human beings. But a tattoo is fixed; it never changes, and that runs counter to the Jewish message of always growing and embracing change. Branding people like cattle only serves to dehumanize us, diminishing the godliness within us. By imitating despicable Nazi practices like branding arms (and for that matter, cremating bodies) aren't we perpetuating the evil rather than remembering it?

There are better ways to perpetuate the memory of the Shoah's victims. And those young'ns who think tattoos are *sooo* cool, who plan to burn a butterfly on their back or a snorting bull on their arm, might pause for a moment first and think about what's on Yeshayahu Folman's arm...and who put it there.

Q—I have always been under the impression that cremation is forbidden by Jewish law. Yet the recent funeral for Amy Winehouse was very Jewish in nature although the singer—who was amply tattooed—had asked to be cremated. Is cremation now accepted in Jewish quarters?

A—The 27-year-old British singer was cremated and yes, she was bedecked with tattoos. I'll focus here on whether it was appropriate for her to have had a traditional Jewish funeral, with a rabbi, *shiva* and all the trappings, when her body was not laid to rest in the traditional Jewish manner.

Unlike other liberalizing trends in contemporary Jewish life, there has been no great clamor for cremation rights. So, the ancient taboo has retained its potency—in theory at least. The practice of cremation is something foreign to Judaism, and that runs across the board, for all denominations. Surely the Holocaust plays into this in our generation (although I've recently heard of some Jews desiring *to* be cremated precisely to show solidarity with Holocaust victims—a practice that in my mind is counterintuitive), but the rationale goes to the heart of what it means to be a Jew. We believe that human beings are created in God's image; there is something about each of us that is of infinite value. Our bodies are therefore sacred and should not be summarily destroyed. If we treat the dead with dignity, the hope is that we will treat the living with the same measure of respect. The Nazis did the opposite, of course, branding people like cattle, crushing them like insects and slaughtering them like sheep.

That having been said, rabbis should always be looking toward the needs of the mourners and in many cases will officiate at memorial services and *shivas*, regardless of how the deceased was interred. There are rulings allowing for the interment of ashes in a Jewish cemetery. Some rabbis might even officiate at that burial and others would officiate, at the very least, at a service taking place elsewhere, before the cremation occurs.

Had I been asked to officiate at Winehouse's cremation, my response, to quote her most popular song, would have been "No, no, no." But I would have done the funeral, and with an immense sadness having far less to do with how she adorned the outside of her body than with the substances she put into it.

There's no denying the tragic nature of this death, even as many of the details remain unknown. Winehouse's honesty and fragility have had a deep impact on her fans and her death should be a wakeup call as to how we revel at watching celebrities self-destruct (see Lohan: Lindsay and Sheen: Charlie).

A death like this should not be fodder for gossip columns. We should strive to salvage a modicum of dignity amidst the media circus that engulfed her soul long before the flames incinerated her body. The real ethical issue here is not how Winehouse's corpse was destroyed after she died, but how so many burdens and pressures conspired to destroy her while she was alive.

Honoring Parents? Healing the Sick?

So many of the Torah of Sinai's fundamental moral laws have taken on added meaning in the *Torah of Auschwitz*. Take the fifth commandment, for example. Honoring parents was difficult enough before people had to decide whether to abandon them to the advancing SS when it was possible to survive by escaping to the forests with the partisans. And then there was Klara, a 92-year-old survivor from Belgium who told Matan Rochlitz in the *New York Times* that she and her boyfriend jumped from a train headed to Auschwitz, leaving her ailing father behind on the train. Many decades later, she met up with a total stranger in Tel Aviv, who had been on that train and was carrying a message from her long-dead father, a message endorsing her act of abandonment. A Gray Zone, if there ever was one.

In the *Torah of Auschwitz*, some bedrock moral certainties have traded in their exclamation points for question marks, while others have gained prominence in the pecking order of *thou shalts* and *thou shalt nots*.

Maimonides, an eleventh-century physician as well as an all-time rabbinic authority, wrote a Jewish version of the Hippocratic oath for doctors:

"The eternal providence has appointed me to watch over the life and health of Thy creatures. May the love for my art actuate me at all times; may neither avarice nor miserliness, nor thirst for glory or for a great reputation engage my mind; for the enemies of truth and philanthropy could easily deceive me and make me forgetful of my lofty aim of doing good to Thy children. May I never see in the patient anything but a fellow creature in pain. Grant me the strength, time and opportunity always to correct what I have acquired, always to extend its domain; for knowledge is immense and the spirit of man can extend indefinitely to enrich itself daily with new requirements. Today he can discover his errors of yesterday and tomorrow he can obtain a new light on what he thinks himself sure of today. Oh, God, Thou has appointed me to watch over the life and death of Thy creatures; here am I ready for my vocation and now I turn unto my calling."

A doctor's prime responsibility is to alleviate pain and protect life. But what of the Jewish physicians in the ghettos and camps who tried as best they could to prolong life even under horrific circumstances and in many situations where their abilities were taxed to the extreme?

Dr. Michael Nevins describes several excruciating scenarios, including these three, in an article for the *Jewish Virtual Library*:

In September 1942 a 22-year-old Jewish senior medical student, Adina Blady Szwajger, gave lethal doses of morphine to several elderly patients and about fifteen infants and children in order to spare them suffering certain death at the hands of the Nazis. While she could hear screaming downstairs as the German and Lithuanian guards were taking the sick from the wards to the trucks, the older children were told that the medicine would make their pain go away. They quickly fell asleep, but since Doctor Szwajger had to flee, it's uncertain whether all the patients died because of the morphine.

Rabbi Shimon Efrata, formerly the rabbi of Bendery (Bessarabia) was deported to Siberia during the war and after the collapse of Germany was appointed rabbi of the surviving community of Warsaw. During his tenure there, he was asked whether a Jew hiding from the Germans in a ghetto bunker must repent for inadvertently smothering a crying infant to avoid detection? His responsum, published in 1961, concluded that Jewish law does not require that the infant be killed; rather, it is optional. If one chooses to die rather than to kill the child, they shall be called holy. However, the individual who did inadvertently suffocate the child should not have a bad conscience for he acted lawfully to save Jewish lives.

In Robert Liften's book, *The Nazi Doctors: Medical Killing and the Psychology of Genocide*, he cites a Jewish doctor who survived Auschwitz:

"At a certain point, he and a few other prisoner doctors were overwhelmed with moribund patients, with suffering people clamoring for relief. They did what they could, dispensed the few aspirin they had, but made a point in the process of offering a few words of reassurance and hope. He found, almost to his surprise, that his words had effect, that 'in the situation it really helped.' He concluded that by maintaining one's determination to try to heal, even under the most extreme conditions, 'I was impressed with how much one could do.'"

Human Dignity and Broadened Concern

Writing for the Parliament of World Religions, Rev. John Pawlikowski wrote in 2014 that three basic perspectives stemming from the Holocaust have become foundational for contemporary ethical reflection:

- respect for basic human dignity must supplant any notion that only correct belief entitles one to fundamental rights;
- our universe of moral concern must be broadened beyond the parameters of our own faith and national communities; and
- acknowledgment of past failings on the part of our religious and national communities is a necessary precondition for development of the internal integrity necessary for genuine and consistent moral commitment.

In addition, studies such as Rab Bennett's volume, *Under the Shadow of the Swastika: The Moral Dilemmas of Resistance and Collaboration in Hitler's Europe*, have advanced research into the ethical decision-making that had to be done during the Holocaust itself.

The Canary in the Coal Mine of "Fake News"

The Holocaust runs rampant on our ability to determine right from wrong; that, in fact, was the intent of the Nazis—to create those "Gray Zones" cited by Primo Levi. In forcing the *Sonderkommando* to work the gas chambers, they forced Jews to carry out the most heinous crimes on their fellow Jews—to save themselves, and thereby to blur the line between perpetrator and victim. Levi wrote, "Conceiving and organizing those squads," he said, "was National Socialism's most demonic crime."

But that which giveth ambiguity also taketh ambiguity away.

Now, just as the concept of objective truth has been once again been placed under attack by a new generation of Nazis and Nazi-enablers, the *Torah of Auschwitz* is riding to the rescue—*for Holocaust denial is the ultimate manifestation of Fake News.*

In fact, the Nazis were the ones who invented the very term "fake news." As Historian Timothy Snyder wrote in an op-ed in the *New York Times*, (Oct. 16, 2019), Adolf Hitler employed the slogan "Lügenpresse," "lying press," in order to malign fact-based journalism; and the *Times*, in a subsequent editorial (Nov. 30, 2019), demonstrated how President Trump's frequent use of the term spread like a virus among authoritarians and would-be strongmen across the world.

Just a week after taking office in January of 2017, the Trump administration chose a symbolic and fitting target for their first major post-inauguration assault on truth (that is, unless you consider the size of the inauguration itself "major"), and it was the Holocaust. Whether or not it was premeditated, what could not be denied was the symbolism and pure cruelty of Sean Spicer's clumsy assertions regarding Bashar al-Assad, Hitler and gas, along with his doubling down on an International Holocaust Day statement that was baldly *Judenrein*.

Spicer said, "We didn't use chemical weapons in World War II. You know, you had someone as despicable as Hitler who didn't even sink to using chemical weapons." And then, after reflecting, he elaborated, saying, "I think when you come to sarin gas, he was not using the gas on his own people the same way that Assad is doing."

On one level, Spicer had a point in comparing Assad's actions, in gassing his own citizens, to Hitler's—but in a manner having nothing to do with gas, and everything to do with the lies and distortions used to cover up the crime. Assad's and Hitler's actions were analogous in this way: Assad's ludicrous claim that the images of suffocating children were staged by child actors was reminiscent of the staged, infamous visit of the Red Cross to Terezin in 1944. The resultant propaganda film of the camp fooled the world into thinking that a notorious concentration camp was the happiest place on earth, filled with tanned, toned and beautiful vacationers, who were, in fact, actors.

The Torah of Sinai affirms that deliberate deception on a scale such as this is a serious violation of the norms of a civilized society. The rabbinic sages wrote (Tosefta Bava Kamma 7:8): "There are seven kinds of thieves—the first of them is the one who deceives people."

At least Spicer later apologized for his outlandish claims, for which he must be given credit. But here is why Sean Spicer's fumbling, bumbling, pathetic comparison of Assad to Hitler matters, despite the apology. And here is why the Administration's steadfast refusal to follow the Spicer route and issue a similar retraction for its infamous *Judenrein* Holocaust Day statement also matters.

Holocaust denial is the canary in the coal mine of Orwellian doublethink, the mother of all fake news, in that it not only defies all standards of empirical science and rejects meticulously documented history, which any act of historical denial might do, but in this case, doing so also attempts to whitewash the greatest moral crime ever perpetrated.

There is, and there never has been, a greater, more bald-faced lie than the denial of the Holocaust. That fact alone warranted an official, immediate White House retraction.

With the rising popularity and enabling of extremist nationalism, Holocaust deniers are enjoying a new popularity. When the Torah of Sinai speaks of the command to remember the evil of Amalek, it is speaking to our generation specifically about keeping alive the memory of the Holocaust, along with other interpretations discussed in prior chapters. And here is one more: The command to remember Amalek is a summons to preserve the essence of *all objective truth.* Holocaust denial is simultaneously an act of both of pure evil and unadulterated falsehood.

The *Torah of Auschwitz* makes clear that the commandment to remember the Holocaust is about keeping alive the essence of all objective truth. The dilution or outright denial of this truth is the nullification of all truth. The Holocaust was objectively, verifiably, utterly—and not alternatively—a fact. That fact is one of the pillars of our epoch, a fundamental truth, and a foundation upon which we are trying to reconstruct a civilized society.

In Judaism, the Big Lie is a Big Sin, and there is no bigger lie than Holocaust denial. In the *Torah of Auschwitz*, the simple act of remembering is an affirmation of honesty in the face of nihilistic cynicism.

Maimonides wrote:

"A person is forbidden to act in a smooth-tongued and luring manner. He should not speak one thing outwardly and think otherwise in his heart. Rather, his inner self should be like the self which he shows to the world. What is in his heart should be the same as the words on his lips" (Hilchot De'ot 2:6).

What a perfect lesson for Spicer's old boss to internalize: The minimizing or denial of the Holocaust-truth is a red line that no public figure should ever be allowed to cross. Once that truth is established, we can begin to work some other basic truths. Facts matter. Words matter. If you are going to lie about the Holocaust even before the inauguration bleachers have been taken down, it should surprise no one that, according to the *Washington Post* Fact Checker, 13,500 lies will pass your lips in your first 1,000 days in office.

For Jews, the pursuit of truth is a fundamental value in and of itself. Judaism is inherently counter cultural, subversive and self-correcting. We don't own the media, but many great journalists happen to be Jewish, because no other religion places inquiry as so fundamental a value that the first Jewish ritual a child performs is to ask a question—four of them, in fact, at the Passover Seder. We ask questions, we demand the highest standards of justice and we do not compromise when it comes to opposing the abuse of power and the pursuit of truth. That is non-negotiable. Real news follows a rigid system of journalistic ethics, with an ironclad commitment to accuracy, independence, fairness, and accountability, and an understanding that words have the power to both harm and heal. There is no new normal when it comes to Jews pursuing truth. This is our *old* normal, our *forever* normal and our *only* normal. But after Auschwitz and in the face of the Trump's *Lügenpresse*-style assault on independent journalism, epitomized by the world-wide attack on the historicity of the Holocaust, what has always been unflinchingly normative must now become a crusade.

The Book of Exodus states that when the Israelites received the Torah they said "*na'a'seh v'nishma*," often translated as, "We will obediently act and *then* we will understand." But the word "*na'a'seh*" connotes active engagement, not blind obedience. In our age of bots and fake news, the *Torah of Auschwitz* reframes this verse to be better understood as, "We will grapple with each word to assess its validity, and *then* we will understand." Each of us needs to be that pain in the butt critiquing social media posts passed along by people we love. On all sides of the political spectrum, the time has long since passed for blindly sharing or retweeting without first being sure that the source is reputable. We need to be the ones to ask, all the time, is this true? *Na'aseh V'Nishma*, the post-Holocaust ethic demands: We will scrutinize and *then* understand.

State-Sponsored Denial: Poland's Holocaust Law

We are also challenged by the Polish government's assertion that Poles were not responsible for the Holocaust—yet as we saw in chapter 7, there were a number (small, admittedly) who brought an angel's grace to Jews seeking refuge. Poland's infamous "Holocaust Law," enacted in 2018, criminalized accusations of Polish complicity in the Holocaust. This is another manifestation of Holocaust denial, this time given the imprimatur of law.

The law has caused a deep rift in Polish-Israeli relations, leading to a full-page plea for understanding by 50 Righteous Gentiles, among them Mirosława Gruszczyńska from Krakow, whom we met in chapter 7.

Some, like Shmuel Rosner in the *New York Times*, have advocated for Jewish tourists to boycott Poland to protest this law. I disagree with that proposal. Poland's denial of historic fact is troubling, but it also not universal. When I visited in 2017, my group received mixed messages rather than outright denial of Polish complicity. For instance, in Warsaw's spectacular new Polin Museum, commemorating a thousand years of Jewish life in Poland, one display speaks with an admirable honesty about the topic, stating, in Polish and English:

"What was the attitude of Poles to the Jewish tragedy? Few chose to risk their lives and the lives of their families by trying to save Jews. Many were simply too preoccupied with everyday hardships of the occupation to concern themselves with the fate of Jews. Some Poles denounced Jews to the Germans or murdered them themselves. How did those on the Aryan side react to the Warsaw Ghetto uprising? Some sympathized with Jews and admired their heroism. Most, however, were indifferent, while others made anti-Semitic comments."

This hardly sounds like a whitewash to me. The museum was created by a unique partnership of the Polish government and the private sector, including Jewish groups. It has been praised universally and is part of an impressive and expanded array of memorials, museums and restored synagogues in Poland.

The Polin Museum also describes the vibrant Jewish life that preceded the rise of the Nazis, when Warsaw was the second largest Jewish city in the world, trailing only New York, and its cultural life was unrivaled. Even now, it is impossible to find a place on the planet that teems with the intellectual ferment that existed among Polish Jews between the wars. We need to learn more about that.

In assessing the complicated historical relationship between Poles and Jews, let's acknowledge that we share quite a bit. While horrible things happened to Jews there, horrible things—admittedly less horrible—happened to Poles too. Jews also need to understand that the most infamous anti-Semitic episodes on Polish soil over the past millennium—like the 1648 Cossack-driven massacre—were not perpetrated by Poles.

And what exactly is "Polish soil," anyway? Poland has been sliced and diced by its neighbors more than just about any other place on earth—except the land of Israel. With empiric Russia on one side and aggressive Germany on the other, and throw in the Hapsburg empire for good measure, I'm not sure we give Poland its due for standing up to oppression as often as it has.

Poles and Jews also share this: one can make a solid claim that the two biggest causes of the downfall of the Soviet Union were the Soviet Jewry movement and the Polish Solidarity movement. And just as "Jew" became a moniker of mockery in Europe, so did "Slav," a term derived from "slave." Poles, who are Slavs, have, like Jews, often been derided as an inferior race and ridiculed by the haters of this world.

As much as Poles need to understand the unique Jewish sensitivities regarding the Holocaust, Jews need to acknowledge that it is a great injustice to call Auschwitz a *Polish* death camp. It wasn't and that mistaken phrase has been repeated often, even if innocently by those viewing the term "Polish" as being purely geographic. When President Obama said, "Polish death camps" in 2012, he later apologized in a letter to Polish President Komorowski, stating that the phrase was intended to describe "a Nazi death camp in German-occupied Poland," stating further, "I regret the error and agree that this moment is an opportunity to ensure that this and future generations know the truth."

When my synagogue's group was being taken through the Resistance Museum, which commemorates the Warsaw uprising of 1944 (during which the Nazis killed over 180,000 Poles), one of my congregants had a spirited exchange with our guide, somewhat reminiscent of the Nixon-Khrushchev "Kitchen Debate" of 1959. Here's how that congregant, Parry Berkowitz, remembers it:

"As I recall the interaction at the Resistance Museum, I challenged our guide for her incessant narrative about the Poles being victimized by the Nazis and the implication, to me at least, that what the Poles endured was somehow equivalent to what the Jews endured. There was no acknowledgement, even tacitly, about the role that many of the Poles played in the persecution of the Jews and how many of the Poles profited from their Jewish friends and neighbors being hauled off to their deaths, or how, when the miraculous few who managed to survive the camps came back to their towns to find their Polish friends and neighbors living in their houses or in possession of their belongings and then claiming rightful ownership and refusing to return the plunder.

"What got particularly under my skin was her response to my challenge. Instead of simply acknowledging that, yes, some of the Poles were not without blame, she instead subtly tried to defeat my premise by citing a worthless, and wholly irrelevant, statistic about the fact that more Poles than any other nationality were represented at Yad Vashem as Righteous Among the Nations, as if to imply that the Poles are all heroes and should be universally lauded for their actions during the war, including her own grandmother, who she claimed also helped Jews. Her statistic about Yad Vashem, while true, was misleading, as I pointed out. The fact that there are more Poles counted as Righteous Among the Nations than any other nationality is just an accident of numbers—there were simply more Jews in Poland than anywhere else. Compared to the overall number of Jews in the population, as a proportion, the number of Poles who did anything is miniscule, and the misleading statistic should not be used to try and demonstrate the universal virtue of the Polish citizenry during the war in the face of the Nazis."

Yad Vashem lists 6,992 Poles among the Righteous Gentiles, and there were likely many more. While the percentage of righteous Poles among the overall population, relative to the three million Jews who lived there, is admittedly very low, I agree with Parry that the guide seemed to write off Polish complicity too glibly. In my mind, however, as I mentioned in chapter 7, the question should not be why there weren't more Righteous Gentiles, but rather how so many could have had the courage to act so boldly at all, overcoming not only fear for the fate of their families, but also centuries of anti-Semitism inculcated by the Church.

Here's something else Jews and Poles share—the concern for an alarming erosion of fragile democratic norms all over the world, through dangerous demagogic tactics of strongman leaders who pit one group against another. What's happening in Poland is also happening in Hungary, and in both countries, our group confronted guides who were terrified to discuss the culpability of their co-nationals during the Holocaust. The rise of governments who refuse to accept responsibility for their actions *back then* is only a symptom of the antidemocratic virus infecting them *now*. It was so sad to see this in Poland; my prior visit in 2010 was very different. That was the week the Polish leadership was killed (somewhat suspiciously) in a plane crash over Russia, and our March of the Living group shared in their grief. That government had been at the forefront of real gains in Polish Jewish relations and the advance of democratic values. That government had built the Polin Museum.

In Poland and Hungary, the far-right wing governments have consolidated power by following a familiar playbook. They demonize the press, co-opt the judiciary and direct anger toward familiar scapegoats. Both Poland and Israel have followed that playbook with regard to the Holocaust Law. It's much easier to stoke old resentments than to nurture peace. Both are playing up the affronts for domestic political gain.

That playbook's principle author is neither Hungary's Victor Orban nor Poland's Andrzej Duda, but their neighbor to the east, Vladimir Putin. So, if Jewish tourists are looking for a place to boycott, how about Russia? No other country has been more responsible for the swirling hatred that is infecting our world, the suppression of free speech, the corruption of the press, the murder of innocents, the exaltation of the cult of personality, and the continuing and as-yet unchecked attacks on America's most sacred institution, the unfettered right to vote.

Those tourists who wish to boycott a country should direct their attention toward the head of the snake. I for one will not consider visiting the land of my grandparents as long as Vladimir Putin continues to spread his venom across the globe.

Poland's Holocaust Law is wrong and should be opposed, vigorously—

and in person. We all need to go there.

And we need to be able to see the good and bad, never whitewashing history's more excruciating truths; but at the same time we should not paint all Poles with the broad brushes of good and evil. We should recognize the moral complexity of the situation.

When the Torah of Sinai stated, "Thou shalt not bear false witness against thy neighbor," it probably had no idea that it was talking about truth in the abstract sense.

The *Torah of Auschwitz* has come along to affix a corollary to the Ninth Commandment. "Thou shalt not bear false witness against thy neighbor— *who died here.*"

The deaths at Auschwitz were not conjured by conspiracy theorists. These murders are objective, verifiable truth, and while ethics can be oftentimes complicated, messy Gray Zones, especially after Auschwitz, moral relativism cannot become the rule to justify future atrocities. There is a morality that transcends both relativism and the strict binary choice of good or evil, and the *Torah of Auschwitz* implores us to explore that domain, so that we will not fall into the trap of perpetual victimhood.

So, to return to our opening question, would I have killed Baby Hitler? Probably not. But neither will I allow his spiritual descendants, the Amalekites of our day, to kill what is true and certain.

The Holocaust happened; there is no alternative to that fact.

Chapter Eleven

THE BOOK OF REFUTATION
Unraveling Racism

On a Thursday morning in August 2016, my synagogue's sacred space was violated. A man from California, deranged by hate, ended a cross-country odyssey targeting Jews right across the street from our parking lot. We were put on lockdown while the police extracted him from his car. A thorough search revealed that the man and car were unarmed. That story was widely publicized in the local and national media.

But here's another story that was not publicized at all. That very same week, late at night—at about 11:00—I was walking back home from my office next door, and I noticed a different car parked at the end of the temple driveway, and a driver getting out. I went over to the driver, my heart beating a little more rapidly, because, well, you know, because of the world we live in. The driver, standing outside the car with the door ajar, held up his phone and said, "I'm having radiator problems and am calling an Uber. Is it OK for me to leave the car here overnight?"

Almost instinctively, I replied, "No. The police are patrolling here constantly and will be suspicious of this car," I added. I gave him directions to the nearest gas station.

There were many reasons for me to be suspicious. I was a little skittish, given what has been going on around the world. Why would he want to abandon the car? Why not call AAA and have the car serviced right then? And besides, he was a stranger. He was different. He was an "other." He didn't belong.

And so, I'm sure the question you are asking is, "What was he?" What *kind* of other? So, I'll tell you.

It was dark, but I could see very clearly:

He had a New York license plate.

He was a New Yorker. And if there's one thing I learned growing up in New England, it's not to trust people from New York.

But what else was he? Inquiring minds want to know. Did he look Middle Eastern? Did he have a foreign accent? Was he a person of color? Did he have a shaved head and a swastika tattooed on his arm? *What* was he?

Well, what was he? A human being, one whose pigmentation may have been a few shades darker than mine—I think… It was dark, you know. To this day, I believe that I would have acted the same way no matter what that pigmentation was. Given my responsibilities, I did not question that I had to get that car out of our parking lot. After all, I have no bomb sniffing dogs. If there were Milk Bones in the car, my dogs would have found them; but bombs, not so much.

I may have done the right thing, but I could have been friendlier. I could have been more helpful to a stranger. And while I firmly believe that I am as colorblind as anyone, I can't be sure of that. I can't be sure of that, because I know something else. I know that I am the product of a society that is struggling mightily to overcome a pathology so inbred, so pervasive and so insidious that it affects us all. It is our greatest challenge.

Merriam Webster defines racism as "a belief that race is the primary determinant of human traits and capacities and that racial differences produce an inherent superiority of a particular race." The key words there are "inherent superiority." People are bigots for all kinds of reasons, but they are *racists* if they feel that the other group is somehow collectively and inherently inferior, whether the rationale is pseudo-science, theology, political expedience or just pure hate. Something about your group is of less value than mine.

In contrast, Jews believe that all human beings are unique individuals created in God's image. That means we are all of equal value in God's eyes. When the Torah of Sinai talks about a "Chosen People," that doesn't mean superior. It might allude to unique responsibilities that Jews have, or perhaps about God's quest for intimacy, in the hopes that such love will inspire us to better love our neighbor; for racism has the power to erode our basic humanity, to *erase* what is good and what is positive. We need to recognize that the toxicity is found in each of us. Racism is a pathology that affects everyone.

Across the world, the handmaidens of hate are joining hands in a most unnatural partnership: ISIS and Aryan Nation, Al Qaida and the alt-right, Hamas and France's National Front, the New Black Panther Party and the far right Israeli Jewish group Lehava. They are all bedfellows spreading racism, bigotry, and fear. It is a moral imperative for us to eradicate it.

The New Second Commandment

The Nazi scourge was fueled by their pseudo-scientific theories about race, which were given the imprimatur of legitimacy by German physicians, medical scientists, anthropologists, psychologists and geneticists. This led to policies that resulted in approximately 400,000 forced sterilizations and over 275,000 euthanasia deaths for those deemed genetically flawed, and then ultimately to the mass murder of Jews and others in the Holocaust. Without the pseudo-science of Nazi racism, there would have been no Holocaust.

Yet when Germany was defeated, somehow the racist virus was not totally wiped out, and in that sense, the Holocaust never really ended. The eradication of racism is, for the *Torah of Auschwitz*, its chief call to arms, and this call begins with a revision of the Torah of Sinai's second commandment.

The original commandment states, "*Thou shalt have no false gods before me.*" The *Torah of Auschwitz* amends that it to add, "*... and the falsest of false gods is the noxious ideology known as racism, which wrongly values some human beings higher than others, and which, when taken to its ultimate end, establishes a particular group as a godlike 'master race' and a single person above them all—and above God.*"

A couple of years ago, I decided to have my DNA analyzed. So, I spat into a test tube (my most expensive spit since Mrs. Allen's class in third grade), mailed it in, and here's what I discovered about my ethnic background:

I am:

97.2 percent Ashkenazi Jewish;

0.8 percent Eastern European—which means Hungarian, Polish, Ukrainian or Russian. I knew there would be a Cossack in there somewhere.

0.2 percent Southern European, which includes Italy, Iberia and the Balkans. No surprise there: 20 percent of the current population of the Iberian Peninsula has Jewish ancestry.

1.7 Broadly European—pointing to some more generalized strands of genetic material going back to the hunter-gatherer days when Europe was settled.

And finally, 0.1 percent... Native American. I'm an amalgamation! *Who knew!*

I'm also 84 percent golden retriever. We all are. We share 84 percent of our *overall* genetic makeup with dogs. With chimpanzees, it's 98.6 percent.

And about 60 percent of our genetic code is shared with your basic banana.

But human beings are in many ways the crown of creation, and genetic researchers have confirmed what the book of Genesis told us long ago—that all humans have common ancestry.

Genesis states that God created diverse kinds of plants and various kinds of animals. But strikingly, as Abraham Joshua Heschel pointed out, the Creation account does *not* say that God created distinct kinds *of human beings*, of varied colors and races; rather it proclaims that God created *one single person*. From a single human being all are descended.

In the Talmud, where Rabbi Akiva says that "Love your neighbor as yourself" is the most important principle of the Torah, Ben Azzai disagrees, saying no: the most important line in the Torah is Gen. 5:1, "These are the generations of Adam." The text sides with Ben Azzai, saying that the fact that all human beings are descended from a single person teaches us that no one can say to his neighbor, "My parent is greater than yours."

Science agrees. When it comes down to it, all of us—all human beings, it turns out—came from the same place: Africa, roughly 200,000 years ago. Genetically speaking, all humans are 99.998 percent the same.

Before Auschwitz, it might have been possible for Jews to view the radical equality promoted by Genesis as a nice concept in theory but of little relevance to those living in perpetual powerlessness. Not anymore.

"It turns out that most white Americans actually do have black blood," says the activist john powell (he spells his name that way). "White blood and black blood have been mixing up for a long time. And so, as we deny the other, we deny ourselves. *Because there is no 'other.'*"

One in five African Americans has Native American roots. In Louisiana, 12 percent of European Americans have some African ethnic ancestry. We are all people of color. Not just color, but colors. There is a veritable rainbow coalition within each of us! I can proudly say that I'm a mutt—a predominantly Jewish mutt, but a mutt nonetheless. We're all mutts—and there is no such thing as race.

The strategy of the racist is to divide and conquer. It's what was done in the nineteenth century to Native Americans who harbored black slaves, and what was done in the twentieth century between blacks and rural whites in the South.

The fastest growing demographic in United States is interracial and inter-ethnic couples, something that was unimaginable just a few years ago, and before *Loving vs Virginia* in the late 60s, in many places it was illegal. Since Judaism transcends all ethnic boundaries, there is no reason for any Jew not to celebrate that. In a just released Jewish population survey, nearly 12 percent of Manhattan's Jews identify as non-white, while in the Bronx, the figure swells to nearly 30 percent.

In writing *Hamilton* for the stage, Lin-Manuel Miranda chose to lie. That is, he intentionally cast the founders of our country as people of color, even though they probably were not. But Miranda wanted to make a larger point—not about that era, but about ours. We are a nation built by immigrants, all of whom were outcasts at one time; and immigrants, as they say in the show, get the job done—all of whom understood that, as George Washington croons, "History has its eyes on us."

After a while, when watching the show or listening to the music of *Hamilton*, an incredible thing happens. You forget about skin color altogether. Mother Theresa said, "One of the realities we're all called to go through is to move from repulsion to compassion and from compassion to wonderment." *Hamilton* has moved us to wonderment.

My DNA study revealed some of my hidden genetic traits. I tend to favor salty snacks over sweet ones. The test also linked me to a certain group of Neanderthals originating in Germany. I'm also genetically marked for hazel eyes, thinning hair, a few freckles, no dimpled chin—oh, and by the way, *fair skin*. Skin color is not racial; rather it results from generations of exposure to ultra violet radiation from sunlight for those living in hotter climates, which increases the production of melanin in the skin, making it darker. It then gets literally baked into one's ethnic heritage.

But it's just one marker among an untold number of markers that tell us so much of what's on the surface and what lies beneath. But while there are markers for skin color predisposition, there is none for race. There is no gene for race. Let me repeat that. The more we learn about the genome, the more scientists conclude: *Race is not genetic.*

Race is an artificial construct, based on faulty theories of Europeans like Johan Blumenbach, a 23-year-old grad student, who in 1775 correlated human character with skull size. The larger skulls, in his mind, correlated to larger brains, which he connected to light colored skin. Spoiler alert—Blumenbach's pigmentation was also white.

Of course, if brain size were truly a determinant of mastery and superiority, we would all be bowing down to whales and elephants, whose brains are much bigger than ours.

These racial theories were in the air precisely at a time when the world economy was expanding dramatically and many nations relied on the slave trade to keep up. It was convenient for them to regard people whom they were treating inhumanely as being less than fully human. *Three fifths* of a human, to be exact. Or to be really exact, three fifths of a *male, white* human. I don't pass judgment on our founding fathers who, after all, were reflecting the tenor of their times; but we must admit that, if pseudo-scientific racism was invented in Europe, it was in America that it was raised to a high art form.

There is little doubt that the racial theories that evolved in the eighteenth century have tainted the soul of humanity more than just about any other system of ideas. Communism killed its millions, true, and millions more have also been killed senselessly in the name of God and religion. But think about the tens of millions of lives destroyed by these misguided theories of racial superiority which justified American slavery, spawned South African Apartheid, led to the genocides of indigenous populations everywhere (including America), and culminated in the *pièce de résistance*—the Holocaust.

The Nazis expanded these warped racial theories not only to include Jews, but to differentiate between subgroups of Europeans; then they added sexual orientation and intellectual disability to the mix. Then they targeted them for sterilization, medical experimentation, slavery or genocide. So, to repeat: if there is one chapter that must be included in our *Torah of Auschwitz*, it is this section, this restatement of the second commandment, which totally debunks these disgraceful, destructive racial theories that formed the ideological underpinnings of the Third Reich.

It's so crazy, on the surface, to call Jews a race. Yet even today, dangerous theories of eugenics are still being propagated by the increasingly mainstreamed White Supremacists, who are virulently anti-Semitic. We must extinguish this particularly treacherous brand of hatred.

I recently participated in a local version of a nationally organized seminar called "Undoing Racism." About 30 of us sat together for three days in a circle and we learned about the roots of the problem and the serious challenges before us. I was one of two clergy attending, and the only Jew. The others were teachers, interns, police officers, firefighters, community organizers, and civic leaders. At one point, those participants with fair skin, about half the group, were asked to be silent, as we listened to those whose pigmentation happens to be darker than mine talk about what it is like to live in their skin. The stories I heard were heartbreaking.

As each person spoke about the profiling—about the discrimination; about a PhD who at an academic conference was mistaken for the maid; about simply passing people on the street and sensing the fear—I thought about how similar the Jewish experience has been, right here in America. In the early part of the last century, Henry Ford and Father Coughlin thought we wanted to take over the world, and Leo Frank's lynching led to the rise of the KKK, which in turn spurred the nativism of the 1920s, which led to our Congress cutting off the flow of Jewish refugees from Europe at the time when we most needed an escape route; and that undoubtedly cost millions of Jews their lives, trapped in Hitler's fortress Europa.

Yes, back in the 30s, for European Jews there was no path to U.S. citizenship. The only available paths led inexorably to the train tracks bound for Auschwitz.

All of that was due to racism—the perception that Jews are somehow an inferior life form.

Abraham Joshua Heschel wrote, "Few of us seem to realize how insidious, how radical, how universal and evil racism is. Few of us realize that racism is man's gravest threat to man, the maximum of hatred for a minimum of reason, the maximum of cruelty for a minimum of thinking."

So how do we undo racism? How do we fight the bigotry that so infects our culture? By proclaiming for all to hear that we are all equal in the eyes of God, that we are all brothers and sisters. We should constantly ask what the Mishna asks: "Is my blood redder than anyone else's?" We are all our brothers' and sisters' keepers.

During the summer of 2019, Trump-era xenophobia hit a new low with the president's race-based attacks on four Congressional women of color, when he suggested in a tweet that they "go back" to the countries they came from. In fact, three of the four were born in America; the fourth is a naturalized American citizen. This was compounded by his repeated use of the imagery of infestation, referring to third world countries as well as neighborhoods in American cities like Baltimore as "rat- and rodent-infested," echoing Holocaust-era claims of Nazis about Jews and their verminous habitats.

In the Talmudic tractate Avot 3:1, Akavya ben Mahalalel, a sage of the founding generation of rabbinic Judaism, gave perhaps the best Jewish comeback ever for those racist, hateful tropes:

> Reflect upon three things and you will not come to sin. Know from where you came and where you are going and before whom you are destined to give account and reckoning. From where have you come? From a putrid drop. Where are you going? To the place of dust, worm, and maggot. Before whom are you destined to give account and reckoning?–before the supremely blessed Holy One.

The rabbis' scientific understanding of human conception and embryonic development was far from complete (though pretty darn good for two thousand years ago), but they sure knew that babies aren't delivered by the stork. Akavya intuited that all humans originate from the humblest of beginnings—a sticky, smelly globule of semen—so no single person stands above all others. His message is one both of lowly beginnings and humble endings too; dust, worm and maggot infestation is not relegated to third world countries or neighborhoods neglected due to generations of institutional racism.

The idea that all people are equal, with each human life being of infinite value, has been at the core of Judaism for many centuries. But, like everything else, it has gained new shades of meaning after Auschwitz. Promoting equality is no longer a Jewish calling card; it has become an urgent calling. Rabbi Irving (Yitz) Greenberg, whose groundbreaking work has greatly influenced my own, has taken another image from Genesis, that humanity was created "in God's image" and applied it to a Holocaust context. Greenberg calls the post-Holocaust generation the beginning of a "Third Era" of Jewish history, a clean break from the Biblical and Rabbinic eras that preceded it. In a monograph, "Perspectives on the Holocaust," Greenberg writes:

> The Holocaust is the most radical challenge to Jewish values and Jewish belief and faith that ever occurred ... It is a total contradiction of everything that Judaism stands for. If there is one belief that, more than any other, characterizes Jewish life, Jewish religion and Jewish practice, it is

in the dignity of man. We speak of the human being in the image of God, of the absolute value of human life. To save one life is like saving the universe. Think of the radical challenge to that statement in the presence of the Holocaust.

The *Torah of Auschwitz* takes that radical challenge and responds with a desperate affirmation of what was already there—it takes the message of Genesis and amps up the volume to rock concert levels. As Greenberg puts it, "...the Nazis' behavior proclaimed the fact that they thought that a Jewish life was not worth one cent."

This is what he means. When the Nazis struggled mightily to finish their genocidal mission in 1944 by wiping out nearly a million Hungarian Jews, they began to run short of Zyklon B, the lethal chemical of choice for their gas chambers. So, to keep up with their diabolical quotas, they cut the gas in half, which in turn tripled the amount of time it took for the victims to die, increasing their suffering exponentially. Even worse, according to testimony of survivors, some children were thrown—while still alive—straight into the furnaces. All to stretch their Deutschmarks and save gas. And the result was a bottom line of less than one cent per Jewish corpse. The best deal ever!

In this new era, where Jews have their own state, what becomes paramount is the ability to exercise power while at the same time promoting sacred values in the secular world. Where in the past Jews could only pray for the defeat of evil forces, now Jews can act. And among the many acts of world repair undertaken, at the very top of the list must be the eradication of the insidious ideology that was employed in an effort to eradicate us.

The Good Swastika

One way to undermine an ideology of hate is to win over the haters, one at a time. Journalist Eli Saslow's recent book, *Rising Out of Hatred: The Awakening of a Former White Nationalist* details how a young white supremacist superstar-in-training, a godson of David Duke named Derek Black, was weaned from his racist ways by an Orthodox Jewish classmate who kept inviting him to Shabbat dinners. Sometimes love wins out, and as David Brooks has written, "Pluralists are always expanding the definition of "us," not constricting it." If we keep on adding to the legions of "us," eventually there will be no more "them."

Another way to undermine an ideology of hate is to corrode its culture from within by subverting its symbols, and that's precisely what we need to do with Nazi racist ideology. Jewish humorists have made a cottage industry of pillorying and mocking Nazi culture, including Hitler himself (thank you, Mel Brooks). But humor isn't the only weapon in our utility belt. So is love.

Let's talk about the swastika—an emblem that the Nazis themselves stole from ancient civilizations and then corrupted. You may recall from chapter 2 that I am not a great fan, nor should I be, of this moniker of fear. But then, in early 2018, I made my first trip to India and Nepal; and along the way, I made my peace with the swastika. Not *that* swastika, that unrepentant symbol of hate seen most recently on the streets of Charlottesville. No, I'm talking about the *original* swastika, the ancient Asian swastika, the one you get when you peel away that nasty layer of red and black paint.

I made peace with the Good Swastika.

Perhaps you can blame it on the incessant, smoky fog of Delhi or Agra's dizzying smell of incense and dung. Perhaps it's because I simply fell in love with a people who steadfastly have refused to abandon their sacred symbol to those who defiled it; who, through their deep faith, have put the hate of the haters to shame. Perhaps it's a product of enhanced sensitivities of the #MeToo era that I came to appreciate how even a symbol can abused.

I don't know, but I did a complete U-turn on this issue, and my making peace with the Good Swastika has helped me on the path to viewing the Holocaust in a more life-enhancing way.

India overwhelms you with fragility and fog. Every billow of smoke from the funeral pyres on the Ganges reinforces the message that life is transitory, a message also driven home by any rickshaw joyride through the marketplace.

Symbols are transitory too, and their transformations can be disorienting. Stars of David are plastered all over Muslim mausoleums like Humayan's Tomb in Delhi—except that they have nothing to do with Judaism. The Mughals adopted the hexagram as a popular architectural motif five centuries ago. So did Buddhists, particularly in meditative mandalas. Some versions of *The Tibetan Book of the Dead* even feature hexagrams with swastikas inside. Take *that*, Adolf!

In India, swastikas are as ubiquitous as samosas. I first saw them at, of all places, Gandhi's grave in Delhi, in a simple decorative pattern lining a security

UNRAVELING RACISM　　165

fence. From that point on, I became acutely sensitive to their presence, which initially caused me to seethe over why the Indian people were being so acutely insensitive to the millions throughout the world whose nightmares had been stoked by that symbol. Had the Himalayas so shielded them from the impact of the Nazi scourge that they weren't even aware of it? Gandhi was killed a few years *after* the Holocaust—so how could this dreaded symbol have been incorporated into a sanctuary for a murdered man of peace?

Security fence at Gandhi's grave

I recalled a time several years back when a bar mitzvah student came to my office with a Pokémon trading card containing a swastika. He asked if it was kosher for a Jew to own it. His grandfather, a Holocaust survivor, had been pained considerably at the sight of this card in the hand of his grandchild.

I pulled a book from the shelf and held up the Pokémon card to a photo of a uniformed Hitler "sieg heiling" the troops. My student looked at the two similar symbols and remarked, "the tentacles face the other way." It wasn't a swastika at all next to the Golbat and Ditto, I told him. It was a *manji*, a Japanese sign of hope, a symbol whose meaning evokes for the Japanese exactly the opposite of what a swastika connotes to those of us in the West. Doing some quick research on the Internet, I was intrigued by the claim that the Nazis deliberately corrupted this 3,000-year-old emblem, transforming an ancient Asian symbol of life into a European monogram of death.

I suggested to my student that as we become more crowded on this shrinking Earth, there still must be a place to respect the belief-space of the other. But at that time, I wasn't willing to give the swastika a pass, noting that while we need to recognize the serenity it brings to the Buddhist, Hindu and Jain, so do our eastern neighbors need to see the pain on the face of my student's grandfather.

But my India trip helped me to accept the Good Swastika without preconditions. I saw how, in India, this symbol brings a sense of warmth and protection to tiny village huts, similar to the role played by the mezuzah in Jewish homes. I also saw how it conveys a feeling of grace and order in public art, in grand squares and vast temples. In Sanskrit, the word connotes well-being; the four arms symbolize sun, wind, water and soil, the basic elements of existence. I also noted how the symbol appears in different colors and variations, but never in the spider-black of the Nazi flag. One could say, with some justification, that it is really is not the same symbol that continues to terrify the other half of the planet, from Auschwitz to Charlottesville. For Indians this symbol hasn't been reclaimed, because they never let it go.

My last stop was the southern port city of Kochi (formerly Cochin), a place noted for the spirit of coexistence that has prevailed for centuries, and the site of an ancient, tiny, Jewish community. One of the synagogues I visited is situated on a hill that also houses a church, a mosque and a Hindu temple. But the most vivid demonstration of coexistence was reserved not for worship spaces, but for two interconnected apartments, side by side in the neighborhood that is called, without a hint of condescension or irony, "Jew Town."

Right down the street from one of the oldest synagogues in all of Asia, the Hindu swastika and the Jewish Star of David coexist side by side, like the proverbial lion and lamb.

Apartments in Cochi, India

Making peace with the swastika does not mean making peace with Nazis past and present, nor with their hateful ideology—nor with their corrupted version of that symbol. Rather, it is a statement of defiance to those who so grotesquely distorted an emblem held sacred by half the world. We should treat it much like we treat the other cultural artifacts smeared and pilfered by the purveyors of the black spider: the priceless stolen artwork, the desecrated Torah scrolls, and the countless academic books the Nazis incinerated.

By reclaiming the Good Swastika, we can render this Nazi perversion as vaporous as those pyres of textbooks in Berlin or the corpses along the Ganges. Yes, everything is ephemeral, and the Nazi incarnation of evil must never be reincarnated. Perhaps our ability to make peace with the Asian swastika—the Good Swastika—can be our way of showing that there is one true way to escape the endless cycles of hatred and death: with coexistence and love. If we can coopt the symbols of hate, maybe we can arrest the hate as well.

What an amazing world that could be if we could come together as one. Where the Manhattan African American, or the Florida Latino, or the Nebraskan Native American, the Iowan farmer—and the Hindu from Varanasi—could all see ourselves as part of the same unbroken line of humanity that stretches all the way back to the Garden of Eden—along with the Stamford rabbi who is 0.1 percent Native American, 84 percent poodle, and just now awakening to an awareness of the kaleidoscope of color that exists inside each one of us.

We can overcome our fear and we can forge such a world. We can love our neighbor and forge such a world. We can embrace the diversity that is embedded within us and implanted among us, and we can forge such a world. We can give help to our neighbor whose radiator overheats, and we can forge such a world.

And we will. I will. Next time, I will.

Because history has its eyes on us.

Chapter Twelve

THE BOOK OF JEWISH UNITY

How the Nuremberg Laws Can

Save the Jewish People

World Jewry is in a state of crisis. Israeli and American Jewry are drifting apart, and within each of those groups we're seeing increased polarization on fundamental issues like the two-state solution, Israel's democratic versus Jewish nature, and the definition of who is a Jew.

Rather than wallowing in malaise, I'd like to propose a solution that could resolve many of these challenges—a Grand Bargain fit for our chaotic times, an innovation worthy of an era of absolute disruption; and this solution comes right out of the playbook of the *Torah of Auschwitz*. For this chapter, let me direct my remarks especially toward my fellow Jews, however you choose to define that group. The rest of you have plenty at stake here too, but bear with me for this one chapter, as I swivel over to the side camera for a more intimate conversation.

We're in trouble. It's not trouble just of our own making, but it's trouble. The concept of Jewish unity has become laughable, except that it's become so painful that it's impossible to laugh. The strained relationship between Diaspora Jews and Israel has reached a breaking point, assisted by a perfect storm of concurrent events:

+ A dramatic decrease of support for Israel among American Jewish young adults, especially among college students, where support is down 32 percent since 2010, as indicated by the 2017 Brand Israel study. This is despite the fabulous success of Birthright Israel in bringing upwards of half a million Jewish young adults on those 10-day free trips over nearly two decades.
+ The Israeli government's repudiation of the American-based non-Orthodox denominations, which has been occurring since the state's beginnings. But the insults and injuries have been compounded recently, by the retraction of an arrangement that would have allowed for egalitarian,

non-Orthodox prayer at the Western Wall, along with controversies over conversion, marriage and many other slights; this has further alienated many Diaspora Jews.

+ The announcement that influential American rabbis with Conservative training will perform intermarriages, a move deemed necessary by many in the Diaspora but equated by many Israelis to a second Holocaust. Intermarriage has become a fact of life for Diaspora Jewry, and the Reform movement's decision in the 1980s to extend the definition of "Who is a Jew" to include those whose father is Jewish, even when the mother is not, has, over time, further exacerbated the split. There is no longer a common definition of "Who is a Jew" that the majority of the Jewish people will accept.

+ Politically, in the 2016 U.S. elections, nearly three-quarters of American Jews voted against a guy that, according to a poll, more than 80 percent of Israelis support.

All of this, and I didn't even mention two states versus one state, settlements, Iran, conversion, or those groups attempting to organize boycotts of Israel or the disputed territories.

While some Jewish leaders are recognizing the urgency of the moment, few are acknowledging how precariously close we are to a permanent rupture. The Israel-Diaspora relationship has itself become a tale of two teams increasingly unable to share the same narratives or acknowledge the same basic truths. That's because the rift has gone tribal.

Pundits bemoan the tribal nature of American culture, where our politics have devolved into a maelstrom of conflicting news channels' social media feeds, generating unyielding allegiance to the "home" team, even when that team is doing verifiable damage to the country. While the Israeli political system has been, to a degree, a tribal enterprise since the earliest days of Zionism, somehow, through it all, Israeli society has been able to pull together at the time of greatest need. The jury is out as to whether that can happen in America.

The last time Israelite tribes tried to unify, it did not end well. King David's empire was ripped apart only one generation after reaching the height of its glory. The 10 northern tribes of this united kingdom split from the two tribes down south, driven away by their own ambition and the excesses of King

Solomon. Jerusalem ceased being the nation's capital for the northerners, and the two sides adapted different names, styles of worship, and alliances. Ultimately both Israel and Judah suffered destruction and dispersion.

Professor Donniel Hartman puts it this way:

> We are a deeply divided people. Divided geographically. Divided religiously. Divided politically. While the nature of all collective life assumes disagreements between fellow members, Jewish peoplehood today is threatened by the intensity and depth of our disagreements. It is especially threatened by the culture of debate and the polarizing way in which we conduct ourselves toward those with whom we disagree. Even more importantly, we need to begin to speak differently about and with each other. The culture of mutual vilification and de-legitimization does not serve any cause. It is increasing alienation from each other, from Judaism, and from Israel.

But there is one thing that unites most Jews, and it's the Holocaust.

Recall those Pew surveys demonstrating that, despite our differences, "Remembering the Holocaust" scores highest by far, garnering the support of nearly three quarters of American Jews and two thirds of Israeli Jews. Nothing else comes close. Not Passover Seders, not fasting on Yom Kippur, not lighting Hanukkah or Shabbat candles, not falafel, not lox and bagels, not Jerry Seinfeld, not Israel itself, not social action, not education, not spirituality and prayer, not custom and law. Not even Gal Gadot.

The Holocaust has given us a common point of departure, a place where we were all present, even if we weren't.

It is said that every Jew, past present and future, stood at Sinai. Well, every Jew stood, metaphorically, in those gas chambers, and it didn't matter whether you were male or female, traditional, liberal or secular, born Jewish, converted to Judaism or married to a Jew. By embracing the *Torah of Auschwitz*, we can come together, Jews of the broadest possible definition, to proclaim to the world that Auschwitz must never happen again.

In Israel Jews are considered a nationality, in America, primarily a faith group. For Jews and Judaism to thrive, we need to be both; for in fact Jews are neither purely a religion nor an ethnic group, but a "people," which combines elements of tribe and tradition. We are a group inextricably tied to an idea, a story, a mission. At this point in time, seven decades after Auschwitz, the group, story and mission all trace back to one place, and that point of departure for most Jews is neither Mount Sinai nor Jerusalem. Jews who are atheist and avowedly secular have little concern for Sinai; unless they are ardent Zionists (or just loved Birthright), Jerusalem doesn't matter much to them either. The ultra-Orthodox have almost nothing in common with secular Jews. But all, including non-European Jews, share a point of departure in a small town in southern Galicia called Auschwitz. Even if we don't share all the same conclusions, Jews of all stripes share the story of Auschwitz.

If Auschwitz has become that common point of departure, that common denominator that most Jews share, perhaps it can also be the source of a resolution to the challenges of disunity.

But for the Jewish people to come together, we must want to do just that. Lip service is not enough—it's not sufficient to say, Beatles-style, "Come together, right now....*over me.*" We've got to come together somewhere in *between* you and me. I believe that we can accomplish that and at the same time demonstrate to the world a new model of inclusivity that respects differences while affirming the overriding need to find common ground.

Those who cry out for Jewish unity but then cower behind old arguments don't really want Jewish unity. The want capitulation. Israelis who bemoan what they perceive as American Jewish materialism, shallowness and willful abandonment of Jewish identity have no idea what it's like to live in a place where Jews and non-Jews routinely partner to explore common concerns together; where, despite some disturbing trends recently, Judaism is seen almost exclusively in positive terms, by Jews and non-Jews, and where Jewish values play an inordinate role in the national conversation. Meanwhile, American Jews who bemoan what they see as Israeli xenophobia, expansionism and arrogance also have no idea what it is like to live under the shadow of hundreds of thousands of rockets aimed at them from just a few miles away, and to live in a place where being Jewish comes as naturally as breathing.

To come together in a way that goes beyond lip service, the Jewish people are going to have reconfigure who exactly we are. We can begin by forging a single, universally accepted definition of "Who is a Jew," an expansive one that promotes peoplehood over religious distinctions and transcends halachic differences, one that will allow each denomination to hold onto its own demarcations but will also transcend them. So, Reform Jews will still be able to accept patrilineal descent and a more lenient path to conversion, while Ultra-Orthodox will still be able to insist on more stringent rulings on everything from conversion standards to bugs in lettuce. Liberal denominations in America will be able to reach out more openly to multifaith and other non-traditional families, while Israelis can determine their own standards of inclusivity—as long as everyone who fits a single, broad based definition of "Who is a Jew" will be able to be fully accepted and included in the big tent of Jewish peoplehood.

The most obvious non-religious definition of "Who is a Jew" for the post-Auschwitz era is the one that we already have, from Israel's "Law of Return"—and the blueprint for that new, trans-denominational inclusive definition of "Who is a Jew" was devised by, of all people, the Nazis. In determining who would be considered a Jew for the purposes of discrimination and eventually death, the Nazis said in the 1935 Nuremberg Laws that anyone with at least three Jewish grandparents was to be considered fully Jewish, but having even just one Jewish grandparent would subject them to discrimination.

The Nuremberg Laws had a devastating impact on German Jewry. Most immediately relevant were two laws—the Citizenship and Blood Laws—that forbade marriages and extramarital sexual relations between Jews and Germans as well as the employment of German women under 45 in Jewish households. The Nuremberg Laws also declared that only those of German or related blood were eligible to be Reich citizens, with others classed as state subjects and denied citizenship rights. These laws were later expanded to include Romanis, Gypsies, and those whom they determined to be racially "black."

Those convicted of violating the marriage laws were imprisoned; later, once the sentences were served, many were re-arrested by the Gestapo and sent to Nazi concentration camps. Non-Jews stopped patronizing Jewish-owned stores and socializing with Jews. Jews were forbidden to work in the civil service or government-regulated professions such as medicine and education. That forced them to take on menial work. If they decided to emigrate, Jews were required to cede up to 90 percent of their wealth. Eventually, all paths to emigration were closed, as the noose was tightened further.

Later at the Wannsee Conference in 1941, the Final Solution was made applicable even for many Jews with just one Jewish grandparent—or none, if they were married to a Jew. But here they weren't just talking about business boycotts and incarceration, they were assessing eligibility to become victims of genocide.

Because of how the Nazis defined Jewish status, many who would have been considered non-Jews by Jewish religious standards were discriminated as Jews. The Nuremberg Laws were the mother of all racist, discriminatory laws. James Q. Whitman, a professor at Yale, has established that Hitler was inspired by U.S. racial policies; and while cause-effect can be debated, both Jim Crow and South African Apartheid can be seen as being part of the Nuremberg "family" of eugenics-based discrimination. Since I've discussed racism in an earlier chapter, let me focus here purely on how the Nuremberg Laws affect Jewish unity.

It is one of the great ironies of human history that the State of Israel intentionally used the very same definition of "Who is a Jew" that was devised by Adolf Hitler. The Law of Return, established in the aftermath of the Holocaust, states that those eligible for automatic Israeli citizenship would include "those born of a Jewish mother or converted to Judaism, plus their non-Jewish children, grandchildren, and spouses, and to the non-Jewish spouses of their children and grandchildren."

It makes perfect sense that the Israelis did this. Israel was created in part as a refuge for those targeted by those restrictions. Israel's Declaration of Independence states:

> The catastrophe which recently befell the Jewish people—
> the massacre of millions of Jews in Europe—was another
> clear demonstration of the urgency of solving the problem of
> its homelessness by re-establishing in Eretz-Israel the Jewish
> State, which would open the gates of the homeland wide *to
> every Jew* [italics are mine] and confer upon the Jewish peo-
> ple the status of a fully privileged member of the comity of
> nations. Survivors of the Nazi holocaust in Europe, as well
> as Jews from other parts of the world, continued to migrate
> to Eretz-Israel, undaunted by difficulties, restrictions and
> dangers, and never ceased to assert their right to a life of
> dignity, freedom and honest toil in their national homeland.

The question arose as to how one would define "every Jew."

That question remains valid today. In some ways it's even more valid, because the prime critique of the Law of Return is that it is discriminatory to allow one group automatic citizenship while denying others citizenship entirely, including many who live in territories controlled by Israel. With Jews no longer facing mortal threats around the world—despite the recent rise in anti-Semitism—and with many living in great prosperity, it becomes harder to defend a policy that appears discriminatory—unless you trace it back to its roots at Nuremberg. The Law of Return is in fact an Affirmative Action plan, compensating not only for the unprecedented discrimination Jews faced under the Nazis, but for the many centuries of persecution that preceded Nuremberg. Yes, the Law of Return is messy, but it is demonstrably necessary—as is the State of Israel itself.

And it is demonstrably necessary for there to be a refuge from persecution for *every Jew*, no matter where they happen to be living or whether or not they be would be considered religiously Jewish by every *other* Jew.

The State of Israel exists to be a home and refuge for all the Jewish people. To quote the Declaration of Independence once again, "This right is the natural right of the Jewish people to be masters of their own fate, like all other nations, in their own sovereign State."

I *belong* to the Jewish people, just as I belong to the U.S. citizenry, and I also happen to *believe* and practice Judaism, a religion based on the covenant at Sinai as interpreted by the classical rabbis. I also subscribe to the interpretation of Judaism that is labeled "Conservative" in the U.S. and "Masorti" in Israel, though I deviate on some issues. But whatever I believe—which also informs how I personally define "who is a Jew," my belonging to the Jewish people implies that I accept the definition of a Jew as laid out in the Law of Return. Not only that, but since Israel's Declaration of Independence includes me as belonging to the Jewish people, I also *belong* to the Jewish sovereign state, and I too am entitled to be a master of my own fate—and to participate actively in the destiny of my people—through my affiliation with that state.

The Declaration mentions that the new country "will be open for Jewish immigration and for the Ingathering of the Exiles," but significantly, nowhere does it require immigration for a Jew to "belong" there, nor does it say anything about military service or philanthropy. It gives me the right—the natural right—to be a master of my own fate through my choosing to affiliate with Israel; and not just me, but even the person who has only one Jewish grandparent who is seeking his or her way back to Jewish peoplehood or away from persecution.

It is very, very powerful that we have a Jewish state that opens its arms so widely to so many, and that the big tent has room for people of all races and ethnic backgrounds, that the doors are open as widely as possible to affiliation with the Jewish people and thereby the Jewish State. It is also very powerful that we have none other than Adolf Hitler to thank for this formula that, as adapted by the Israeli government, holds to key to the reunification of the Jewish people.

Thank you, Adolf!

So here goes:

I propose that we create a class of Jewish "citizenship" that will reinvent Jewish peoplehood, revitalize all streams of Judaism, minimize differences on conversion, strengthen Israeli democracy, boost pro-Israel pride on college campuses and possibly even put the Jewish state on the path to reconciliation with its neighbors.

I believe that a "Law of Return," Nuremberg-based definition of Jewish identity can be the foundation that can repair the fraying relationship between Israel and Diaspora Jewry and between Jews of differing religious streams, between religious and secular, liberal and conservative and all the other fault lines that are ripping us apart. Rather than giving Hitler a posthumous victory by our dissolving into irrelevance through infighting and apathy, we can achieve Hitler's ultimate posthumous defeat by using his plan for a Final Solution as a blueprint for a worldwide Jewish renaissance.

Take *that*, Adolf.

With that law as our baseline, we can begin to forge a trans-denominational, post-tribal and more inclusive Jewish people. In an interconnected world where globalization has obliterated boundaries, the Jewish people can become the first truly global citizenry, albeit one whose heart beats solidly in Zion. There could be no more powerful statement about what it means to be Jewish—or to have any national identity at all—in this ineffaceably singed post-Auschwitz era.

A century ago, the early Zionist essayist Ahad Ha'am, in his classic treatise, "The Wrong Way," challenged both Theodore Herzl and the religious establishment by simultaneously affirming an enduring Diaspora and the centrality of Zion as the heart of a renascent (and primarily secular) Jewish culture. Only an approach such as his, affirming the equality and mutuality of all Jews, whether they live in Jerusalem or Johannesburg, will enable us to unify the tribes of Israel.

Step one of my Grand Bargain would be to extend "Jewish citizenship" to anyone, anywhere, covered by the Law of Return, along with all current Israeli Jews. A Jewish citizen might not be recognized universally as a Jew according to rabbinic law, but he or she will be eligible for something of potentially much greater value than an ark opening at the local synagogue.

Step two: Give these "Jewish citizens" the right to participate in Israeli democracy—in exchange for a real demonstration of commitment, but one that does not have to include moving to the Promised Land. That could mean actually voting in Israeli elections or something less radical, but it must be more meaningful than representation in the virtually powerless House of Lords that the World Zionist Congress has become. If Jewish citizenship is to have real meaning, there is no substitute for the right to be involved in the selection of representatives of the Jewish state. Other bodies claiming to represent the Jewish people are democratic and representative, but they have all the clout of the Mickey Mouse Club.

Think how this idea would galvanize Diaspora Jewry and transform its relationship with Israel into what it most needs to be right now: a partnership of equals. Jewish citizens would be able to participate in forging a future for the Jewish people, taking them from the sidelines and thrusting them right into the middle of the action.

Dual citizenship is the norm in many free countries. Fully belonging to the Jewish people should mean more than the right to lobby, rally, retweet and donate. Jewish citizenship would entitle us to directly affect the future of the only Jewish state the world has seen for 2,000 years, a place that we love and wish to cultivate. Dual citizenship would clarify that Diaspora Jews and Israeli Jews have a stake in each other, that the relationship is not one of mere convenience; and that despite our occasional infatuation with other partners, like evangelicals on the right and radical BDS on the left, solidifies the permanence of this marriage.

What, short of actual *aliyah*, would qualify Jews for this enhanced level of citizenship? I would suggest a period of national service on behalf of the

Jewish people. Each applicant would need to spend a certain amount of time in Israel, beginning, for many, with a Birthright trip, which would now have a weightier function. Some basic Jewish literacy requirement might also be considered, along the lines of the literacy test that Meghan Markle, the Duchess of Sussex, needed to take before becoming a British citizen and marrying Prince Harry. According to the New York Times, that citizenship test is filled with tough, nitpicky questions about the 1284 Statute of Rhuddlan and the popularity of the sandwich spread Marmite. It's noteworthy that the Duchess will still maintain her American citizenship, even as a British royal, and presumably be able to vote in both countries.

A Jewish literacy test might include questions about whether it is kosher to put Jell-O on a bagel (it depends, but who would want to?) and just who were Maimonides, Bar Kochba, Shabbtai Zvi (Google them) and Leonard Bernstein, as well as questions about modern Zionism and Israel—and (my Hebrew school teachers would be so happy) maybe some Hebrew language too, or Yiddishisms like *mensch*. Having this test be a requirement for enhanced Jewish citizenship (as opposed to the provisional citizenship achieved through the Nuremberg standards) could revolutionize Jewish literacy throughout the world. That alone could save the Jewish people. But the Law of Return would grant everyone, even those who don't take or fail the test, full status as non-voting citizens of the Jewish people.

Many questions naturally arise. Let me deal with a few of them here:

Is it fair to offer benefits of citizenship to those not living in the "home base" and paying taxes there?

Children of American immigrants to Israel can attain American citizenship and vote in American elections even if they *never actually live* in America, and American expats are generally allowed to use foreign taxes paid as a credit against their U.S. tax obligation. Something similar could be considered for Jewish citizens living in the Diaspora. Perhaps annual federation pledges and synagogue dues could become part of the mix, on a sliding scale that is fair and affordable. One could still be a citizen of the Jewish people without paying a penny, but any additional benefits would require a concomitant commitment. So, to repeat: Diaspora Jews wishing all the benefits of official, enhanced Jewish citizenship would be required to earn the privilege.

What about army service?

About 35 percent of Israeli Jewish women avoid conscription, as do 27 percent of eligible men, primarily on religious grounds. Yet they get to vote, and some replace military service with the kind of national service that I am proposing. In addition, many Diaspora Jews already serve in the Israeli army without making aliyah. And of course, Israel's Arab citizens do not serve in the army or do national service, and do vote in elections.

But whether or not they serve in the Israel Defense Forces, aren't all Israelis on the "front lines"?

Increasingly, Diaspora Jews on the right and left are being called upon to fight existential battles for Israel's physical survival, with such activities as lobbying Congress about Iran, foreign aid, or fighting the Boycott, Divestment and Sanctions movement; and for its soul, by spearheading fights for pluralism, minority and women's rights, and advocacy for the two-state solution. Increasingly, terrorism and anti-Semitism threaten Jewish communities everywhere. Cyber-hate has dramatically shrunk the distance between us as it is increased the danger for all. No one can be a spectator anymore and the need to draw the two communities closer together has never been more essential.

What about accusations of dual loyalty?

Haters are gonna hate. Why should Jews face questions of dual loyalty when dual-citizen French, Irish, and Italian Americans do not? American Jews need to get over this.

How could Diaspora Jews vote for candidates they haven't heard of or pass judgment on issues that do not affect them directly?

My sister has lived in Israel since the Carter administration, yet she votes absentee in American elections all the time. One could easily ask whether it is fair that, according to published estimates, 30,000 expats living in Israel voted in an American election in 2016 that could ultimately determine whether LGBTQ couples will be entitled to marry in Kentucky or whether a pregnant teen in Louisiana will be forced to carry to term? My answer to that is: Yes it *is* fair, because on some level, those 30,000 have chosen to cast half their lot with the U.S. And I choose to cast half my lot with the Jewish people's only state in 2,000 years. It's true that I can't completely unpack the complexities of Israeli politics or feel what it's like to have tens of thousands of enemy rockets permanently aimed toward me. At the same time, no one living outside the U.S. can possibly understand what it's like to live in America right now.

In the summer of 2018, I led a congregational trip to Israel. During a guest presentation, one of the members of the group (OK, it was me) asked how it is that Israelis could be so loyal to President Trump. The speaker's reply was a version of the standard fare Diaspora Jews have heard for generations:

"While you are choosing to sit back and watch from the sidelines, we Israelis are putting ourselves on the line daily, in the roughest of neighborhoods. So, when someone comes along and acts so supportively, we can turn a blind eye to a few indiscretions. Nobody's perfect, after all."

My reply must have shocked him:

"Can you even begin to fathom the enormity of the battle we are waging right now? We are fighting for freedom of the press, for oppressed refugees, traumatized children and victimized women. We are fighting for our planet. We are fighting for the future of democracy itself. And, oh, by the way, we are fighting for you. Israel's Trump-enabled anti-democratic slide is as much an existential danger as any external enemy. Because I love Israel, I fear that she will pay a very steep price when the Trump nightmare ultimately ends. So, while every day I pray for those who are defending Israel's borders, you should also say a little prayer for us. While Israelis have been spending the summer skirmishing with Hamas and praising foreign autocrats, we Americans—Democrats, Republicans and Independents—have been fighting in the trenches of democracy's Last Best Hope.

"So please don't lecture me about sitting on the sidelines."

Just as I don't question that my American-Israeli cousins have a profound interest in what goes on here, so should they recognize that I have a deep stake in what goes on there, a personal stake, and one that has been certified by Israel's own Declaration of Independence and endorsed by its Law of Return.

But isn't Judaism a religion and not a political entity?

As we've been discussing, Jews have always been both a people and adherents of a faith, but the idea of religion divorced from peoplehood is relatively recent, pushed by Napoleon, nineteenth-century German reformers and mid-twentieth-century American suburbanites. For most Jews today, it is peoplehood that matters most. That includes the 62 percent of American Jews who told Pew that being Jewish is mainly a matter of ancestry and culture (only 15 percent said "religion"). When 94 percent of all American Jews say they are proud to be Jewish, most are thinking about being part of a people—a people, I would add, with an idea.

What would David Ben-Gurion say?

Back in 1950, Israel's prime minister and American Jewish leaders came to an agreement that the State of Israel would not claim to speak on behalf of all the Jewish people. When Prime Minister Benjamin Netanyahu went to Congress in 2011, he stated explicitly, "I speak on behalf of the Jewish people and the Jewish state." I don't know who died and made him king, but he definitely wasn't voted into that position, nor was he speaking on behalf of this Jewish person. Then, when he returned to Congress in 2015, in a move that was widely condemned as partisan and divisive by American Jews, causing what has turned into a deep fissure in Israel's bipartisan support, he referred to "Jewish people" no fewer than eight times.

Prime Minister Netanyahu has often ignored the 1950 memo, but under my Law of Return-based proposal, the prime minister truly would represent world Jewry, just as the American president still represents those American expats living in Ma'aleh Adumim—and did I mention that all of them get to vote absentee in American elections?

Ben-Gurion would say that my plan is an abandonment of the Zionist dream of universal aliyah. But after calming down with a glass of tea and turning his visionary gaze ahead seven decades, he would see that the Jewish people today are hopelessly split and mass aliyah is a pipe dream. Bipartisan support for Israel in American politics is waning dramatically, and Israel's democracy is in jeopardy. Desperate times require desperate measures, and it's not hard to imagine that the most visionary individual in modern Jewish history might give this idea sincere consideration.

Ben Gurion might have wavered, and other Diaspora negators would have too; but I'm absolutely convinced that Theodore Herzl would have supported this plan. After all, he had a weakness for outlandish plans, some of which actually came to fruition.

OK, wouldn't Judaism become corrupted by politics?

Have you seen the Knesset? Have you seen some of our American Jewish organizations at work? Judaism can never be completely divorced from politics, but Jewish citizenship would go a long way toward fostering the exchange of ideas and empowering the development of creative Jewish visions. If you are asking whether American Jewish life would become more Israel-focused, the answer is yes; and I believe that's a good thing. With some actual skin in the game, American Jews would all be encouraged to engage with Israel constructively rather than throwing their hands up and dissociating from it.

And speaking of dissociating, an entire segment of Jewish Israelis, the Haredim, chooses to reject key symbols of statehood. See what happens in a room of ultra-Orthodox when Hatikva is played or the memorial siren sounds on Yom Hashoah. A 2018 poll released shortly before Israel's seventieth birthday showed that only 17% of Israeli ultra-Orthodox celebrate Independence Day and only 36% thought Holocaust Remembrance Day is a day of mourning. Yet they who completely reject the very fact of Jewish political sovereignty participate fully in choosing Israel's leaders and shaping its policies.

How would this affect pluralism and conversion?

This plan places world Jewry on a trajectory toward unity rather than further disengagement. With Diaspora Jewry now part of the electoral equation, thereby marginalizing rejectionist groups that have held veto power for too long, we could begin to collaborate on thorny issues like conversion, patrilineal descent, and non-Orthodox and women's prayer groups at the Western Wall. Old compromises could be dusted off, including conversion-related proposals of the Neeman Commission of the late 90s and the more recent Western Wall compromise. At the very least, Diaspora and Israeli leaders would be talking about solutions rather than ignoring the problem. And while my idea would require lots of massaging before it could be implemented internationally, the idea of using the Law of Return to create a more inclusive definition of "Who is a Jew" can be beneficial to Jewish unity here in America, too.

Would the Israeli right ever agree to this?

While this plan could cost current parties some power, there's a solid chance that those Diaspora Jews who take on the responsibilities of enhanced Jewish citizenship will skew right, both politically and religiously, because they would be more motivated and better organized than the progressives. But all Israelis should understand that the more Diaspora Jews sign on to this, the more the burdens of the Jewish future will be shared and the less isolated Israel will be.

It's interesting that in October 2018, a right-wing Knesset member proposed an idea strikingly similar to mine. Speaking at a roundtable about Israel-Diaspora relations at the General Assembly of the Jewish Federations of North America, Bezalel Smotrich of the Jewish Home party said, "I think that the Jews of the world, whoever spends at least two weeks a year in the State of Israel, should have the right to vote for the Knesset. I will now propose such a bill. I think this will greatly strengthen the ties between us."

As for progressive Diaspora Jews, at last they would have a chance to feel that their concerns are being heard, and that they could help construct an Israel consistent with the visions of its founders, not as spectators but as builders. Nearly 22,000 American Jews voted for the Reform Movement representatives in the 2015 World Zionist Congress elections. Imagine how many would be drawn to vote for an election of far greater consequence.

What about Israeli minorities?

Israeli Arabs might reasonably be concerned at this demographic bump of voting Jews, just as the Palestinians were petrified by the mass immigration of Russian Jewry in the 1990s. I would hope that the opportunity would be seized to imagine innovative ways to create two states for two peoples with two thriving diasporas.

This is a lot to swallow, so let's simply chew on these questions for a while: What would it mean for Diaspora Jewry to have more than a vicarious involvement in the Jewish people's boldest collective venture since the Talmud? What would it mean for American and Israeli Jews to view themselves as full partners, and for the varieties of Judaism emerging from each community to be embraced and shared? What would it mean for Diaspora Jews who now shun Israel to suddenly realize that they can be part of the solution? What would it mean for both Israeli and Diaspora Jews to embark on a massive, Birthright-esque project to promote Jewish literacy—which all sides desperately need—and global volunteerism representing the Jewish people?

What would it mean for Jews to speak of unity—and actually mean it?

Now, I have no illusion that my idea will be quickly accepted, but this is not an all-or-nothing proposition. When I first proposed it, in an op-ed syndicated internationally by JTA, which subsequently won an award for commentary from the Religion News Association, the response from the Jewish world was, shall we say, tepid, at first; and then on my blogspace at *Times of Israel*, downright nasty. I guess that means I struck a nerve. Maybe the idea of world Jewry voting in Israeli elections will be too hard for most people to swallow; in which case, that part of my plan might be modified or tabled for the time being. Maybe the bar to qualify for enfranchisement needs to be set very high. These things would need to be hammered out through negotiation—I personally love the idea of national service.

But the fact remains that since Birthright Israel was imagined two decades ago, world Jewry has been twiddling its thumbs while its two main communities have been drifting apart like polar ice sheets passing in the night. No one has proposed anything bold enough to reverse that trend, and in fact the opposite has been happening. Israeli politicians continue their unabated onslaught of insults directed against American Jews, and American Jews continue to respond by caring less and less about Israel. Those destructive trends must be reversed.

Is this really a pipedream? Perhaps; but I would like to put Sheldon Adelson and George Soros into a room with Michael Steinhardt, Ron Lauder, Lynn Schusterman and a Bronfman or two, close the door and tell them to get this done. Ok, *ask* them. And then it will be no dream, with or without the pipe.

Israel, like the Holocaust, has now passed the 70-year barrier. Time to think big. It is time for the Jewish people to reimagine what a nation can look like—a pliable one that can exist both within and outside its borders. It is time for those Jews living in America, who overwhelmingly claim to be proud to be Jews—to the tune of 94 percent, according to Pew—to put up or shut up, by refusing to flush 3,000 years of heritage down the toilet, and by refusing to give up on the only Jewish state the world has known for two millennia. And it is time for those living in Israel to give up their delusion that they can manage just fine without their annoying brothers and sisters across the sea. It is time for those concerned about some mythical ethnic "purity" to understand that diversity is our strength and that assimilation through intermarriage is not another Holocaust.

If they would have been chosen to die at Auschwitz, we are duty-bound to welcome them with open arms.

We don't know where it will all end up, but it is time for all concerned to understand that the historical anomaly of having a once-every-two-millennia thriving Jewish state exist at the same time as the most successful Diaspora community ever, is one to relish and not to abhor—and to relish as equals.

We can have the last laugh on the Nazis. From out of Nuremberg comes the Torah, and the message of Unity from the Valley of the Shadow of Death. Let the Nuremberg Laws, turned on their head, lead us from our people's darkest hour to an unparalleled Jewish renaissance.

Chapter Thirteen

THE BOOK OF BEARING WITNESS

Kaddish for a Shoe

Can you say Kaddish for a shoe?

I found myself asking that question in 2010 when I heard the sad news that a fire had destroyed some shoes.

Now normally, losing a few shoes in a fire is not such big news, but these weren't just any shoes. These were the shoes warehoused in a barracks at Majdanek, a thousand of them, destroyed by a flash fire believed to be accidental.

Majdanek, the infamous death camp on the outskirts of Lublin, called by a *New York Times* war reporter "the most terrible place on earth," is the one death camp that has remained virtually unchanged since the day of its liberation. The Nazis didn't have time to destroy the evidence because the Soviet Army swooped in so quickly. And of all the exhibits there, the barracks filled with shoes leaves the most indelible impression. Now the shoes and their rightful owners have been reunited on high. Having visited the site just months before, in April, I felt a very personal, deep sense of loss when I heard about the fire.

Can you say Kaddish for a shoe?

I'm thinking of one shoe, one that grabbed my attention. It was red, a child's shoe—tiny. All the rest were dusty and grey, but this one retained its color, as if to call attention to the innocence of the child who wore it and the uniqueness of every victim.

Primo Levi has stated that in the camps, death began with the shoes. As feet began to throb from infection from days and days of marching and the pain from the sores that became fatally infected, the shoes became instruments of torture. But now the shoes play a different role entirely.

The Yiddish poet Moshe Shulstein writes:

> *I saw a mountain*
> *Higher than Mt. Blanc*
> *And more Holy than the Mountain of Sinai*
> *On this world this mountain stood.*

such a mountain I saw—Jewish shoes in Majdanek...
Hear! Hear the march.
Hear the shuffle of shoes left behind—that which remained.
From small, from large, from each and every one.
Make ways for the rows—for the pairs—
For the generations—for the years.
The shoe army—it moves and moves.
We are the shoes, we are the last witnesses.
We are shoes from grandchildren and grandfathers,
From Prague, Paris and Amsterdam,
And because we are only made of stuff and leather
And not of blood and flesh, each one of us avoided the hellfire.
We shoes—that used to go strolling in the market
Or with the bride and groom to the chuppah
We shoes from simple Jews, from butchers and carpenters,
From crocheted booties of babies just beginning to walk ...
Unceasingly we go. We tramp.
The hangman never had a chance to snatch us into his
Sack of loot—now we go to him.
Let everyone hear the steps which flow as tears.
The steps that measure out the judgment.

Columnist Michael Berenbaum adds, "The shoes of Majdanek are rotting. They smell. The rot and the smell tell us of the distance that stands between that time and our time. They bear witness to the erosion of time, which we do not want to couple with the erosion of memory."

The shoes bear witness; and a thousand of those shoes are now no more. But these shoes are not the last witnesses.

For now, we must stand in their shoes.

For Jews, the most repeated verse of the Sinai Torah is the one from Deuteronomy 6 known as the *Sh'ma*:

Hear O' Israel, the Lord is our God, the Lord is One!

For the sake of argument, let's set aside any post-Holocaust theological issues for the time being as we unpack that seminal verse.

When you look in a Torah scroll at this sentence, one thing becomes immediately clear, even to a person who does not read Hebrew. Two letters are larger than the rest, the final letters of the word *Sh'ma* and *Echad*—the *ayin* and the *daled*.

שְׁמַע יִשְׂרָאֵל יְהֹוָה אֱלֹהֵינוּ יְהֹוָה אֶחָד

No one really knows why this is. One possibility is to make sure not to mispronounce those two words. The *daled* at the end of *echad*, for instance, can easily be misread as a *resh*, which would change the word from *echad* to *acher*, from the word "one" to "another."

Hear O Israel, the Lord our God *is another God*, sort of distorts the meaning.

But commentators have also speculated that the reason for the two enlarged letters has something to do with the word that you get when you put the *ayin* and *daled* together. And that is the word "*Ayd*," or "witness." There is something about the *Sh'ma* that calls on each of us to bear witness.

But bear witness to what? And how? And why?

Unlike a blessing in Hebrew, there is no place to say "*Amen*" after the *Sh'ma*. Typically, it's enough to hear the cantor say a blessing and all we have to do is acknowledge it by saying "*Amen*." And in that way, we have fulfilled the responsibility of saying that prayer. Not so with the *Sh'ma*. Each person must actively recite it, usually in full voice, so that we can hear ourselves affirm divine unity, each of us bearing witness to it on our own.

There is a response to the *Sh'ma*, but it's not "*Amen*." It's that verse that was recited in the days of the temple when the people heard the High Priest pronounce that most sacred of names, on the holiest moment of the year, on Yom Kippur, in the most mysterious place, the Holy of Holies. "*Baruch shem k'vod malchuto l'olam va'ed*"—Blessed be the Name of the One whose glorious sovereignty is forever and ever." Traditionally this verse is recited silently after that first line of the *Sh'ma*. Except on Yom Kippur. This is the day when we can feel the awe, this is the one day when we are close enough to the source of all life and meaning, that we can sense, even if only for an instant, the clarity of our mission—our place in the scheme of things. So, we can say OMG! to what we have seen.

The response to the *Sh'ma* is more than an *Amen*. *Amen* is what bystanders say. *Amen* is the polite applause after a chamber concert. *Amen* is the nod of agreement after a sermon or the broad smile after a bar mitzvah speech. *Amen* is a letter to the editor, or clicking "like" on Facebook.

Amen is what spectators do.

The *Sh'ma* is for witnesses.

In saying the *Sh'ma*, we are walking in the steps of all those who said it before us or who will after us. Our kids or grandkids at bedtime. Jacob's children at their father's bedside—assuring their dad, whose name was Israel, "*Sh'ma Yisra'el*—Listen, Dad, Israel, your God and our God, they're one and the same. We'll carry on."

And when we say the *Sh'ma* we are bearing witness to martyrs, who, from Roman times onward, had these sacred words on their lips while meeting their demise. Rabbi Akiva and the others in the first century, to the martyrs of the first Crusade in 1096, the victims of the Spanish Inquisition, the massacres of Polish Jewry in 1648, the Czarist pogroms and the Holocaust.

Rabbi Akiva was sentenced to death for studying Torah. The Romans tortured him by scraping off his flesh with a giant comb. As he was being tortured, Akiva recited the *Sh'ma* and his students asked how he could praise God while in such pain. Rabbi Akiva replied: "All my life, I strived to love God with all my soul. Now that I can fulfill it, I do so with joy!"

With his dying breath, he sanctified God's name by crying out the words of *Sh'ma*.

So, when we say the *Sh'ma*, we aren't just remembering the martyrs. We're bearing witness to their suffering and their triumphs. We're saying, for all to hear, that their story has become our story.

I know that it might seem unnecessarily dour to talk about martyrdom in the concluding chapter of a book designed to show how the Holocaust can bring about positive change. But having seen the death camps and massacre sites in Poland and beyond, I've come to a greater understanding of what it means to be a witness; and there is no way to end this book other than to discuss, in depth, the responsibility that role entails.

In a stirring speech given at the White House in 1999, Elie Wiesel said, "Fifty-four years ago to the day, a young Jewish boy from a small town in the Carpathian Mountains woke up, not far from Goethe's beloved Weimar, in a place of eternal infamy called Buchenwald."

He was finally free, but there was no joy in his heart, and he assumed there never would be again. Liberated by American soldiers, Wiesel remembered their rage at what they saw. And he stated that even if he lives to be a very old man, he will always be grateful to them for that rage, and for their compassion. "Though he did not understand their language, their eyes told him what he needed to know—that they, too, would remember, and bear witness."

On the *March of the Living* in 2010, my group heard the story of Judy Altmann, a survivor returning, with us, to the camps for the first time. In fact, we *lived* her story. We were with her as she discovered for the first time where her sister most likely perished—at Belzec—and she brought a small group to the barracks where she was imprisoned at Auschwitz-Birkenau. One teen took it upon herself to, "adopt" Judy's story, to carry that story with her once Judy is no longer with us. This teen's promise epitomizes what it means to be a Jewish witness, merging the *ayin* of *Sh'ma* and the *daled* of *echad*. The letter *ayin* comes from the Hebrew word "eye," and *daled* from the word *delet*, door. That teen will become Judy's eyes and will open doors though which a new generation will enter her story.

Judy Altmann on the March of the Living, 2010

For Jews, that's a true witness protection program—but we need to bear witness to more than just the horrors of the Holocaust.

We Were There

Several years ago, I had the honor of hearing Representative John Lewis speak. He was very powerful, talking to a group of college students about the need to be involved, to bear witness to the Civil Rights struggles of his generation. Lewis was one of 10 speakers at Martin Luther King's March on Washington in 1963 and is now the last surviving speaker. There was urgency in his voice that mirrored Wiesel's. We have now become witnesses, I thought, as he described vividly the bridge in Selma, the barking dogs and the police, Sherriff Clarke fending them off with a gun in one hand and a cattle prod in the other, and the deaths of the freedom riders in Mississippi, among them Jews. The shared suffering of the Civil Rights era rang out to me when Lewis concluded his lecture by saying, "We may have come over in different ships, but now we're all in the same boat."

And so, as filtered through the *Torah of Auschwitz*, that passage from Deuteronomy known as the *Sh'ma* has taken on added meaning, reminding us that we are all now *edim*, (witnesses), and not merely to tragedy, but also to the majesty of the cosmos, to the miracle of life, to the eternal lessons of the Jewish experience and to the unity of all humanity.

Theologian Art Green asks, why does the *Sh'ma* say "*Adonai Eloheynu*," "The Lord OUR God?"

Adonai, he states, was what was there before each of us came into existence. *Adonai* becomes *Eloheynu*—OUR God—for the brief instant that our lives flash across the screen. But then we let it go, and it is *Adonai* once again, endless being. Our individual existences are merely the blink of an eye, but we are linked to an eternal life force. We are eternal witnesses to its power, and to the role that our people have played in the unfolding of the divine drama.

Just think about that and read the phrase as Green would—*Sh'ma Yisrael...Adonai-Eloheynu-Adonai...echad*. Each of us is living in that one narrow window of time, that brief, fleeting moment of *Eloheynu*, shoehorned in between the two *Adonais*—the eternities that preceded our birth and that will follow. For this brief moment, we inherit the mantle of being a witness to all that has come before, of all that becomes ours, of all that sanctity becomes *Eloheynu*. What are we going to do with that fleeting, priceless gift?

Yes, much of the Jewish experience has been painful, but that has given us the unique ability to feel others' pain because we ourselves have felt it. We have the responsibility to love the stranger, as the Torah instructs us three dozen times, because we were strangers in the land of Egypt. We have that certain instinct, that radar, to detect prejudice, an instinct that many others lack. We can bear witness to all suffering, because we have felt that pain.

A perfect example of that was when the Supreme Court welcomed its third sitting Jewish justice, Elena Kagan. Nice Jewish girl. Earned her street cred as a 12-year-old in the Upper West Side by having a run-in with her rabbi, and as result became Lincoln Square Synagogue's first bat mitzvah. For many, the most revealing moment in her confirmation hearings came when Senator Lindsey Graham asked where Kagan had been on Christmas Day of 2009. His purpose was simply to find out her views on the failed terror attack on an airliner that occurred that day. But in asking that question, he unknowingly pushed that button that Jews all know so well, the button of the witness, and that radar kicked in, and she responded in the perfect Jewish manner—not to up the ante with defensiveness, but to diffuse a volatile situation with humor.

She said, "Like all Jews, I was probably at a Chinese restaurant."

I have no way of knowing what the senator was thinking, but I know exactly what Elena Kagan was thinking; which is exactly what I would have thought, and exactly what Woody Allen thought in Annie Hall when he got upset every time someone asked him *"D'Jew* want to go out to eat?" She poked fun at a question that was insensitive, though not deliberately so, and her joke pointed to a coping mechanism that has been employed by Jews and other non-Christians to deal with feelings of being outsiders on December 25.

Brilliant.

Neurotic, but brilliant!

Being a witness has its burdens, and one is, I suppose, neurosis. Kagan had no reason to be defensive in that hearing. She had just been nominated to the Supreme Court! As a Jew and as a woman, that is truly remarkable.

But still, she is a witness. And her response to that question, along with many others, indicated that she takes that role seriously, as her subsequent rulings have borne out. Even at a time when Jews are at the pinnacle of power, we must remember that we were slaves, the consummate outsiders. Not our ancestors. *We* were the slaves. For a Jew, there is no such thing as history, there is only an ever-evolving present, a story that we are writing even as it unfolds before us. From a God's-eye view, our moment of existence is infinitesimal. But from our perspective, our ability to bear witness is eternal.

We are the authors, we are the main characters and we are the storytellers. That is what it means to bear witness.

In Israel you really can sense the timelessness of the Jewish story and what it means to be witnesses to it. That's what I love about being there; every moment connects you to history. Once when I was leading a group in Israel, we were headed north and the bus driver decided to veer from the road-most-traveled and take an alternative route to our destination. (The bus driver was a pain in the neck, but that's another story.) So, we were meandering through the Jezreel Valley and passed right alongside Mount Tabor, a steep hill that sticks out of the otherwise flat farmland. You might recall that this is the place where in the book of Judges, Deborah defeated the Canaanite King Sisera when, after a sudden downpour, all his chariots slid down the mountain in the mud.

So just as we were passing this sacred, storied site, a sign on the road stated plainly and without a hint of irony, "Slippery when wet."

I'm sure it *is* slippery when wet! It was for Sisera, 3,000 years ago. We know! We read the book! And that sign, in the same language as the original story, bears witness to that fact, and links all of us something that happened long before we were born. But the past doesn't come alive through the sign itself. It comes alive through our *reading* the sign. We are the eyes and the doorway, the *ayin* and the *daled*, the AYD, the witness, making the story of Deborah spring to life.

Bearing witness goes beyond being part of key moments in world history. It means to take those experiences and channel them into wisdom. If you take the word AYD and reverse the *ayin* and the *daled*, you get "DA," to understand.

The child who brings matzah to school during Passover, bearing witness and sharing wisdom (and usually most of the matzah), regaling classmates about slavery in Egypt rather than wasting lunch hour discussing last night's ballgame or the latest exploits of the Kardashians. With each crunch, he is bearing witness to a deeper understanding of God's redemptive power, the pain of the Israelite slave, and what it means to live a holy life.

Our task is to discern the call of our age, to respond, to dig beneath what Art Green calls the "complex, civilizing masks of language," to lead ourselves to that primal scream that goes beyond words, the kind of unfiltered, pure message that one hears in the shofar's call or in a wordless *niggun* (melody); something that can penetrate deeper, a place more ancient—deeper within us than words can reach. We need to respond to that call of the *Sh'ma*: Listen—Listen to that call; listen to that primal whistle. Listen to the Oneness that hides beneath all apparent divisions; to the heart that is beating next to you, to voices raised and souls reaching upward, yearning for Oneness.

For Jews and others who take on the responsibilities of the *Torah of Auschwitz*, it is our responsibility to bear witness to the truth, no matter how uncomfortable that may be. And it is our responsibility, as a people who stands in Covenant, to open ourselves up to the flow of divine love and to bring light and blessing to the lives of others. That is what it means to bear witness.

In our day, we also must bear witness to the dangers that surround us. Having seen firsthand the product of unconstrained hatred, it is our responsibility as Jews to alert the world to the similar dangers percolating elsewhere.

Because we are the heirs to Auschwitz, our voice projects a moral resonance that cuts through the noise.

The Anne Frank Rule

In my house, we have the Anne Frank Rule.

One night during a school vacation, my family was engaged in a stimulating round of "Apples to Apples"—that popular game where a rotating judge picks a descriptive card (like "refreshing," or "feh!") and other contestants select cards that they hope the judge will consider the best possible match (like "Passover" and "Alan Dershowitz"). Naturally, we were playing the Jewish version.

I've found this game to be a very helpful tool in navigating through the complex choices of Jewish identity. Echoing the randomness of such choices, "Apples" effortlessly shuttles us from lox to Leviticus and from Moses to Jackie Mason; from the sublime to the ridiculous. This reflects a randomness experienced by younger Jews as they shuffle various pieces of the Jewish identity puzzle through their psychological playlists.

This particular game was one of our all-timers. It came down to the final hand, with my two kids and me each having a chance to win. With the game on the line, we doubled the stakes and pulled out two descriptive cards: "odd" and "offensive."

Ethan and Dan played "Crown Heights," "my bedroom," "J-Date" and "Dennis Prager." I suppose any of those could have been the best match. But I held the trump card in my hand. You see, I had just drawn "Anne Frank." We have a little rule in my family, one suggested to us by a close friend. Whoever plays the "Anne Frank" card automatically wins that hand. No questions asked. The idea is that it would be offensive to Anne's memory, and by extension, all Holocaust victims, for Anne to lose to, say, "Joan Rivers" or "potato kugel."

But here, the exact opposite would be occurring. Anne would win for matching "odd" and "offensive." How could we shame her in this way?

I succumbed to that logic and pulled back the card. I lost the battle but won the war, as my family then engaged in a dialogue about how, just as Anne's is no normal card, the Holocaust is not just any old piece of the Jewish identity puzzle.

The "Anne Frank Rule" applies to our culture writ large just as it works for "Apples to Apples." Once the Holocaust is invoked in an argument, it usually is game, set and match—but only when the subject is raised at the proper time and by the proper person, and only if it is not overused. The Holocaust offers numerous potential lessons that can be applied to contemporary situations, but it's debatable as to which analogies "work." Comparing any concession in international negotiations to the appeasement at Munich, for instance, is a tactic that has been so overused that its potency has been drained (Google "Netanyahu" and "Munich," for instance, and you get over 960,000 results). So the Holocaust card, like the Anne Frank card, must be played sparingly and with due deliberation.

When the Holocaust-related term "Concentration Camps" was used in July of 2019, in describing the crowded and squalid detention facilities used by the Trump administration for asylum seekers and other refugees at the U.S.-Mexican border, the U.S. Holocaust Museum cried foul. I winced a bit myself. But in an essay for Slate, Yale historian Timothy Snyder explained how and when Holocaust analogies are not only appropriate, they are necessary.

"Analogizing is not some mysterious operation: It is how we think. Every time someone asks you for advice about a situation beyond your personal experience, or every time you are faced with an unfamiliar choice, your mind makes analogies with what you do know. Then you ask questions that allow you to clarify similarities and differences. At some point, you have understood and can act. 'Never again' is nothing other than an invocation of that process. We start from what we know about the present and make our way back to the 1930s and 1940s. Once we understand something about the history of the Holocaust, we make our way forward again, seeing patterns we would have missed. If we notice a dangerous one, we should act. Without this effort, though, 'never again' becomes its own opposite: 'It can't happen here.' . . . *To forbid analogies makes the Holocaust irrelevant to future generations* [italics mine]. If an American child can identify with Anne Frank, an American child might ask hat it is like for immigrant children to be separated from their parents. To forbid analogies is to forbid learning, and to forbid empathizing . . . The point of historical comparisons is not to seek a perfect match—which can never be found—but to learn how to look out for warning signs."

The use of the Shoah in conversations about refugees is completely appropriate, especially in light of the hundreds of thousands of Jews who were turned away at the door to freedom, including—it must be noted—the family of Anne Frank, whose father Otto sought to bring his family to America. Had she survived, Anne Frank would have turned 90 in June of 2019—and she could have lived a perfectly uneventful, happy life in Hoboken.

Holocaust analogies should be used sparingly, to be sure, but when used appropriately, there is no question as to who has the moral authority to play that card. Jews do.

I've never been a big fan of calling the Jews a "chosen people." Still, I never saw the concept as a signal of superiority, but rather as a summons and a responsibility, to bring Sinai's vision of holiness, justice and love to the world. In the *Torah of Auschwitz*, chosenness still calls on us to strive to repair the world, as it did at Sinai; but now our moral voice has been amplified 10 times over by historical experience. When Jews invoke Auschwitz, the world listens—because we were there. Many hate us for that, especially if they idealize fascism. Others admire us. But everyone listens.

When we embrace Auschwitz, we hold the Anne Frank card close to our vest, play it when necessary, and appreciate the moral power of our message.

The Dance of the Witness

When I led services in 2010 for the *March of the Living* teens in the synagogues of Poland, it was almost as if the dead were calling out to us. Europe is filled with dead synagogues. Beautiful, restored—but still dead. Back in the 1930s, the chief rabbi of Krakow, who preached precisely where I was standing, was firmly convinced that Polish Jewry was ascendant. "There... the Jewish people came into its own," wrote Abraham Joshua Heschel of the Poland of that era. "It did not live like a guest in somebody else's home, who must constantly keep in mind the ways and customs of the host. There Jews lived without reservation and without disguise, outside their homes no less than within them."

The Jews of Palestine were small in number at that time, American Jews were too assimilated, and Soviet Jewry was being crushed by the Communists. But Poland is where the best and brightest studied Torah in glittering yeshivot, where three million Jews lived a vibrant life, separate from but unbothered by their neighbors. Poland was the great meeting place of Hasidic fervor of Galicia, the Talmudic expertise of Lithuania and the western scholarship of German Jewry. It all came together in Poland, arguably the most vibrant Jewish community in all of history.

The Jews of Poland must have thought it would last forever.

So as I stood there in front of my *March of the Living* group at the Tempel Synagogue, that large ornate structure tucked between the narrow little alleyways of the Kaszimierz, the Jewish quarter with few Jews, I speculated out loud with the teens what it meant to be a witness. I asked them to realize that, just as in their synagogues back home, the pews they were sitting in once belonged to someone who sat in that same place, every Shabbat, every Rosh Hashanah and every Yom Kippur. In the fall of 1942, the place was full on Yom Kippur. And the next year, they were all gone, following the liquidation of the Krakow ghetto in March of 1943—a scene emblazoned in our consciousness by Steven Spielberg in the movie *Schindler's List*. That horrible scene was witnessed by Schindler on horseback from the top of the hill, when amidst the tumult the camera focuses our attention on a single victim, a little girl.

And what we remember most about the girl from the movie is her shoe. Her red shoe.

I asked the teens to think of that one individual while we said the mourner's Kaddish. The person who sat in that pew. And then we danced. We danced to the melody created by Shlomo Carlebach* in memory of those victims, the *Krakower Niggun*. And at that moment we became living witnesses.

Witnesses don't sit on their butts and listen passively while succumbing to a spiritual numbness. Spectators do that. Witnesses pray with intensity. Witnesses sing with fervor. Witnesses perform acts of selflessness and courage. Witnesses stand arm in arm with those who marched at the bridge in Selma and with those who suffered Egyptian slavery.

Witnesses slide in the mud on Mount Tabor and lift a Torah at the Western Wall. Witnesses cry with the parents of terror victims and mass shootings and scream to Congress about the fate of refugees. Witnesses march in to hear John Lewis speak about how he marched out.

But most of all, witnesses dance.

So we danced, and the walls of the Tempel Synagogue came alive. Then days later, we danced again at the synagogue in the eastern Polish town of Lancot, also dead and lovingly restored, and our voices echoed so loud that a Polish woman came in off the street asking how we could be singing so loud when her whole country was in mourning for their president. "We're not singing," she was told by Judy Altmann. "We are praying."

Carlebach's *Krakower Niggun* begins with a vision, one that he had as he sat in the pews of the Krakow synagogue, of the Jews of the city boarding the trains, their belongings and loved ones snatched from them. The darkness of the ovens suddenly gave way in his vision to a bright light. And the victims: instead of being limp corpses, they were dancing in joy.

I have that same vision now, about the 1,000 shoes of Majdanek. The victims are no longer barefoot. Their sores have healed. The infections have gone away. The shoes don't even smell anymore. They fit perfectly. And somewhere, a little girl, like Cinderella or like Dorothy in Oz, tries on her long-lost slipper, smiles, jumps for joy, and is home.

Now we must be their eyes. Their *aynayim*. And we must stand in their shoes—their ragged, dusty shoes, the shoes of Majdanek—and dance their

* Bringing up Shlomo Carlebach carries some risk in light of serious #MeToo accusations made against him. Carlebach's flaws cannot be overlooked, but he appears in this book because any discussion of the world of post-Holocaust Judaism would be incomplete without his contributions.

dance. And we stand in their place. We are their eyes and we stand in their shoes—we are their witnesses—and we will open the door, the *delet*, to their future, and our own.

After a death, the traditional time of intense mourning for Jews is seven days—*shiva* in Hebrew. At that point, the bereaved family arises from their low chairs and leaves the house walking up and down the street, symbolically re-entering the world.

The Torah of Sinai includes the most hopeful of prophecies in chapter two of Isaiah:

"The Lord will mediate between nations and will settle international disputes. They will beat their swords into plowshares and their spears into pruning hooks. Nation will not take up sword against nation, nor will they train for war anymore."

The Holocaust counters with that more menacing image indelibly burnt into my soul back when I was forced to watch *Night and Fog* while in Hebrew school:

"And they shall turn their fat into soap and their skin into lampshades."

But the *Torah of Auschwitz*, tying together threads of narrative, synthesizing fact, memory, and the inextinguishable human instinct to overcome the darkness, reclaim hope and choose life, looks squarely at the soap and lampshades, without denying them, and asks:

What now? How can we reconcile Hitler with Isaiah?

We reconcile the two by rising from *shiva* and turning Hitler's demise into a more lasting victory for humankind. Conceding that we can no longer count on divine assistance to settle international disputes—and in fact bowing to the knowledge that it is downright dangerous to see divine purpose in the course of international events—we are called upon to roll up our sleeves and start learning how to meld swords into plowshares on our own.

David Grossman, author of the searing novel *See Under: Love*, who is from my post-Holocaust generation, writes eloquently in his 2008 collection, *Writing in the Dark: Essays on Literature and Politics*, about growing up among survivors in Israel and in particular, of his dilemma on what to tell his own child:

> About two decades ago, when my oldest son was three, his pre-school commemorated Holocaust Memorial Day

as it did every year. My son did not understand much of what he was told, and he came home confused and frightened. "Dad, what are Nazis? What did they do? Why did they do it?" And I did not want to tell him. I, who had grown up amid the silence and fragmented whispers that had filled me with so many fears and nightmares, who had written a book about a boy who almost loses his mind because of his parents' silence, suddenly understood my parents and my friends' parents who chose to be mute.

I felt that if I told him, if I even so much as cautiously alluded to what had happened over there, something in the purity of my three-year-old son would be polluted; that from the moment such possibilities of cruelty were formulated in his childlike, innocent consciousness, he would never again be the same child.

He would no longer be a child at all.

As I stood in front of my Hebrew school students on Kristallnacht 2018, I felt very differently. To paraphrase Ecclesiastes, there is a time for speech and a time for silence, a time to traumatize kids with movies about lampshades, a time for cryptic, fragmented whispers—*and a time to openly explain precisely what happened and why it is so important for us to become living witnesses.*

A couple of months later, I took my synagogue's teen group to the Museum of Jewish Heritage in Manhattan. Its full name is "Museum of Jewish Heritage: A Living Memorial to the Holocaust." It's been called that for a long time, but quite recently, the term "living memorial" took on a whole new meaning. As I would have guessed, my teens were very interested in the Holocaust memorabilia and the personal stories of their guide, who was a second-generation survivor. But they were blown away by what awaited them on the upper floor. There they met two survivors—actually 3-D facsimiles of two survivors, a man and a woman, both aging but not impaired, and both equipped with voice recognition technology and the answers to just about every question the kids threw at them:

What was your bar mitzvah like?

They recalled in greater detail than I can recall my own bar mitzvah. It was Holocaust by hologram. For the kids it was a revelation and fun. For me, it was astonishing and just a little bit spooky. These survivor's stories will now achieve immortality, and in their own voices. By better enabling a new generation to hear them—even to interact with them—they have become their own witnesses.

Thus far, only a small number of survivors have been interviewed for this project, called "New Dimensions in Testimony (NDT). They are among the 55,000 who have given video testimony for the Institute's Visual History Archive. Josh Grossberg, a media liaison to the USA Shoah Foundation describes the process: "They all come to Los Angeles for about a week, and they sit under a dome of lights surrounded by more than 100 cameras. And we go through the process of asking them 1,500 or so questions. It takes several days... For us it wasn't only about the technology. I know the technology is pretty cool when you look at it. For us, it's all about telling stories."

But what interested me most was how my teens responded. The hologram was cool, the stories instructive, and the situations described painful, tragic and heroic. But as close as it came to a real encounter with a survivor, there was still a yawning gap between virtual and real. You can't really care for an image. The very fact of needing to talk to an image was itself a stark reminder of the scarcity of real witnesses left. Only a few years ago, most of the docents at this museum were first generation. Not anymore. The transition from real to virtual can help to transmit the facts, but it can't inculcate the feelings. And a witness needs to *feel* the story in order to be able to retell it.

Below is a letter written by Jack and Barbara Levitz of Peekskill, N.Y. to their teenage granddaughter, Yaffa Englander, as she embarked on the 2019 March of the Living. It perfectly embodies the aspiration that the Holocaust, which rests at the core of contemporary Jewish existence, can inspire compassionate, positive, life-affirming action.

> Dear Yaffa,
> Because of your kind heart and sweet *neshama*, we expect that the *March of the Living* has been an "emotional roller-coaster" for you. This experience is very likely a significant step in your personal growth toward being an even better informed and committed Jewish leader and educator. We hope that this excursion through lived-history is deepening your understanding and knowledge of the Holocaust and

impacts you in indelible ways. The following are concepts that your experience brought to mind for us that you may now wish to contemplate as prospective lessons learned:

Not to *fear* but to *fear* complacency

Not to *hate* but to *hate* inhumanity

Not to *be sad* but to *be saddened* by the extent of loss

Not to feel *different* but to have *different* expectations of acceptance

Not to be *intolerant* but to *not tolerate* injustice

Not to *forget* but be wary how quickly so many *forget* to remember

Not to be *discouraged* but be *encouraged* by the *courageous* acts of so many

Not to be weighed down by *hopelessness* but lifted up by *hopefulness*

Not to *humiliate* but show *humility*

Not to be *narrow-minded* but be thoughtfully *mindful*

Upon your return from Poland and Israel, per-haps we can further explore these ideas together from the perspective of your current experience.

Sent to you with serious thought and much love,

From Grandma and Grandpa

Here's an excerpt from Yaffa's reply:

"As I sat surrounded by symbolic gravestones for the thousands of communities wiped off the map by this particular death camp, Treblinka, your words provided me with an acute sense of humanity, dignity, and righteousness in your call to action. In a place like that, it's easy to get caught-up in the personal and communal feeling of tragedy—your message enforced that with each negative action, there is a positive parallel act that can have a truly extraordinary effect."

The Passover Haggadah speaks of Four Children who ask about the Ex-odus from Egypt. Back in the latter part of the twentieth century, Rabbi Yitz

Greenberg suggested that we add a fifth child, the one who did not survive to ask. Perhaps now there is a sixth, and this child is alive and well and sitting at our Seders, eager to understand how something that happened not so long ago affects her own life, and how that very real event, freshly blanketed by a thin layer of springtime moss and a bed of sunflowers, can be synthesized with the story of Moses, the plagues, the miracles of Sinai and that omniscient artist formerly-known-as-God.

That child wants to be a witness but doesn't know how. That child is moved deeply at times by the stories, but can't totally connect. That child also wants to move on, to flourish in a loving world, to find rich, contemporary meaning in ancient rituals and resonant relevance in new ones.

Counting in decades rather than days, we have now reached the end of *shiva* for the Holocaust. It is time to re-engage with the world, to be prepared to re-enter history, or perhaps to enter it for the first time—not as victims, but as witnesses. It is time to descend from the mountain of shoes, bearing in our arms the *Torah of Auschwitz*, much as Moses bore the two tablets of stone from Sinai's peak. The prevailing message is life-affirming, despite the suffering recorded in its chronicles. The events are now history, but the question before us is not how to keep the anguish immediate while a new layer of green covers the bloodied, sacred ground. It is rather, how do we render its lessons indelible by allowing it to raise us from the bloody, muddy, mossy muck? How can we acknowledge that the time to weep has yielded, as always, to a time to dance—not with the shadow of Amalek, but with an eternal life-force, with renewal and hope—while acknowledging that these tears will never completely go away? How can we enable the anguish and the anger to be absorbed into the realm of ritual and story, despite the pain, despite the continued presence of anti-Semitism and hate in our world, and thereby enable the Holocaust to become transcendent and ever-present?

Once that happens—and as I hope I've demonstrated, it is truly beginning to happen—we will rise completely and joyously from our mourning bench, and the shoes of Majdanek will lie dormant no more. And the Jewish people, and so many others too—will join in an eternal dance.

Appendix:

A digest of "mitzvot" from the *Torah of Auschwitz*

1) The *Torah of Auschwitz*, a series of sacred teachings and practices that enable us to confront the darkest demons of seven decades ago. At the same time, **this narrative is filled with positive and life-affirming lessons** that can have an enormous impact on not just the Jewish people, but the entire world.

2) Jeremiah, in chapter 31, envisions the creation of a "**New Covenant**," and this passage is used by Christians, Jews and Muslims to validate their post-biblical additions to the sacred canon. But the prophecy fits even better as a harbinger of the *Torah of Auschwitz*, in this mashup of relevant verses: "Behold, I will bring them from the north country, and gather them from the uttermost parts of the earth, and with them the blind and the lame, the woman with child and she that travails with child together; a great company shall they return hither...Behold, the days come, says the LORD, that I will make a new covenant with the house of Israel, and with the house of Judah; not according to the covenant that I made with their fathers in the day that I took them by the hand to bring them out of the land of Egypt...**And there is hope for your future, says the Lord.**"

3) The *Torah of Auschwitz* that is now emerging will feature Anne Frank's wisdom as its book of *Proverbs* and Elie Wiesel's *Night* as its book of *Job*. **Auschwitz was the Nazis' attempt to extinguish the human spirit. The *Torah of Auschwitz* has reignited that sacred torch.**

4) The *Torah of Auschwitz* **has taken root** to the point where it now is no longer joined at the hip to Zionism.

5) The *Torah of Auschwitz* stands, like the Jewish people itself, as a **living refutation of Hitler's pathological nihilism.** To remember the Holocaust without a social conscience is not to remember it at all. As Elie Wiesel said in his Nobel acceptance speech, "Wherever men or women are persecuted because of their race, religion, or political views, that place

must—at that moment—become the center of the universe."

6) *Choose Life!* Here's where the *Torah of Auschwitz* veers from the Torah of Sinai's path. The *Torah of Auschwitz* teaches that "Choose life!" calls upon us *literally* to choose life in the face of death, to seek the path that will engender survival, despite any odds, and that survival itself is victory. It goes beyond simply making each moment of life as full as possible, as Psalm 90 implores: "Teach us to count our days that we may gain a heart of wisdom." The *Torah of Auschwitz* goes beyond that, imploring us simply to add to life by continuing to live, and thereby make our lives into a statement of persistence and courage.

7) So the *Torah of Auschwitz* interprets that verse from Psalm 126 anew: *Those who procreate in tears shall witness the end of their suffering, as they reap the sweet joy of their first fruits, and against all odds, a life imbued with hope continues with a new generation.* And we can now understand Deuteronomy 30:19 from the perspective of the survivor: "Choose life, so that you and your children may live." For the survivor, the directive is to choose life in the most literal sense, by having children.

8) Psalm 16 is calling on us to place *Auschwitz itself* before us always. No, not the place of death and destruction, but the place of renewal and hope, the place that now exists to forever remind us where hate ultimately leads, the place visited by more people every year than were killed there, the place of pilgrimage for heads of state and leaders of all faith traditions—and a place where thousands of Jewish youth congregate every year for Jewish youth's annual Spring Awakening, the *March of the Living*. That Auschwitz.

9) In the *Torah of Auschwitz*, Rywka Lipszyc is our new Elijah, a prophet who attained his status in Jewish folklore in large part because in the Bible he is never recorded to have died. Rywka is now the one to visit every Seder, even if she is still underage for the wine.

10) What the *mezuzah* was to the Torah of Sinai, the swastika has become to the *Torah of Auschwitz*, in a perverse, inverse fashion—a talisman of fear rather than a sign of our escape from the Destroyer, who in Egypt passed over those doorposts marked in lamb's blood. Jews mark that bloody spot with a *mezuzah*, while anti-Semites scrawl a swastika. One chases evil away, the other invites it in.

11) The *Torah of Auschwitz* commands us to come face to face with our

darkest impulses, the hatred that persists toward the Other—and the fear that persists within ourselves.

12) In the *Torah of Auschwitz*, **the *mezuzah* has been transformed from a security blanket into a time capsule,** a herald of heroism from a dark past, beckoning us toward a brighter future.

13) In the Torah of Sinai, on the seventh day, God rested. **In the *Torah of Auschwitz*, at the conclusion of the seventh decade, the dead began to rest in peace.**

14) **Never Forget (*Zachor*) became perhaps the rallying cry and first commandment of the *Torah of Auschwitz*, alongside its corollary, "Never Again."**

15) The *Torah of Auschwitz* emphasizes *zachor*, not as a call to punish the villains—even those who reside within our psyches—or simply to remember the Holocaust as a singular event. Rather it is a call *to remember the victims*—each individual—and not merely the victims of the Holocaust itself. **Our task is to ensure that *never again* should a cry from the depths of despair, danger and loneliness go unheeded—from *anywhere and anyone*.**

16) The call to remember, ***zachor*, is not simply a call to preserve the memory of one dark chapter in history, but *to preserve historical memory*, period.** *Never forget* means to remember always that there is an authentic basis for experienced truth, that *facts matter* and we should be accountable to them.

17) **The commandment *zachor*, as filtered through the *Torah of Auschwitz*, has come to mean that we've got to remember and to cherish the uniqueness and sanctity of every human being,** down to even the smallest shreds of their existence—every strand of hair, every single letter of every name. Which, incidentally, is why Nazis hate Jews—then and now. While Nazis have always been more about numbers, Jews have always been more about names. The second book of the Torah is called "*Shmot*," "names."

18) In the *Torah of Auschwitz*, **a mitzvah that nearly equals the one to "Choose life" in importance is that every lost or abandoned person must be found.**

19) In Leviticus 19:14, the Torah of Sinai says that we should not place a stumbling block before the blind. But the *Torah of Auschwitz* says, *Yes,*

you should place these stumble stones everywhere a victim lived, to remove blinders from the eyes of those who try to forget their suffering. The *Torah of Auschwitz* commands, **You should place a stumbling block before the blind**—those blind to the suffering of others.

20) **The *Torah of Auschwitz* asks us to go beyond just reciting names. We need to learn their stories.** But in this hyper-visual era, where a picture is worth a thousand words and an Instagram a thousand Tweets, we need to go one step beyond even that: We need to remember faces too.

21) **The experiences of the Holocaust can help us confront a dizzying world where everything has been turned on its head**; where everything we thought was true turns out not to be; when "new normals" become what's normal. The *Torah of Auschwitz* instructs us never to stop dreaming of the destination, even as our inner GPS seems to be constantly recalculating the route.

22) But here's where the *Torah of Auschwitz* takes over and raises *Pikuach Nefesh* (the mitzvah to save a life, even if it means breaking a commandment) to the next level. **Adaptation, once a grudging concession to reality, has now become a *mitzvah*.** Once an exception to the rule, it has become the rule.

23) The *Torah of Auschwitz*, which reflects Jewish historical experience with a Darwinian twist, says that **Judaism must be flexible enough to save *itself*,** to remain relevant in a radically changing world—while remaining true to its core values.

24) The *Torah of Auschwitz* compels us to eradicate those boundaries. I believe we have entered a world of connection rather than separation and distinction. **We are moving, in a sense, from *Kosher to Kesher*.** These nearly identical Hebrew words signify the old ways and the new. The laws of keeping Kosher are, like the rest of the Sinai laws of holiness, built on distinction, on drawing lines of separation. *Kesher*, on the other hand, is the Hebrew word for connection, calling on us to dissolve distinctions.

25) The Torah of Sinai says, "*God is One*," referring to that ineffable name proclaimed only by the High Priest on Yom Kippur Day, as he hoped for the expiation of Israel's sin. And the *Torah of Auschwitz* responds, **"We are One," with that word being the final, ineffable cry of battered bodies and intertwined souls;** and still we await the expiation of *God's*

sin. The final letter of *Echad*, the *daled*, trails off into silence, opening the door—*delet*, in Hebrew—to eternity, as the doors to the gas chambers were pried open and the bodies were heaped in piles.

26) When the *Torah of Auschwitz* cries "Echad," it is far less concerned with the embroiderer than with the tapestry itself. It is not dwelling on God's essence but rather on the Oneness of humankind. When we speak of our being "one," we're not merely speaking of a virtual oneness, a cyber community or a soulful connection, but a physical connection too: body and soul, spirit and sinew; *Rikma Enoshit Echat*—sharing our very real and very fragile earth, the same heating air, the same rising oceans, the same parched soil. **We are all inextricably connected.**

27) The *Torah of Auschwitz* states, "Love the stranger, because not only do you know how it feels to be a stranger who is hated, but you also know how it feels to be a stranger who is loved—by someone who was a stranger to you." And it says, "Don't merely love your neighbor as yourself; cultivate kindness in yourself and accept grace from others. **Love your neighbor, because you have been loved by your neighbor.** And through that love, your faith in humankind has been restored.

28) **"We are caught in an inescapable network of mutuality, tied in a single garment of destiny."** Those words of Martin Luther King perfectly capture the essence of the *Torah of Auschwitz*.

29) Adam's and Eve's family was resettled to the east. Unlike the Torah of Sinai, **the *Torah of Auschwitz* begins not in paradise, but way, way east of Eden; with hell, not paradise, as its starting point, and it traces the journey back home, back to the Garden**—a journey that in 1945 took the survivors through fire and water and scorched earth, far more lethal than the flaming swords of the *cherubim*.

30) **The earth is ours and we are utterly responsible for all that happens to it**— all of it—the people, and the flowers, too. The flowers at Dachau have become a symbol of God's ultimate helplessness and our ultimate responsibility. We still pray, though no longer for divine intervention, but in gratitude for the basic tools provided us: warm summer days, rain in its season, the miraculous ecosystem. We look to heaven for resolve but for little else, for "the earth has been given to humankind." That is the environmental message of the *Torah of Auschwitz*.

31) **The *Torah of Auschwitz* compels us to continue our unrelenting ques-**

tioning and not to give up on God so easily, whether or not God has given up on us.

32) In the *Torah of Auschwitz*, **the path back to God is littered with shattered dreams, flavored with a strong sense of the absurd mixed with a pinch of wonder.** We remain attuned to the possibility of an orderly universe, despite all that we have witnessed.

33) The *Torah of Auschwitz* **sees art as a path toward a restoration of the Sacred,** as we join Betzalel in continuing to defy the darkness by designing sanctuaries, making music, writing poetry and dancing.

34) While the *Torah of Auschwitz* might give us glimpses of the artist-formally-known-as-God, **the focus always returns to us.**

35) **The realm of ethics must be a major component of the *Torah of Auschwitz*.** While moral dilemmas are hardly new and predate the Holocaust by many centuries, since Auschwitz we've entered a brave new world of complex choices. The ethical tenets of the Torah of Sinai, highlighted by the Golden Rule, need now to be retrofitted to reflect the impossible, "Sophie's Choice" scenarios described by Elie Wiesel, Primo Levi, the partisans, the *Sonderkommandos*, those who gave up their children, and those who ran away from their elderly parents to save themselves. Even the actions of the notorious *Judenrat*, who betrayed their fellow Jews hoping simply to survive, only to find themselves meeting the same fate, deserve to be addressed from an ethical standpoint. Primo Levi spoke of the Holocaust yielding a complex set of ethical dilemmas that he called the "Gray Zone," because rarely are the solutions black and white.

36) Here's a case where the Torah of Sinai and the *Torah of Auschwitz* come into direct conflict. **One form of "tattoo" (wearing tefillin) commands us to aspire to the triumph of life; the other marks humankind's deep descent to the realm of death.**

37) So many of the Torah of Sinai's fundamental moral laws have taken on added meaning in the *Torah of Auschwitz*. Take the fifth commandment, for example. Honoring parents was difficult enough before people had to decide whether to abandon them to the advancing SS when it was possible to survive by escaping to the forests with the partisans. **In the *Torah of Auschwitz*, some bedrock moral certainties have traded in their exclamation points for question marks,** while others have gained prominence in the pecking order of *thou shalts* and *thou shalt nots*.

38) Now, just as the concept of objective truth has been once again been placed under attack by a new generation of Nazis and Nazi-enablers, the *Torah of Auschwitz* is riding to the rescue: **Holocaust denial is the canary in the coal mine of Orwellian doublethink, the mother of all fake news**, in that it not only defies all standards of empirical science and rejects meticulously documented history, which any act of historical denial might do, but in this case, doing so also attempts to whitewash the greatest moral crime ever perpetrated.

39) The *Torah of Auschwitz* makes clear that the commandment to remember the Holocaust is about **keeping alive the essence of all objective truth and the pursuit of fact-based truth as a fundamental value.** The Book of Exodus states that when the Israelites received the Torah they said "*Na'a'seh v'nishma*," often translated as, "We will obediently act and *then* we will understand." But the word "*na'a'seh*" connotes active engagement, not blind obedience. In our age of bots and fake news, the *Torah of Auschwitz* reframes this verse to be better understood as, "We will grapple with each word to assess its validity, and *then* we will understand."

40) When the Torah of Sinai stated, "Thou shalt not bear false witness against thy neighbor," it probably had no idea that it was talking about truth in the abstract sense. The *Torah of Auschwitz* has come along to affix a **corollary to the Ninth Commandment. "Thou shalt not bear false witness against thy neighbor—*who died here.*"** The deaths at Auschwitz were not conjured by conspiracy theorists. These murders are objective, verifiable truth; while ethics can be oftentimes complicated, messy Gray Zones, especially after Auschwitz, moral relativism cannot become the rule to justify future atrocities.

41) **The eradication of racism is, for the *Torah of Auschwitz*, its chief call to arms,** and this call begins with a revision of the Torah of Sinai's second commandment. The original commandment states, "*Thou shalt have no false gods before me.*" The *Torah of Auschwitz* amends that it to add, "*... and the falsest of false gods is the noxious ideology known as racism, which wrongly values some human beings higher than others, and which, when taken to its ultimate end, establishes a particular group as a godlike 'master race' and a single person above them all—and above God.*" If there is one chapter that must be included in our *Torah of Auschwitz*, it is this

section, this restatement of the second commandment, which totally debunks these disgraceful, destructive racial theories that formed the ideological underpinnings of the Third Reich.

42) **The Holocaust has given us a common point of departure, a place where we were all present, even if we weren't.** It is said that every Jew, past present and future, stood at Sinai. Well, every Jew stood, metaphorically, in those gas chambers, and it didn't matter whether you were male or female, traditional, liberal or secular, born Jewish, converted to Judaism or married to a Jew. **By embracing the *Torah of Auschwitz*, we can come together**—Jews of the broadest possible definition—to proclaim to the world that Auschwitz must never happen again.

43) And so, as filtered through the *Torah of Auschwitz*, that passage from Deuteronomy known as **the Sh'ma has taken on added meaning, reminding us that we are all now *edim*, (witnesses)**, not merely to tragedy, but also to the majesty of the cosmos, to the miracle of life, to the eternal lessons of the Jewish experience and to the unity of all humanity.

44) In the *Torah of Auschwitz*, **chosenness still calls on us to strive to repair the world, as it did at Sinai; but now our moral voice has been amplified 10 times over by historical experience.** When Jews invoke Auschwitz, the world listens—because we were there. Many hate us for that, especially if they idealize fascism. Others admire us. But everyone listens.

45) The Torah of Sinai includes the most hopeful of prophecies in chapter two of Isaiah: "The Lord will mediate between nations and will settle international disputes. They will beat their swords into plowshares and their spears into pruning hooks. Nation will not take up sword against nation, nor will they train for war anymore." The Holocaust counters with that more menacing image indelibly burnt into my soul back when I was forced to watch *Night and Fog* while in Hebrew school: "And they shall turn their fat into soap and their skin into lampshades." But the *Torah of Auschwitz*—tying together threads of narrative, synthesizing fact, memory, and the inextinguishable human instinct to overcome the darkness, reclaim hope and choose life—looks squarely at the soap and lampshades, without denying them, and asks: *What now? **How can we reconcile Hitler with Isaiah? We reconcile the two by rising from shiva and turning Hitler's demise into a more lasting victory for humankind.***

Notes

Chapter One

On the impact of the 1970s TV mini-series *Holocaust*, see an academic paper by Josh Niemtzow of Emory University, "The Realization of Comprehensive Holocaust Education in West Germany."

"Conscience is a Jewish invention. It is a blemish, like circumcision.... There is no such thing as truth, either in the moral or in the scientific sense. I am freeing men from the restraints of an intelligence that has taken charge; from the dirty and degrading modifications of a falsehood called conscience and morality." This quote of Hitler comes from Hermann Rauschning, president of the Senate of Danzig during the years 1933–1934. He is said to have recorded a number of remarks by Adolf Hitler. See "The Dictatorship of the Conscience," an academic paper by Bernard N. Schumacher, The Catholic University of America Press, Volume 15, Number 2, Spring 2017, pp. 547-578.

"New Survey by Claims Conference Finds Significant Lack of Holocaust Knowledge in the United States," Conference on Jewish Material Claims Against Germany, 2018. http://www.claimscon.org/study/

For more on the Holocaust breaking through in popular culture, see an article by Adam Rosenberg in *Mashable*, April 26, 2017, "Call of Duty: WWII won't ignore the Holocaust anymore" https://mashable.com/2017/04/26/call-of-duty-wwii-holocaust-interview/#2jUDdKTH7iqP. Also see a New York Times article from Sept. 9, 2017 by Jonah Engel Bromwich: "Secret Hitler, a Game That Simulates Fascism's Rise, Becomes a Hit."

Jacob Neusner's notion of a "Judaism of Holocaust and Redemption" is succinctly explained in his 1993 op-ed in the *Los Angeles Times*, "Back to the Fold, Not to the Faith: Since the Six-Day War, formerly indifferent Jewish intellectuals discovered not the Torah, but Jewishness." https://www.latimes.com/archives/la-xpm-1993-04-25-op-27068-story.html. I also relied heavily on class lecture notes for Neusner's undergraduate course at Brown, "Religious Studies 68: American Judaism."

The oft-cited 2013 Pew Survey, "A Portrait of Jewish Americans," can be found at https://www.pewforum.org/2013/10/01/jewish-american-beliefs-attitudes-culture-survey/

Chapter Two

For more on Yisrael Kristal, see Ofer Aderet's article, "World's Oldest Man, Auschwitz Survivor Yisrael Kristal, Dies at 113," *Ha'aretz*, Aug 12, 2017. A parallel case is the story of Shoshana Ovitz, who survived Auschwitz, settled in Haifa, had four children, and in August of 2019 celebrated her 104th birthday at the Western Wall, surrounded by about 400 descendants. https://www.timesofisrael.com/holocaust-survivor-marks-104th-birthday-at-western-wall-with-400-descendants/

Aside from Riwka's, a number of wartime diaries with similarity to Anne Frank's have surfaced. See "Before Anne Frank, there was Renia Spiegel" (*Washington Post*, Sept. 8. 2019): "In July 30, 1942, Renia, then 18, was summarily executed by the Nazis after they discovered her hideout in the city of Przemysl in southeastern Poland. More than half a century later, her translated diary—strikingly similar in some ways to that of Anne Frank but long kept locked in a vault—is finally set to be published in the United States. The scheduled release of "Renia's Diary: A Holocaust Diary" …comes at a critical time, as nationalism and right-wing populism have drawn comparisons with the 1930s—including in the United States, where Renia's sister Elizabeth Bellak fled with her mother after World War II."

On sweetness and the Mokum carrot, see Dan Barber's interview with Krista Tippett on her radio program *On Being*. "Driven by Flavor," original air date: December 9, 2010. https://onbeing.org/programs/dan-barber-driven-by-flavor/.

Some good background on the Jewish community of Budapest can be found in a thin volume written by Linda Vero-Ban, who is also the wife of Rabbi Tamas Vero of the Frankel Leo Synagogue. Both have been building the Jewish community there since they were teenagers. The book, *Jewish Community Life in Budapest*, was published in English by Bee Jewish Books in 2015, and is available at www.beejewishbooks.com

The stone tablet found at the Oświęcim synagogue is described in detail on pages 26 and 138 of the companion guide to the permanent exhibition of the Galicia Jewish Museum in Krakow, *Rediscovering Traces of Memory: The Jewish Heritage of Polish Galicia*, (Indiana University Press, 2009). The tablet is a *Shiviti*, a Jewish meditative device designed to focus prayer on God and Jerusalem.

Chapter Three

The incident in my synagogue's parking lot was the subject of considerable news coverage when it happened, and later on in my own work, including, "When a Jew Does It," which appeared in *The Washington Post* on March 24, 2017.

Maimonides in fact includes Amalek in **three** of his 613 mitzvot, which includes the commandment to wipe out Amalek's descendants; to remember what Amalek did to the Jewish people; and not to forget Amalek's atrocities and ambush on our journey from Egypt.

On the invisible fence keeping deer from straying over the German-Czech border, see "Czech deer still avoid Iron Curtain" BBC News, April 24, 2014. https://www.bbc.com/news/world-europe-27129727

On Michael Flack's poetry and other young poets of Terezin, see https://dissidentpoetry.wordpress.com/tag/terezin/

Leonard Fein's quote is from "Days of Awe," an article he wrote for the first issue of the magazine *Moment*, in 1982, during Israel's first Lebanon war. For a generation, Fein was the leading prophetic voice of American Jewry, and *Moment*, which he edited, became the prime mouthpiece for progressive Jewish ideas.

Chapter Four

The story of Honi, the Jewish Rip Van Winkle, is found in the Talmud, tractate Taanit, p. 23a.

For more on the significance of 70 years in the Jewish tradition, see Jill Jacobs' article in the *Forward*, "70 Years Represents a Lifetime," April 18, 2018. https://forward.com/opinion/399020/70-years-represents-a-lifetime/. She notes that 70 years is the length of the first exile and adds God's promises in the book of Jeremiah, "When Babylon's 70 years are over, I will take note of you, and I will fulfill to you my promise of favor, to bring you back to this place." Jacobs adds:

> Seventy years, in Jewish tradition, represents a lifetime. As the psalmist wrote, "The span of our life is 70 years." At 70, one reaches *seivah*, meaning old age, though the word is associated with wisdom. According to the Talmud, the carob tree,

which appears in several rabbinic stories as a source of sustenance and even miracles, takes 70 years to bring forth fruit.

I want to acknowledge one of my prime mentors on this topic, Prof. David Roskies, whose book, *Against the Apocalypse: Responses to Catastrophe in Modern Jewish Culture*, (Cambridge: Harvard University Press, 1984) challenged the view of the Holocaust as a unique event standing outside history, without analogy or precedent. While in its scope it is unique, the responses to the Shoah follow familiar patterns. Jews have had all too much practice in dealing with world-shattering catastrophes, and even during the Holocaust itself, Jews found themselves making reference to prior devastations. One focus of his has been the liturgy of destruction, and his *Nightwords: A Liturgy on the Holocaust* (New York: CLAL, 2000) remains the definitive attempt to integrate Shoah themes into the format of traditional Jewish lamentation.

The article on the Netflix roast of Anne Frank: "Sick and Unacceptable: Netflix's Satirical 'Roast' of Anne Frank Draws Fire" (Ha'aretz, May 29, 2019). "Host Jeff Ross—sporting a yellow armband with a Star of David—kicks off the series' third episode with a monologue in which he explains why Frank deserves a roast, as a solo clarinet plays "Hava Nagila" slowly and mournfully. "I only kid the ones I love, and Anne Frank is close to my heart," Ross says. "When we talk about the Holocaust we always say 'Never forget,' yet genocides continue to take place all over the world."

Chapter Five

Read more about the *stolpersteine* (stumbling stones) at http://www.stolpersteine-gelsenkirchen.de/stumbling_stones_demnig.htm. Created by artist Gunter Demnig, they tell the casual walker that the building they are passing housed people who were rounded up and taken away to be murdered because of their ethnicity, religion, politics or sexual persuasion. These modern-day *mezuzahs* of memory have collectively become the single biggest Holocaust memorial in Germany and beyond, located in over 600 municipalities. Each inscription begins with the words, "Here lived…"

If you are interested in having a name recitation memorial ceremony in your community, you can download victims' names from the Yad Vashem website, at https://www.yadvashem.org/downloads.html#pot. Names can be accessed alphabetically, by country or by age. The database is extensive.

Livia Bitton Jackson's essay, "Blond Braids at Auschwitz," can be found in the Spring 1995 edition of *Lilith*, http://www.lilith.org/shop/download/v20i01_Spring_1995-08.pdf, and in its entirety in the collection *Different Voices: Women and the Holocaust* by Carol Rittner and John Roth (Paragon House, 1993).

Before Hitler came to power, 16,000 Jews lived in the Bavarian Quarter of Berlin's Schöneberg district. It was often referred to as the Jewish Switzerland because it was an affluent neighborhood of physicians, businessmen, lawyers, and artists. Holocaust historians have identified the names of 6,000 Jews from Schöneberg who were deported or killed. This decentralized memorial consists of 80 two-sided plaques on 80 lampposts throughout the neighborhood. The stark contrast between an innocent-looking everyday item on one side, and the official Nazi statute on the other, shocks passersby. The signs force us to realize that the Holocaust did not happen all at once. The process of dehumanization took years, and it began with the little things. See a map of the signs at http://www.stih-schnock.de/bilder/transparency_1933_fl_.jpg and http://www.stih-schnock.de/bilder/transparency_1993_fl_.jpg.

Read more about the Bavarian Quarter in an interview with the memorial's creators that appeared in the *New York Review of Books* in 2013: "Jews Aren't Allowed to Use Phones: Berlin's Most Unsettling Memorial," by Ian Johnson.
https://www.nybooks.com/daily/2013/06/15/jews-arent-allowed-use-telephones-berlin-memorial/

Zelda Schneurson Mishkovsky, an Israeli poet best known as simply "Zelda," died in 1984. This poem might be her most famous, and it forms a perfect coda to this chapter (in Israel, it is often recited on Yom Hashoah). You can hear a classic rendition of the poem put to music, sung in the original Hebrew by Chava Alberstein, at https://youtu.be/ECtbWpCraE8

> **"Everyone has a name"**
> Everyone has a name
> given to him by God
> and given to him by his parents.

Everyone has a name
given to him by his stature
and the way he smiles
and given to him by his clothing.
Everyone has a name
given to him by the mountains
and given to him by the walls.
Everyone has a name
given to him by the stars
and given to him by his neighbors.
Everyone has a name
given to him by his sins
and given to him by his longing.
Everyone has a name
given to him by his enemies
and given to him by his love.
Everyone has a name
given to him by his holidays
and given to him by his work.
Everyone has a name
given to him by the seasons
and given to him by his blindness.
Everyone has a name
given to him by the sea and
given to him
by his death.

Chapter Six

Kenneth Miller's works on evolution and religion include *Finding Darwin's God: A Scientist's Search for Common Ground Between God and Evolution*, (New York: Harper, April 3, 2007) and *The Human Instinct: How We Evolved to Have Reason, Consciousness, and Free Will*, (New York: Simon & Schuster, April 17, 2018).

I discuss *Pikuach Nefesh*, whereby Jewish laws can be broken in order to save a life, in another context in an article I wrote for the Religion News Service in March, 2018: "As a rabbi, I will violate the Sabbath to help save lives from gun violence." https://religionnews.com/2018/03/20/as-a-rabbi-i-will-violate-the-sabbath-to-help-save-lives-from-gun-violence/

Charles Krauthammer, "Phony Theory, False Conflict," *The Washington Post*, November 18, 2005. Here's more searing commentary excerpted from this article by a major conservative thinker:

> Let's be clear. Intelligent design may be interesting as theology, but as science it is a fraud. It is a self-enclosed, tautological "theory" whose only holding is that when there are gaps in some area of scientific knowledge—in this case, evolution—they are to be filled by God. It is a "theory" that admits that evolution and natural selection explain such things as the development of drug resistance in bacteria and other such evolutionary changes within species but also says that every once in a while God steps into this world of constant and accumulating change and says, "I think I'll make me a lemur today." A "theory" that violates the most basic requirement of anything pretending to be science—that it be empirically disprovable. How does one empirically disprove the proposition that God was behind the lemur, or evolution—or behind the motion of the tides or the "strong force" that holds the atom together? In order to justify the farce that intelligent design is science, Kansas had to corrupt the very definition of science, dropping the phrase "*natural* explanations for what we observe in the world around us," thus unmistakably implying—by fiat of definition, no less—that the supernatural is an integral part of science. This is an insult both to religion and science.

Hear Rabbi Irwin Kula's discussion of disruptive innovation and Judaism on the podcast, *Judaism Unbound*, at https://www.judaismunbound.com/podcast/2017/1/24/episode-53-draft-title-irwin-kula.

See *The Innovator's Dilemma: When New Technologies Cause Great Firms to Fail (Management of Innovation and Change)*, by Clayton Christensen,

(Boston: Harvard Business Review Press. Reprint edition, January 5, 2016).

Chapter Seven

Hear a lovely rendition of *Rikma Enoshit Echat* sung by the Israeli musician Roni Dalumi at Yad Vashem on Yom Hashoah, at https://youtu.be/8nJ9shRntRw

As alluded to in the text, I cannot in good conscience put into this book the "shocking and ineffable photos" of the intertwined bodies of the victims. You can see some at http://www.auschwitz.dk/Nyiszli.htm, along with the testimony of Dr. Miklos Nyiszli, a Jew who had to sort through the corpses in order to survive. The first photo on that web page, a latticework of limbs, is what inspired this chapter, which first took the form of a Kol Nidre sermon—part of me dies every time I look at it.

Nyiszli, whose direct supervisor was the infamous Josef Mengele, details an incredible story in his memoir, *Auschwitz: A Doctor's Eyewitness Account*, (New York: Arcade Publishing, 1993 (translation), pp. 114-120), in which, at the bottom of the 3,000 dead bodies piled up, they found a girl who was still alive—barely.

> I grabbed my instrument case, which was always ready, and dashed to the gas chamber. Against the wall, near the entrance to the immense room, half covered with other bodies, I saw a girl in the throes of a death rattle, her body seized with convulsions. The gas kommando men around me were in a state of panic. Nothing like this had ever happened in the course of their horrible career. We moved the still-living body from the corpses pressing against it. I gathered the tiny adolescent body into my arms and carried it back to the room adjoining the gas chamber, where normally the gas kommando men change clothes for work. I laid the body on a bench. A frail young girl, almost a child, she could have been no more than fifteen. I took out my syringe and, taking her arm—she had not yet recovered consciousness and was breathing with difficulty—I administered three intravenous injections. My companions covered her body which was as cold as ice with a heavy overcoat. One ran to the kitchen to fetch some tea and warm broth. Everybody want-

ed to help as if she were his own child. The reaction was swift. The child was seized by a fit of coughing which brought up a thick globule of phlegm from her lungs. She opened her eyes and looked fixedly at the ceiling. I kept a close watch for every sign of life. Her breathing became deeper and more and more regular. Her lungs, tortured by the gas, inhaled the fresh air avidly. Her pulse became perceptible, the result of the injections.

The rest of the story of this girl can be found at that website and in the book.

The righteous of all nations have a share in the World to Come. See the rabbinic commentary known as Tosefta, 13:2, and the debate between Rabbi Eliezer and Rabbi Joshua on whether Paradise is reserved for Jews only, or whether Gentiles may partake of the reward as well. Rabbi Joshua's view, that "the righteous of all peoples have a share in the World to Come," holds sway and has never been refuted. For more background on this topic, see https://www.myjewishlearning.com/article/the-world-to-come/, where you'll find an essay by Rabbi Louis Jacobs, "The World to Come."

Ray Allen's moving essay on his visit to Poland, "Why I Went to Auschwitz" from *The Player's Tribune*, August 3, 2017, can be found at https://www.theplayerstribune.com/en-us/articles/ray-allen-why-i-went-to-auschwitz

Chapter Eight

Regarding Adam's first sunset, which terrified him, see Babylonian Talmud, Avodah Zarah 8a and Midrash Genesis Rabbah 12:6. Of this incident, Elie Wiesel wrote, "God gave Adam a secret—and that secret was not how to begin, but how to begin again."

Some additional reflections on Noah's flood and Hurricane Sandy, excerpted from a Rosh Hashanah sermon that I gave in 2013:

> In the *Zichronot* (Remembrance) section of the *Musaf* service on Rosh Hashanah, we read how God remembered Noah and his family in the ark, and we hear the refrain, "*v'zacharti et briti.*" God remembers the covenant. Long before Sinai, well

before Abraham, the rainbow was the first covenant—the first time where God and humanity entered into a contractual relationship. And it was over caring for the planet. The Great Flood was supposed to be the last time God would cause such unfathomable destruction—the last time we could pin such a thing on God. The appearance of that rainbow marked a key moment in the human story: the instant when God turned the wheel over to us. That was the *brit*—the deal—that God pledged to remember. If you read the text of Genesis 9, whether you are a rabbi versed in midrash or a Bible-thumping preacher who takes the passage literally, there should be no disagreement at all. Noah's flood was God's doing. But the text makes it clear as can be that subsequent Superstorms would not be divinely orchestrated. Run-of-the-mill thunderstorms—Okay. They are truly what rabbis and insurance companies would call "acts of God." But not Sandy. God did not flood out the New York Subways. God did not submerge the roller coaster on the Jersey shore. Hurricanes that follow the natural order of things, the kind we had until the mid twentieth century, those are acts of God. Mega storms that defy all historical precedent; those are on us. As outrageous as it sounds, from a Jewish theological viewpoint, we caused Sandy. We caused climate change. We broke the earth. We own it. And we have to fix it.

Chapter Nine

See Rabbi Yitz Greenberg's "Perspectives On the Holocaust," (CLAL, 1986), where he writes (p.12), "It's not so much that one cannot be a liberal or a secularist anymore; or Orthodox or traditional anymore; it's that each one must be shattered...After the Holocaust, it is not so important what position you take, as long as you're ashamed of it."

For more on Rabbi Zalman Schachter-Shalomi's concept of paradigm shifts as they relate to the Holocaust, see "The Spirituality of the Future" by Rabbi Zalman Schachter-Shalomi—https://theshalomcenter.org/node/1395. "Paradigms shift at crisis points: one third of Jewry was destroyed with Auschwitz, and something fundamental in the world was destroyed with Hiroshima and Nagasaki; something about the old was destroyed. So we recognize that being Jewish after these events can no longer be a matter of simply following the past."

See the "Wise Men of Chelm" entry in *YIVO Encyclopedia of the Jews of Eastern Europe*: http://www.yivoencyclopedia.org/article.aspx/Wise_Men_of_Chelm

It is thought that the use of Chelm as a locale for such folk stories began during the eighteenth or nineteenth century, became stabilized, and then remained a constant feature in Jewish folklore. It is unclear why Chelm was the locus for these stories. Some have speculated that it was a result of a rivalry with another town. Others claim that Chelm earned its reputation purely by chance. With no documentary evidence denoting the history of the use of Chelm as a center for Jewish morons, the city's folkloric status is based solely on conjecture.

Is there a biblical source for "Man plans, God laughs?" Some see a connection to Proverbs 16:9—*A man's heart devises his way; but the LORD directs his steps.* Or Psalms 33:10—*"The Lord brings the counsel of the nations to nothing; he frustrates the plans of the peoples."* No matter what the source, Jews have been struggling with an oppositional God for a long time—just about as long as God has been struggling with a "stiff necked" obstinate people.

Rabbi Abahu's theory of multiple universes can be found in *Midrash Genesis Rabbah* 3:7.

Rabbi Judah b. R. Simon said: "*Let* there be evening" is not written here, but "*And* there was evening"; hence we know that a time-order existed before this. Rabbi Abahu said: "This proves that the Holy One, blessed be He, went on creating worlds and destroying them until He created this one, and declared, 'This one pleases Me; those did not please Me.'"

See how this idea of multiple universes gained traction in traditional Jewish sources, in the blog posting *"A thousand worlds and this,"* by Professor Clémence Boulouque, October 18, 2017: https://tif.ssrc.org/2017/10/18/a-thousand-worlds-and-this/.

There's more to the Red Sox story, which I covered in my piece for the *New York Jewish Week*, "The Eclipse of the Curse," written in 2004 just after the World Series. See the original article at https://www.joshuahammerman.com/2008/03/eclipse-of-curse.html

My 14-year-old son Ethan informed me, just after the Red Sox fell behind the Yankees in the ALCS, three games to zero, that he had challenged God that if the Red Sox didn't win the World Series this time, he would become an atheist. Imagine your child telling you this when no team in history had ever come back from the kind of deficit the Sox were facing. He was asking for a miracle. No, he wasn't merely asking, he was threatening God. And it worked. It worked so well that I found myself becoming more and more troubled by the theological implications of victory. If the Sox lose, my kid becomes a hardened skeptic, like the rest of us. But if they win because of this audacious wager, he could sink into a fundamentalist morass, totally convinced that God can be manipulated magically. And if the Sox win again? At that point he would become so smug as to render him indistinguishable from a Yankees fan.

Chapter Ten

As mentioned previously, that famous Hitler quote, which is widely said to have appeared in *Mein Kampf*, comes from Hermann Rauschning, president of the Senate of Danzig during the years 1933–1934.

To find the current tally of President Trump's lies while in office, check the *Washington Post*'s factchecker database at https://www.washingtonpost. com/graphics/politics/trump-claims-database/?utm_term=.520f2115f13c

The Ethics Centre excerpt on baby Hitler, posted by Matthew Beard, is reprinted with permission. See https://ethics.org.au/the-problem-with-killing-baby-hitler/.

Chapter Eleven

Rabbi Yitz Greenberg's seminal essay, "The Third Era of Jewish History: Power and Politics (CLAL, 1987) can be found at

http://rabbiirvinggreenberg.com/wp-content/uploads/2013/02/ 3Perspectives-Third-Era-1987-CLAL-3-of-3.pdf.

My op-ed, "The Good Swastika," which inspired this section, was first published by the *Religion News Service* on January 26, 2018. https://religionnews.com/2018/01/26/the-good-swastika/. This article was part of a three-column submission that earned me first place honors for "Excellence in Religion Commentary" at the 2019 Religion News Association Awards.

Chapter Twelve

The division between American Jews and Israeli Jews could not be more pronounced, especially in regard to President Trump. In mid-2019, the American Jewish Committee released simultaneous surveys of American, Israeli, and French Jews. In Israel, 79% of Jews somewhat or strongly approved of the way President Trump is handling U.S.-Israel relations, compared to just 36% of American Jews. Meanwhile, the president earned an overall unfavorable rating from 71% of American Jews. You can find the survey at https://www.ajc.org/survey2019. These numbers solidify my observation that the relationship between the Israeli and American Jewish communities is deteriorating rapidly—and that remembering the Holocaust has become our most deeply shared priority, the very linchpin of Jewish identity, and the starting point for reconciliation and potential unity.

The Donniel Hartman quote comes from p. 10 of the sourcebook for a course created by the Shalom Hartman Institute: *iEngage: Israel's Milestones and their Meanings The Legacy of the Past and the Challenge of the Future—A special iEngage Series to mark 50 years since the Six-Day War and 70 years since Israel's establishment.*

My proposal on universal Jewish citizenship has been floated in a number of places. It's even won recognition from the Religion News Association. When I introduced it to the Israeli public in my *Times of Israel* blog, https:// blogs.timesofisrael.com/let-jews-everywhere-vote-in-israeli-elections/, it went quasi-viral. The comments were quasi-unkind. I mean they were brutal, which told me I had struck a nerve. And sure enough, similarly radical ideas are being floated by others, including Tal Keinan's *God in the Crowd: Twenty-First Century Judaism* (New York: Penguin Random House, 2018). Keinan expands the role of the Israeli president to become, in effect, the president of the Jewish people, whose office would administer Jewish holy sites, set standards for conversion, birth, marriage and burial in state cemeteries, among other things. His office would require senior representation of the major streams of Judaism: Reform, Conservative and Orthodox (pp. 281-282). I like it, and I hope the Jewish establishment will have the courage to act on it. But I don't think it goes far enough.

Chapter Thirteen

Moshe Shulstein's Yiddish poem was translated by Mindele Wajsman and Bea Stadtler and appeared in *From Holocaust to New Life: A Documentary*

Volume Depicting the Proceedings and Events of the American Gathering of Jewish Holocaust Survivors, ed. Michael Berenbaum (American Gathering of Jewish Holocaust Survivors, 1985).

A traditional folktale from the 1700s by the Jewish teacher, Jacob ben Wolf Kranz, the Maggid of Dubno, helps to ease us to the close of this book. It can be found, among several other places, in *The Hungry Clothes and Other Jewish Folktales*, by Peninnah Schram. This version was taken from an article in the *Seattle Times*. https://www.seattletimes.com/seattle-news/the-story-of-the-kingrsquos-diamond-and-a-rabbirsquos-scratch/

There was once a king who owned an enormous and very beautiful diamond. Every day, the king took the diamond from its jewel-encrusted box and looked with awe as the gem transformed sunlight into magnificent, shimmering kaleidoscopes of color. It made him very happy. One day, the king accidentally dropped the diamond. It grazed the side of its box, and then fell heavily to the floor of the throne room. Picking it up, the king found a long, jagged scratch down one side of the stone. Horrified, he immediately called upon his royal jewelers to repair the gem, but they were unable to do so. The king then called upon other jewelers from other lands near and far, but none were able repair the diamond as the king wanted. Finally, a pauper appeared at the palace and said that he could repair the king's jewel. The king and his advisers were wary at first, but then, realizing they had nothing to lose, they invited the pauper to proceed. The pauper retreated into a cell, and after working for an entire week, he emerged and handed the king his diamond box. Sitting upon, his throne, the king opened the box, smiled with delight and held up for the jewel for all to see. The pauper had not removed the jagged line at all. Instead, he had etched an image of a rose onto one end of it, leaving the scratch as the stem of the beautiful flower.

Some wounds won't go away, but if we handle them right, they can make the wounded even more beautiful than before.

Bibliography

Ackerman, Diane. *The Zookeeper's Wife: A War Story*, New York: W.W. Norton, 2008.

Auslander, Shalom. *Foreskin's Lament*. New York: Riverhead Books, 2008.

Casey, Maura. "The Twists and Turns of Defining a Crime," *The New York Times*, Feb. 20, 2000. https://www.nytimes.com/2000/02/20/nyregion/the-twists-and-turns-in-defining-a-crime.html

Berenbaum, Michael, editor. *From Holocaust to New Life: A Documentary Volume Depicting the Proceedings and Events of the American Gathering of Jewish Holocaust Survivors*. New York: American Gathering of Jewish Holocaust Survivors, 1985.

Fackenheim, Emil. *The Jewish Return into History: Reflections in the Age of Auschwitz and a New Jerusalem*. New York: Schocken Books, 1978, 23-24.

Frankl, Viktor E. *Man's Search for Meaning*. Boston: Beacon Press, 2006.

Friedman, Shalom. *Living in the Image of God: Jewish Teachings to Perfect the World—Conversations with Rabbi Irving Greenberg*. New York: Jason Aronson, 1998.

Greenberg, Rabbi Irving. "Perspectives on the Holocaust." *CLAL*, 1986.

Hartman, David. "Auschwitz or Sinai?" *Shalom Hartman Institute*, 1982 https://hartman.org.il/Blogs_View.asp?Article_Id=394

Lipszyc, Rywka. *Rywka's Diary: The Writings of a Jewish Girl from the Lodz Ghetto*. New York: Harper, 2015.

Magid, Shaul. *American Post-Judaism: Identity and Renewal in a Postethnic Society*. Bloomington, Indiana: Indiana University Press, 2013.

Neusner, Jacob. *American Judaism: Adventure in Modernity*. Englewood Cliffs, New Jersey: Prentice-Hall Inc., 1972.

Neusner, Jacob. "The Implications of the Holocaust," *Journal of Religion*, Vol 53 No. 3, July 1973, 293-308.

Roskies, David. *Against the Apocalypse: Responses to Catastrophe in Modern Jewish Culture*, Cambridge: Harvard University Press, 1984.

Rubenstein, Richard. *After Auschwitz: History, Theology and Contemporary Judaism*: New York: MacMillan Publishing, 1966.

Volavková, Hana. *I Never Saw Another Butterfly: Children's Drawings and Poems from Terezin Concentration Camp 1942-1944*. New York: Schocken

Books, 1987.

Wiesenthal, Simon. *The Sunflower: On the Possibilities and Limits of Forgiveness.* New York: Schocken Books, 1970 - English translation.

Wiesel, Elie. *Legends of Our Time.* New York: Schocken Books, 2004

Wiesel, Elie. *The Night Trilogy: Night, Dawn, Day:* New York: Hill and Wang, 2001.

Zornberg, Avivah. Genesis: *The Beginning of Desire.* Philadelphia: JPS, 1995.

Acknowledgements

This book began with two journeys to Eastern Europe, and I am grateful to all my fellow travelers who made each trip possible. In 2010 I went on the March of the Living, thanks in no small part to the encouragement (and funding) supplied by Dr. Hesh Romanowitz of blessed memory. I'm also grateful to his wife Sheila Romanowitz, who was among the first to read an early version of this book.

Our 2010 group of teens (which included my son Dan) was escorted by Judy Altmann, a remarkable human being who survived both Auschwitz and Bergen Belsen. Stricken with typhus, Judy was barely alive when she was liberated by the British Army in 1945. This was her first time back at Auschwitz, but she remembered every inch of the camp, even showing the teens the barracks where she was held.

Her father's last words to her before Mengele separated them were, "Judy, you will live." Thanks to her youthful energy and knowledge of six languages,

Judy Altmann

she did. Judy remains a captivating speaker to groups in our community and well beyond, especially to youth. "If you see any injustice in the world, stand up. Don't just say it doesn't concern me," she says to her rapt audiences. "If more people had done that, more Jews would be alive today." And she adds, "I certainly have all the reasons in the world to hate. But hate destroys you, not them. Use your energy for good things and for better things."

The 2017 congregational tour was an adventure that my wife Mara and I shared with a cross section of community leaders and close friends, including Peter and Betsy Kempner, Sari and Alan Jaffe, Gary Lessen and Lois Stark, Eileen Rosner, Judith Aronin, Parry Berkowitz and Devra Jaffe-Berkowitz, Susan and Art Greenwald, James and Elissa Hyman, Susan Frieden, Eric Frieden, Stephanie Goldpin, Charles Siegel and Marty and Lisa Glinsky.

Congregational tour in front of the Warsaw Ghetto memorial

Without them, this trip—and this book—could not have happened.

In truth, my entire congregation has helped me to develop and refine these ideas—in group discussions, casual conversations and feedback from the 2017 High Holiday sermon cycle where many of these themes were first articulated. My congregants remain fellow travelers in so many respects.

Special thanks to Barbara Krasner of Olswanger Literary Agency, and to Anna Olswanger, for their dogged belief in the importance of this book, and to Larry Yudelson of Ben Yehuda Press and his team for seeing this vision through to publication. Special thanks as well to Laura Logan for her editing expertise.

So many friends, relatives, students and teachers have walked this path with me—too many to mention. I most especially want to thank Andrew Aisenberg and Paul Klein for helping me discover the ins and outs of Berlin; my sons Dan and Ethan for making their dad proud of them every single day; my pups Chloe, Cassidy and Casey for not barking quite so loud when I was completing this book; and most of all, Mara. I'm in awe of her infinite capacity to love all creatures, whether two- or four-legged—and I feed off of that. I couldn't imagine having taken this life-journey without her.

DISCUSSION QUESTIONS FOR "EMBRACING AUSCHWITZ."

Chapter 1:

1. *For most of my life, I felt that the Holocaust took up far too much Jewish bandwidth, that it smothered joy and suffocated Jews with guilt and resentment. It posed questions that were unanswerable. It eclipsed centuries of Jewish achievement and it brought out the worst in people. It gave us an excuse to hate—and it gave our children the excuse to opt out of being Jewish altogether. Who would want to be part of such a hopeless, hapless people?*

   Do you agree that the Holocaust has been overemphasized in Jewish life? Has its impact been primarily negative? Has the Holocaust been a positive force in the development of your religious/cultural identity?

2. One criticism of the "March of the Living" and similar programs is that it has fostered an attitude of victimization among impressionable teenagers. Has the Holocaust's treatment in Jewish education circles been primarily negative and parochial, or has it emphasized the universal lessons of the event?

Chapter 2:

1. *After seven decades of grief for what was lost—and so much was—Yisrael's tale of triumph over tragedy, of life over death, is an early indication that the Holocaust narrative is beginning to shift, from a story of abject despair to one of astonishing, incredible and miraculous (though not necessarily divinely ordained) survival. Yisrael Kristal might be Exhibit A that, for the Jewish people, at least, what doesn't kill us makes us stronger.*

   Do you believe that the mere fact of survival is heroic? What of "survivor's guilt," which has haunted Holocaust survivors for decades? Has that guilt begun the process of melting away–into something more akin to pride?

2.   *And we can now understand Deuteronomy 30:19 from the*
     perspective of the survivor: "Choose life, so that you and
     your children may live." For the survivor, the directive is to
     choose life in the most literal sense, by having children. Here's
     one more way the commandment from Deuteronomy 30, to
     "choose life," plays out in the Torah of Auschwitz: through
     the survival of Yisrael—not Yisrael Kristol the individu-
     al—but through Israel the collective, the Jewish people.

How do you interpret the commandment to "choose life?" To what degree
is your interpretation influenced by the Holocaust? To what degree is it reflected in your personal life journey?

3.   *We are all survivors—and maybe God is a survivor too.*
     But after Auschwitz, perhaps the God of Psalm 16, the
     one whom we place before us, is survival itself, that life
     force that drives us to breathe and to love and to find
     hope among the ashes, if only we will choose life.

Can you imagine God in this way, as a life force?

4.   *In the Torah of Auschwitz, perhaps Auschwitz itself must be the*
     place where a true divine vision can best be seen—not the Aus-
     chwitz that existed in 1944 but the Auschwitz that today exists
     for the sole purpose of remembering that prior incarnation.

Can Auschwitz ever be transformed into a symbol of the triumph of that
life force, despite all the horrific things that occurred there?

Chapter 3:

1.   *Long before the Holocaust, Jews were already a glass-half-empty*
     people. Born of slavery, perpetually exiled and perennially hated,
     there is good reason for Jews to be prone to cynicism and despair.
     We have a dark side and it is not something that can be easily
     exorcised—this is a major lesson of the Torah of Auschwitz.

Do you feel that the Jews too often succumb to pessimism and negativity? Can this be exorcised? Has it been?

2. *Even as we struggle to forge a feel-good vision for a new age, we will never stop dancing with Amalek. Perhaps that is for the best, because we've gotten pretty good at it, and we can teach others how to keep those dark forces of resentment and victimization in check.*

Do you agree with this assertion?

Chapter 4:

1. *It has been axiomatic in Jewish history that approximately seven decades after an enormous disaster has occurred (and there have been many), new, creative expressions of faith surface as a new generation comes of age. It's uncanny how often this "seven-decade rule" has borne itself out.*

Does this rule play itself out in individual lives as well, that great disruptions—say, the death of a parent or spouse, or a financial loss, or a health setback—are often followed by times of great creativity?

2. Jews break a glass at weddings to recall one of our saddest moments, the destruction of the temple. Rituals have developed to memorialize the Holocaust, such as the lighting of a yellow yahrzeit candle on Holocaust Remembrance Day. But as yet we've not, for the most part, brought Holocaust memorial rituals into everyday activities and sacred moments that are not in and of themselves connected to the Holocaust. Can you think of ways Jews (and others) can do that? Should we?

Chapter 5:

1. *The Jew has an obligation to remember, but then to shed the confining casing of resentment and despair, and to transform the disaster into an embrace of life and a relentless pursuit*

of justice and dignity for every human being. For a Jew is responsible not merely to be a witness, but to dream, to imagine a better future—despite the darkness that surrounds us.

Do you agree? Do most Jews agree?

2. *The Hebrew word for soul, neshama, has the word shem— name—right at its heart. Jews are, after all, Semites—descendants of Noah's son Shem—so Jews are literally "Name-ists." And the hater of Jews is, by definition, an anti-Shem-ite—the "Denier of names." One who defiles God is one who perpetrates what is called a "Hillul ha-shem," a desecration of the Name; and one who dies the holiest of deaths, as a martyr, dies, "AL Kiddush hashem," in an act of ultimate sanctification of the Name. To be named is to be—and even more, to be holy.*

What are the ways that totalitarian regimes try to deny the basic humanity of their enemies (and quite often, their own people as well)?

3. How does this chapter's reinterpretation of the command, "Zachor!" (Remember!) stray from the original meaning. Name several ways this commandment has been reinterpreted in light of the Holocaust and discuss whether it has become the most important commandment, aside from the mandate for saving life itself.

Chapter 6:

1. *The experiences of the Holocaust can help us confront a dizzying world where everything has been turned on its head; where everything we thought was true turns out not to be; when "new normals" become what's normal.*

How can the experiences of the Holocaust—the testimony of witnesses, the poetry, the essays, the philosophy of people like Elie Wiesel, Primo Levy and Viktor Frankl—inform those experiencing the enormous disruptions of the early 21st century, including technological change and most recently the coronavirus crisis? Do we experience these more recent disruptions differently, having "been" through the Holocaust?

2. *There is no greater task for post-Holocaust Jews than to teach humans how to live with hope and dignity, like Naftali Stern and those who prayed with him on that fateful Rosh Hashanah in 1944. How to rise above the raging torrent, how to survive with grace and love, and how—as I learned so painfully on a cold night in Krakow—to appreciate the regenerative powers of each breath and to never stop growing.*

Apply those lessons to your life experience. What lessons of perseverance, hope and dignity can you teach the world?

Chapter 7:

1. *We are moving, in a sense, from Kosher to Kesher. These nearly identical Hebrew words signify the old ways and the new. The laws of keeping Kosher are, like the rest of the Sinai laws of holiness, built on distinction, on drawing lines of separation. Kesher, on the other hand, is the Hebrew word for connection, calling on us to dissolve distinctions. "We are not leaving Kosher behind, but now we need to look at it through the prism of Kesher; because in the end, we are all one human tissue, as we were at Auschwitz."*

This is among the more radical assertions made in this book. With a world-wide battle intensifying between forces of nativism, xenophobia and other strains of radical nationalism (as opposed to good old-fashioned national pride) and those seeing the underlying connections between all people, I clearly stand on that latter side. I also assert that the *Torah of Auschwitz* does as well. What do you think? Has Judaism—along with other faith traditions—evolved to a point where we've begun the journey from Kosher to Kesher?

2. *Many people bemoan the fact that more gentiles, in Poland and Hungary especially, didn't do more to save Jews. There is some*

validity to that, but I am amazed that anyone would have risked
their lives to help a people who, since early childhood, they had been
taught to despise, who, they had been taught for many centuries,
had killed their god. Anti-Semitism was thoroughly ingrained in
their culture and especially in the church. But still, some were able
to bypass centuries of prejudice and get right back to the core values
that spawned Christianity in the first place. Something was able
to cut through it all, something innate and good, and it led thou-
sands of people to acts of incomprehensible risk and selflessness.

It's far easier for me to take this glass-half-full approach to righteous gentiles, focusing less on their rarity than on my amazement over the fact that
there were any at all. Especially when compared to other situations—like
Egypt in Exodus, when no one raised a finger to help the Israelites. Where
do you stand on this issue?

Chapter 8

1. *Before the Shoah, when the earth still belonged to God, we, who*
   had once experienced Paradise firsthand, could only imagine Eden's
   opposite. As David Grossman writes in his masterful novel, See
   Under: Love—"We always pictured hell with boiling lava and
   pitch bubbling in barrels," until the Nazis came along, "show-
   ing us how paltry our pictures were." Now, nothing is left to the
   imagination. The earth is ours and we are utterly responsible for
   all that happens to it; all of it—the people, and the flowers, too.

Has God ceded control over the destiny of the earth to humanity?

2. *"Es brent…It is Burning" is a Yiddish poem–song written in 1936*
   by Mordechai Gebirtig. The Yad Vashem website states, "The song
   became a prophetic song of the impending Holocaust, describing
   the burning of the Jewish shtetl. The poet calls upon the Jews not
   to stand idly by, but to be proactive and put out the fire that is
   consuming their precious town. They should extinguish the fire and
   demonstrate to the world that they can take care of themselves."

This song calls on Jews to take matters into their own hands, before it is too late. Would you say that the Jewish people or others have become more proactive in the decades since the Holocaust? Have our politicians learned to take the long view?

Chapter 9:

1. *We are drawn to theological speculation as moths to a flame. Some say we have a "religious instinct," asserting that if there were no God we would be compelled to invent one. Whether or not that's true, it's worthwhile to explore new ways to imagine God, ones that do no shame to the memory of the abandoned martyrs.*

Do we try too hard to salvage God's reputation after cataclysmic events, especially this one? Would we be better off simply leaving God out of the conversation for a generation or two?

2. Do any of the ideas offered here resonate with you? Have you come up with a theology of your own that takes the Holocaust seriously?

Chapter 10:

1. *The Torah of Auschwitz makes clear that the commandment to remember the Holocaust is about keeping alive the essence of all objective truth. The dilution or outright denial of this truth is the nullification of all truth. The Holocaust was objectively, verifiably, utterly—and not alternatively—a fact. That fact is one of the pillars of our epoch, a fundamental truth, and a foundation upon which we are trying to reconstruct a civilized society.*

If you could put together a top ten list of self-evident truths, along the lines of the Declaration of Independence's "we hold these truths…" would the fact that the Holocaust happened be right at the top? What else would be on that list? Would these truths have to be scientifically verifiable—or can they rely on faith? Why is it important to have such a list?

2. Would you have killed baby Hitler?

Chapter 11:

1. *Abraham Joshua Heschel wrote, "Few of us seem to realize*
    how insidious, how radical, how universal and evil racism
    is. Few of us realize that racism is man's gravest threat to
    man, the maximum of hatred for a minimum of Reason,
    the maximum of cruelty for a minimum of thinking."

How is it possible that racism still exists after the Holocaust? It seems
like the world took a deep breath after witnessing genocide first-hand (and
doing nothing to stop it), spent a couple of worthy decades coming up with a
Universal Declaration of Human Rights, spawning a United Nations, liberating some colonies and creating states like Israel, and then eventually getting
around to ridding the world of Jim Crow and South African apartheid. That
was a pretty good half century, but we are far from rid of racism. Why is it
that so many of the questions on the U.S. Census form revolve around an
artificial construct called race?

2. Can a symbol of hate like the swastika be reclaimed by its original owners
as a symbol of love? Can you design a new symbol of global unity and equality, along the lines of the ubiquitous "Coexist" bumper sticker?

Chapter 12:

1. *Rather than giving Hitler a posthumous victory by our dissolving*
    into irrelevance through infighting and apathy, we can achieve
    Hitler's ultimate posthumous defeat by using his plan for a Final
    Solution as a blueprint for a worldwide Jewish renaissance.

So what do you think? Can using the Nuremberg Laws, one of the most
racist, anti-Semitic acts of legislation in history—as filtered through the
Law of Return—turn the tables on the Nazis and be the ultimate slap in
Hitler's face?

2. Do you have a better idea? Or is the unity of the Jewish people no longer relevant?

Chapter 13:

1. *For Jews and others who take on the responsibilities of the Torah of Auschwitz, it is our responsibility to bear witness to the truth, no matter how uncomfortable that may be. And it is our responsibility, as a people who stands in Covenant, to open ourselves up to the flow of divine love and to bring light and blessing to the lives of others. That is what it means to bear witness.*

What does it mean to you to bear witness to the Holocaust? Will that change in another generation or two? In a thousand years, how will the Holocaust be recalled?

2. *How can we acknowledge that the time to weep has yielded, as always, to a time to dance—not with the shadow of Amalek, but with an eternal life-force, with renewal and hope—while acknowledging that these tears will never completely go away? How can we enable the anguish and the anger to be absorbed into the realm of ritual and story, despite the pain, despite the continued presence of anti-Semitism and hate in our world, and thereby enable the Holocaust to become transcendent and ever-present?*

That's the question I leave you with.

I invite you and perhaps your class or book group to continue this conversation, by emailing me at joshuah@tbe.org.

About the Author

Joshua Hammerman, a celebrated rabbi and award-winning journalist and blogger, has served Temple Beth El in Stamford, Connecticut, for over three decades.

He is the author of *thelordismyshepherd.com: Seeking God in Cyberspace* and *Mensch-Marks: Life Lessons of a Human Rabbi —Wisdom for Untethered Times*. He also contributed to the children's book *I Have Some Questions About God* and the collections *Text Messages: A Torah Commentary for Teens* and *Peace in Our Cities: Rabbis Against Gun Violence*.

Rabbi Hammerman was a past winner of the Simon Rockower award, the highest honor in Jewish journalism. In 2019, he was awarded first prize by the Religion News Association for excellence in commentary.

His articles have appeared widely, as a regular columnist for *The New York Jewish Week* and featured blogger for the *Times of Israel*, along with the Jewish Telegraphic Agency, the *Forward*, the Religion News Service, the *New York Times Magazine* and *Washington Post* and elsewhere.

During his time at Temple Beth El, Rabbi Hammerman has been president of the Interfaith Council of Southwestern Connecticut and the Stamford Board of Rabbis, a chaplain for the Stamford Police, and a member of the pastoral advisory committee of Stamford Health Systems. He has been a member of the faculty of CLAL, the National Jewish Center for Learning and Leadership. In addition, he has been heavily involved in many Jewish think tanks. He has been a champion of inclusiveness and innovation in synagogue life, focusing on creating an oasis of warmth, love and mutual respect, while at the same time, challenging congregants—and himself—to reach ever higher in setting spiritual and ethical objectives.

Rabbi Hammerman was ordained at the Jewish Theological Seminary in 1983 after receiving a master's degree in journalism from N.Y.U. and a B.A., magna cum laude, from Brown University, where he twice won the university's prestigious Bishop McVickar Prize in Religious Studies.

Rabbi Hammerman is an avid fan of the Red Sox, Patriots and all things Boston; he also loves a good, Israeli hummus. He lives in Stamford with his wife, Dr. Mara Hammerman, a psychologist. They have two grown children, Ethan and Daniel, along with Chloe, Casey, and Cassidy, three standard poodles. Many of his articles and essays can be found at his website, joshuahammerman.com.

www.ingramcontent.com/pod-product-compliance
Lightning Source LLC
Chambersburg PA
CBHW022006080426
42733CB00007B/489